Thomas Aquinas

On Human Nature

Thomas Aquinas

On Human Nature

Edited, with Introduction, by
THOMAS S. HIBBS

Hackett Publishing Company
Indianapolis/Cambridge

Copyright © 1999 by Hackett Publishing Company, Inc.
All rights reserved

Printed in the United States of America

1 2 3 4 5 6 7   03 02 01 00 99

Cover design by Listenberger Design & Associates
Interior design by Meera Dash

For further information, please address

Hackett Publishing Company, Inc.
P. O. Box 44937
Indianapolis, Indiana 46244–0937

Library of Congress Cataloging-in-Publication Data
Thomas, Aquinas, Saint, 1225?–1274.
    [Sentencia libri De anima. English. Selections]
    On human nature / edited, with introduction, by
Thomas S. Hibbs.
       p. cm.
    Selections from the author's Sentencia libri De anima, and
Summa theologica.
    Includes bibliographical references (p.   ).
    ISBN 0-87220-455-3 (cloth).—ISBN 0-87220-454-5 (pbk.)
    1. Aristotle. De anima.   2. Soul.   3. Psychology—Early works to 1850.
I. Hibbs, Thomas S.   II. Thomas, Aquinas, Saint, 1225?–1274.
Summa theologica. English. Selections.   III. Title.
B415.T5713 1999b
128—dc21   98-50832
                                     CIP

CONTENTS

INTRODUCTION

The human soul, St. Thomas Aquinas writes, exists "on the confines of [the] spiritual and corporeal" (ST, I, 77, 2). The human person is thus a microcosm of the whole universe, a little world, in whom the perfections of both the spiritual and the material orders coincide. Aquinas adopts Aristotle's account of human beings as composites of soul and body, wherein soul is related to body as form to matter. This is the so-called hylomorphic theory of human nature. Composed of matter and form, human beings are akin to all other natural substances. But, since the highest capacity of human soul, the intellect, is an immaterial power, human beings are peculiar examples of matter-form composition. Nowhere else do we find an immaterial power united to a body.

Aquinas's position eludes categorization in terms of the fundamental modern and contemporary alternatives of dualism and materialism. Nor does it help to depict hylomorphism as a compromise or middle position between dualism and materialism. The latter are closer to one another than either is to Aquinas's account. Dualism and materialism are united in rejecting the very notion of soul as animating, organizing, and directing principle of the body. Descartes's emphatic rejection in his *Meditations* of the body as constitutive of who we are as human beings set the terms of debate over human nature well into this century.[1] Although Descartes, perhaps the most important modern proponent of dualism, eventually comes round to noting that mind and body are somehow united and constitute one being, he nowhere countenances the language of soul. Hobbes, who denies that there is anything immaterial in human beings and thus provides us with a classical articulation of materialism, is often thought to be diametrically opposed to Descartes. But he is equally unsympathetic to the Aristotelian conception of the soul as animating principle of the body.[2] He describes life as "but a motion of limbs," and treats human beings as complicated machines.[3] The consequences are immediate and striking. Freedom and coercion are indistinguishable, and reason is but a slave of the passions. In contemporary philosophy, debates over mind and body

---

[1]See *Meditations*, II, trans. by Donald Cress (Indianapolis: Hackett Pub. Co., 1993).   [2]For an examination of influential modern philosophers that takes the repudiation of soul as central to the history of modern philosophy, see Pierre Manent, *The City of Man*, trans. by Marc A. Le Pain (Princeton, N.J.: Princeton University Press, 1998).   [3]*Leviathan*, introduction, ed. E. Curley (Indianapolis: Hackett Pub. Co., 1994).

usually focus on the question of whether mental states are reducible to physical ones, that is, whether thought is reducible to physiological processes. Often overlooked is the question whether there is anything distinctively human about the body. Without the language of soul or some viable substitute for the notion of the body as informed, the danger is that the body will be denigrated as merely biological.[4] The selections from Aquinas in this volume focus not only on the relationship of soul and body or on the nature of the intellect and human knowledge, but also on the peculiarly human characteristics of our bodies and bodily passions.

For Aquinas, the study of the soul is the primary avenue into the study of human nature. It is the crucial, pivotal inquiry of philosophy, providing us with self-knowledge and urging us to realize and perfect our nature in pursuit of the goods of knowledge and virtue. Aquinas subscribes to Aristotle's teaching on the appropriate order of philosophical pedagogy. The student is to begin with the propaedeutic disciplines of logic and mathematics and then move through natural philosophy to ethics and politics and on, finally, to metaphysics. Where does the study of human nature occur? It is the culminating inquiry of the philosophy of nature. Aristotle's approach to human nature, accordingly, differs markedly from that which takes its point of departure from the mind-body problem. In an essay that deftly deploys Aquinas's commentary to explicate Aristotle, Martha Nussbaum and Hilary Putnam write,

> The mind-body problem . . . starts from a focus on the special nature of mental activity—therefore from just one part of the activity of some among living beings. . . . Aristotelian hylomorphism, by contrast, starts from a general interest in characterizing the relationship, in things of many kinds, between their organization or structure and their material composition. It deals with the beings and doings of all substances. . . . It asks two questions in particular. . . . How do and should we explain or describe the changes we see taking place in the world? . . . What is it about individuals that makes them the very things that they are?[5]

Since soul is to body as form is to matter and form is defined in relation to its proper matter, soul must be understood in relationship to body. From its mode of defining, the study of the soul pertains to natural philosophy,

---

[4]For an instructive exception, see Leon Kass, "Thinking about the Body," in *Toward a More Natural Science* (New York: The Free Press, 1985), pp. 276–298.
[5]"Changing Aristotle's Mind," in *Essays on Aristotle's De Anima*, ed. A. Rorty and M. Nussbaum (Oxford: Clarendon Press, 1992), pp. 28–29.

which investigates substances composed of matter and form (Commentary on the *De Anima*, Book I, Lecture 1). For St. Thomas Aquinas as for Aristotle, the study of the soul embraces all living things and investigates their natures by attending to their habitual modes of operation. Far from setting human beings in opposition to nature, it depicts them as part of nature and proceeds to underscore what is peculiar to the human species.

As Aquinas notes in his commentary, the inquiry of the *De Anima* is pivotal in three respects (Commentary on the *De Anima*, Book I, Lecture 1). First, the study of what human nature is and its proper activities is a prelude to the study of the human good in the disciplines of ethics and politics. Second, metaphysics, the discipline at the pinnacle of philosophy, answers to the natural, human desire to know, an orientation that is disclosed in the study of the soul. Third, without the knowledge, established in the *De Anima*, of the immateriality of the human intellect and the nature of its operation, we would not even be able to begin thinking about the nature and activity of the separate substances and God. Thus, we would not be able to do metaphysics. If the study of human nature is for Aquinas crucial to philosophical inquiry, it is also central to theology.[6] The *Summa Theologica*, from which most of the material in this volume is derived, is a decidedly theological text; yet in the excerpts we have included in this volume, there is virtually no argument that depends upon properly theological or revealed doctrines. Still, the guiding influence of theology is reflected in the order of proceeding. How is this so?

We are already familiar with the order appropriate to philosophical pedagogy, which begins from what is most evident to us and first in our experience (natural philosophy) and proceeds toward what is first in the order of nature or being (metaphysics). By beginning from God, theology reverses this order and takes as its point of departure what is first in being and last in our experience. (ST, I, 2). Theology, then, treats the coming forth of things from God in creation and culminates in the return of all things to God through Christ and the sacraments. By far the largest segments of Aquinas's theological writings are devoted to the created order

---

[6]For other texts, which are not included in this volume, where St. Thomas considers human nature, see *Questions on the Soul*, trans. with an introduction by James H. Robb (Milwaukee: Marquette University Press, 1984); *Aquinas Against the Averroists: On There Being One Intellect*, Latin text with English translation, notes, and interpretive essays by Ralph McInerny (West Lafayette, Ind.: Purdue University Press, 1993); and *Summa Contra Gentiles*, Books II and III (Notre Dame, Ind.: University of Notre Dame Press, 1975).

of nature, in which human nature occupies a crucial place. Aquinas traces the complexity of human beings (in contrast to the simplicity of lower, embodied creatures and of disembodied angels) to their being situated at the juncture of the material and the immaterial. Human beings contain the perfections of both orders (ST, I, 77, 2).

One of the advantages of beginning with the commentary on the *De Anima* is that in it we can follow Thomas's patient introduction and clarification of the Aristotelian vocabulary that pervades the more theological discussion in the *Summa Theologica*, where he rarely pauses to explain the original context in Aristotle's own texts.[7] Another reason for studying the commentary is that the theological order of proceeding can mislead readers who are unaccustomed to Aquinas's complex pedagogical style. Since theology begins with what is prior by nature although last in our experience, the treatise on human nature begins with the soul and then turns to its union with the body (ST, I, 75–76). A reader might hastily infer from this that we could know the soul prior to, and in isolation from, the body or that we could have some sort of immediate, introspective access to the nature of the intellect. All of these inferences are explicitly denied by Aquinas in the same treatise (ST, I, 87, 1–4), but if the difference between the philosophical and theological modes of proceeding go unnoticed, readers might come away thinking that Aquinas has more in common with Descartes than with Aristotle.

---

[7]This is not to say that Aquinas should be viewed as merely a commentator on Aristotle or that his commentaries are obviously superior to those of other medieval philosophers. How to interpret Aristotle was a much vexed question in the thirteenth century, and Aquinas's interpretation is but one of many. Aquinas is distinctive in that he devoted a great deal of time to careful expostion of entire texts of Aristotle. He did this not just in his early years, but even as his prominence rose and as he composed his most mature works. For example, Aquinas composed *The Commentary on the De Anima* while he was working on the *prima pars* of the *Summa Theologica;* for the dating of these and other works, see Jean-Pierre Torrell, *Saint Thomas Aquinas, Volume I: The Person and His Work* (Washington, D.C.: The Catholic University of America Press, 1996), pp. 327–361. The selections from the commentary that we have included will allow the reader to ascertain, first, Aquinas's interpretation of key passages from the *De Anima* and then to examine how these teachings inform and/or are transformed by their use within a more independent writing of Aquinas, the *Summa Theologica.* For an argument that takes the commentaries to embody Thomas's philosophy, see James Collins, "Toward a Philosophically Ordered Thomism," The New Scholasticism 32 (1958), pp. 301–326. For an opposed position, see Mark Jordan, *The Alleged Aristotelianism of Thomas Aquinas* Gilson Lecture 15 (Toronto: PIMS, 1992).

Readers familiar with Descartes's *Meditations* will, upon encountering Aquinas's writings on human nature, immediately note the difference in tone between the two. Aquinas's approach is far removed from Descartes's anxious quest for absolute certitude. Of course, to some readers, Aquinas's apparent indifference to skeptical worries seems naive and uncritical. While these are controversial issues about which much should be said, it is worth considering a question not frequently asked by modern critics of Aquinas: How might he view the Cartesian preoccupation with skepticism? From the perspective of Aristotle and Aquinas, the approach looks awfully contrived and artificial; instead of focusing on human beings actively engaged with things in the world, it offers us an abstract mind trying desperately to find entry into the world. Aquinas would urge, moreover, that reasonable doubts are always local, never global; they are formulated against a set of background assumptions that could never all at once be successfully put in question. If doubt were to become truly global, it would be fatal.

These divergent characterizations of the nature of the intellect and its relationship to things repose upon a more fundamental disagreement, a dispute over whether human nature and human understanding are susceptible to analysis in terms of what Descartes calls clear and distinct ideas. In his investigation of human things, Descartes seeks a certitude formerly achieved only in mathematics. By contrast, Aquinas echoes Aristotle's caution against demanding the same degree of certitude in all inquiries and insists upon a plurality of methods. At the very outset of the *De Anima*, Aristotle notes that knowledge is desirable for two reasons: (a) because of the certitude gained and (b) because of the nobility of the object known. When we cannot have both, we should prefer the dim knowledge of noble objects to a certain knowledge of less dignified objects (Commentary on the *De Anima*, Book I, Lecture 1). Not doubt, but wonder is the abiding inspiration for philosophy. And the goal is not certitude or power but wisdom, rooted in the natural human longing to behold the ultimate principles of the whole of being.

Following Aristotle, and in contrast to Descartes, Aquinas urges a methodological retreat in our pursuit of self-knowledge. The indirectness of human self-knowledge and its pivotal role in the transition from the natural to the divine can be seen in the very order of questions in the *Summa*. In the discussion of human knowledge, Aquinas moves from an examination of how the soul knows corporeal things beneath it, what are its mode and order of knowing, and what it knows in material things (ST, I, 84–85) to how it knows itself (ST, I, 87) and then to how it knows what is above itself (ST, I, 88). There is no possibility of gaining immediate, introspective access to the intellect or the soul. The route to self-knowledge is indirect, oblique. To understand the essence of any species, we must begin with the objects naturally pursued by members of the species in question, then move back from these to examine the activities, powers, and, finally, the essence. For all the achievements of philosophy, we remain mysteries to ourselves.

The manner of defining the soul further underscores the distinctiveness of Aquinas's Aristotelian method. The definition of the soul as the "primary actuality of a physical body potentially alive," accords with the stipulation that in the definition of a form, we must state its proper subject (Commentary on the *De Anima*, Book II, Lecture 1). The definition brings technical precision to the insight that the soul is the actualizing, animating, and organizing form of the body, and that we cannot understand one without the other. And yet the intellectual soul presents certain problems for understanding the union of the human soul and body in terms of the union of form and matter. In the culminating sections of his *De Anima*, Aristotle compares sensation and understanding. Although there are important similarities between the two, telling differences emerge. The intellect so differs from sense that it must be an immaterial power, whose operation transcends every bodily organ. Wherever he discusses the immateriality of the intellect, Aquinas adduces a standard set of arguments—(a) that it knows sensible things in abstraction from the here and now, (b) that it apprehends the universal and not just the singular, e.g., not just water but what it is to be water, (c) that, unlike sense, its objects are not limited to a set of contraries, and (d) that it is self-reflective. All these arguments find their initial articulation in the section from the commentary on Book III, Lectures 7 and 8 of the *De Anima* that we have reprinted. Aquinas also spells out Aristotle's argument on behalf of the subsistence of the intellect. The conclusion follows from the coupling of the immateriality of the intellect with the premise that whatever has an operation proper to itself, subsists (Commentary on the *De Anima*, Book III, Lectures 7–10).

The impeccable logic of the argument for the subsistence of the intellect conceals a host of problems. From the vantage point of Aristotle's philosophy, the separate subsistence of the intellect is deeply troubling. Both Aquinas and Aristotle insist that even if the intellect operates independently of bodily organs, it still needs the body to present it with an object. Here and in the *Summa Theologica*, Aquinas affirms the intellect's orientation toward and dependence on phantasms, that is, sensible images, for every act of knowing (ST, I, 84, 7). The intellect's transcendence of the limits of material conditions in its very act of knowing sensible substances seems simultaneously to allow for the intellect's separate existence and to undercut the possibility of its knowing anything in such a disembodied state.[8] Thus does the study of soul generate seemingly insuperable difficulties. When Aquinas comes to address these issues in the *Summa*, he underscores their philosophical intractability (ST, I, 89, 1).[9] He asserts that the separated soul knows by turning not to phantasms but to "pure intelligibles." Yet he immediately adds that the separated existence of soul is "not in accord with its nature" and that it receives species only by an "influence of the divine light." These assertions leave the reader wondering whether an exclusively philosophical solution to this issue is possible. It seems that, according to Aquinas, a satisfactory resolution can be had only from the perspective of theology, with the revealed teachings on the resurrection of the body and the graced elevation of the intellect to the vision of God. Attention to the successes and limits of Aristotle's philosophical inquiry is instructive on two points. First, it makes clear that Aquinas's preoccupation with the question of the separate existence of the intellect is not manufactured from extraneous theological concerns. Second, we see how the careful formulation of philosophical problems sets the stage for a positive engagement of philosophy by theology.

But Aquinas does not immediately advert to a theological argument. Instead, he attempts to clarify the underlying philosophical assumptions and principles. Indeed, the tension between soul as form and soul as subsistent pervades the opening questions of the treatise on human nature (*de Homine*), which begins where the commentary on the *De Anima* concludes. Soul as form underscores our kinship with other animals, whereas the soul's subsistence points to our similarity to angels. Aquinas pairs an ascending, philosophical account of humans as the pinnacle of the animal kingdom with a descending, theological account of human souls as the lowest and weakest of spiritual substances. Some deem these approaches fundamentally incompatible and conclude that Aquinas is trying to carve out an impossible middle position between Plato and Aristotle. No quick resolution of these issues is possible; all we can do here is to urge the

---

[8]See Deborah Modrak, "The Nous–Body Problem in Aristotle," *Review of Metaphysics*, 44 (1991), pp. 755–774.　　[9]See Anton Pegis, "The Separated Soul and Its Nature in St. Thomas," in *St. Thomas Aquinas 1274–1974: Commemorative Studies*, Volume I (Toronto: PIMS, 1974), pp. 131–159.

reader to attend to Aquinas's supple, analogical use of terms.[10] This consideration is particularly evident in his account of the subsistence of the intellectual soul. The technical terminology for what exists in its own right is "this particular thing" (*hoc aliquid*). Because of the argument just stated, Aquinas holds that the soul is subsistent. But he adds the qualification that properly and completely something can be called *hoc aliquid* only if it both "subsists and is complete in nature" (ST, I, 75, 2, ad 2, and Commentary on the *De Anima*, Book II, Lecture 1). It seems that we have grounds for attributing the former but not the latter to the soul. In contrast to an angelic intellect, then, the human intellect is a *hoc aliquid* in only a diminished and analogical sense. To highlight the difference, Aquinas proceeds to argue that the soul is not in the same species as an angel, chiefly for two reasons: first, the intellect's mode of knowing differs markedly from that of the angel, and, second, the soul itself is not in any species whatsoever, since it is but part of a composite (ST, I, 75, 7). We are not disembodied intellects but rational animals; thus, the genus to which we belong is the genus animal. For Aquinas the impossibility of reducing the account of human nature to univocal concepts reflects the complex phenomena of human nature.

Aquinas was acutely aware of plausible alternative accounts of the relationship of soul and body. As he notes, some suppose that because the intellect is immaterial, it cannot be the substantial form of a material body. Instead, it is related to the body as mover to moved. This position has the apparent advantage of explaining the interaction of the soul with the body without immersing it in matter. Some who find this view congenial posit a number of souls as mediators between the body and the intellect (ST, I, 76, 3). An individual human being would be alive by the vegetative soul; animal by the sensitive soul; and man by the intellectual soul. Aquinas counters that the multiplication of souls has the awkward result of rendering any particular human being only accidentally one. "Animal" would be predicated of "man" accidentally, not essentially. By contrast, Aquinas recurs to Aristotle's definition of the soul as a first actuality, giving being and unity to the body. The substantial form is derived from the highest power of the soul, which contains virtually what belongs

---

[10]As we have already noted, Aquinas does not think it is possible for us to reduce our philosophical language to univocal significations, at least not without doing violence to our experience and our understanding. For Thomas on analogy, see Ralph McInerny, *Aquinas and Analogy* (Washington, D.C.: The Catholic University of America Press, 1996).

to lower souls (ST, I, 76, 4). Being contained by and ordered to the highest power in human beings, the lower powers are not the same in human beings as they are in inferior animals. They are transformed and elevated by their participation in the intellectual soul. One substantial form, the intellectual soul, gives being and unity to the whole.

In his treatment of human knowledge in the *Summa Theologica*, Aquinas spends a good deal of time combating a view that he attributes to Plato and his followers. As Aquinas sees it, Plato confuses the mode of our understanding with the mode of being of things. Aquinas is careful to locate Plato's view within its historical context, as a response to the position of the early natural philosophers who held either that there could be no knowledge because the objects of knowledge are sensible things, always in flux, or that knowledge is a matter of the physical elements in us hooking up with the physical elements in things (ST, I, 84, 1). Wanting to save the character of knowledge as universal, immaterial, and immobile, Plato posits the existence of a separate order of Forms corresponding to our ideas. Aquinas objects that this assumption fails to salvage knowledge of sensible things, which are singular, material, and mobile, and that it renders the union of soul and body inscrutable. What is missing in Plato is a more radical reflection on the nature of our intellectual operation and its relationship to its proper objects, the natures of sensible substances. More specifically, what is missing is the intellectual operation of abstraction performed by the agent intellect (ST, I, 84, 6). For Aquinas, the intellect is both passive, that is, receptive of sensible things, and active upon them (ST, I, 79, 2–3). Our knowledge of sensible things which is at first vague and general, is made precise and specific by actively engaging with sensible things, by persistent questioning of them. Aquinas compares the active or agent intellect (*intellectus agens*) with a light that illuminates sensible things and renders what is potentially intelligible actually intelligible.

Technically and precisely, Aquinas states that understanding is the result of the intellect's abstracting the intelligible species from the phantasm, an image of the sensible thing. Abstraction explains the modal difference between the thing known, a sensible singular, and knowledge, which is universal, extending beyond this or that instance to all things sharing the same nature. The language of abstraction can be confusing, if we think of it in physical terms as a stripping away of a material surface to arrive at an intelligible or spiritual core. On this picture, the agent intellect's operation would resemble that of a construction crane, extracting the intelligible species from experience. Abstraction is no such mechanical process. It is an "active power to consider the nature of sensible things without considering their individuating conditions," that is, the conditions that pertain to them as this or that instance and not just as members of a species (ST, I, 85, 1, ad 4). Thus, we can consider the nature of a cow while disregarding the fact that this cow is here before us now and has a certain color, weight, and so forth. This possibility does not mean we can imagine a universal cow, but rather that the intellect can distinguish in the image what is essential from what is accidental. In so doing, the intellect apprehends what is universally true of all cows, their common nature. In defining natural substances, be they human beings or cows, we must include flesh and bones but not this flesh and these bones. Abstraction salvages what Plato's doctrine could not: our knowledge of sensible things.[11]

In a variety of ways, then, Aquinas underscores the intellect's natural orientation to sensible singulars. Indeed, he makes his own Aristotle's teaching (a) that the intellect is a potency made actual only by its interaction with things and (b) that knowledge is not by contact of knower and known or by the presence of a similitude of the latter in the former but by an identity of knower and known. Still, to speak of the intelligible species as a mean between intellect and thing presents a potential problem.[12] In an article that asks whether the species is related to our intellect as what is understood or as that by which we understand (ST, I, 85, 2), Aquinas insists that the primary object of our knowledge is the nature of sensible things. The species is the means by which (*quo*) we know things rather than what (*quod*) we know. Aquinas's language might seem to imply that we first inspect the content of our consciousness and then look to the external world to confirm that the content accurately reflects external things. The most obvious problem with this procedure is that it traps us in an infinite regress. If what we encounter first is always the content of our consciousness, the way things have affected us, then the turn from the species to the world will always be frustrated by the fact that we will once again encounter an image or likeness of what exists outside us. One can

---

[11]Criticisms of abstraction are a staple of the philosophical literature. For an incisive early modern critique, see the Introduction to Berkeley's *A Treatise Concerning the Principles of Human Knowledge* (Indianapolis: Hackett Pub. Co., 1977). Berkeley's target is Locke, and the reader is invited not only to weigh Berkeley's criticisms but also to consider whether Locke's version of abstraction is interchangeable with that of others, notably Aquinas.   [12]On this issue, see John O'Callaghan, "The Problem of Language and Mental Representation in Aristotle and St. Thomas," *The Review of Metaphysics*, 50 (1997), pp. 449-541.

see here how the view of Descartes and Locke on the temporal priority of ideas in our coming to know external things quite reasonably generates both Hume's skepticism about whether we can know the external world at all and Berkeley's claim that "to be is to be perceived" (*esse est percipi*).

Aquinas nowhere asserts that we first know the species and then through it, know the thing. In terms of temporal order, the species can be known only after we know the thing, by a reflective act that accompanies our knowing of things. In that reflective act, we simultaneously know the thing and know that we know it.[13] In the latter, we acknowledge that our intellect has been informed by the nature of the thing. This acknowledgment is congruent with Aristotle's dictum that we know activities by first knowing the objects of those activities. If the species is not an instrumental means of knowing things, one might wonder whether it would not be safer to eliminate the language of species altogether. Would it not be less misleading to speak simply of an intellect and a thing, or better, of an intellect knowing a thing? Why posit the species or concept as a third thing? The response is that the concept is not a thing, but is the very activity of the intellect as it is informed by the thing in the act of knowing it. Indeed, the Latin term *conceptum* can have our meaning of "concept," but it can also mean "thing conceived." The latter is more in accord with Aquinas's use.

If Aquinas's view of knowledge gives rise to technical and substantive difficulties, his view of the will has seemed utterly implausible to some. Aquinas's emphatic statement that the will necessarily desires happiness (ST, I, 82, 1) sounds excessively constricting to modern ears. According to Aquinas, the only sort of necessity that is repugnant to our voluntariness is that of force or coercion (ST, I-II, 10, 2). We are masters of our own actions by free choice of means, not by determining ultimate ends for ourselves. In what, then, does our freedom consist?

Some have wanted to see in Aquinas's assertion that the will moves the intellect an inchoate acknowledgment of the autonomy of the will. Aquinas does indeed note that, whereas the intellect moves the will by proposing ends to it, the will moves the intellect to the exercise of its own act (ST, I, 82, 4) and is even capable of moving itself (ST, I-II, 9, 3). The role of the will in the exercise of intellectual acts is rightly seen as an important Augustinian contribution to Aquinas's generally Aristotelian

---

[13]See Frederick Wilhelmsen, "The 'I' and Aquinas," and "Modern Man's Myth of Self-Identity," in *Being and Knowing* (Albany: Preserving Christian Publications, pp. 183–196 and 197–212).

view of human action. It allows Aquinas to reflect on the ethical conditions of our exercise of our intellectual powers in ways that Aristotle never does. Nowhere, however, does Aquinas countenance anything more than a relative, and carefully circumscribed, autonomy of the will. In fact, he derives freedom of the choice from the "free judgment" of reason (ST, I, 83, 1). Accordingly, most interpreters of Aquinas trace human freedom to the indeterminacy of reason, to its ability to consider a number of aspects of any object, its various desirable and undesirable features, and thus to revise its judgment about the goodness of any particular object.

What is common and deficient in these two approaches to human freedom is their essentially negative character. They accent the indeterminacy of intellect or will or both. Yves Simon coins the term "superdetermination" as a more apt description of Aquinas's view of freedom. The reason the will cannot be compelled by any particular good is that it has a natural orientation to what Aquinas calls the good in common (*bonum in communi*). The good in common is not an abstraction or an aggregate but rather the universal good containing intensively all particular goods. Thus, the will's "inexhaustible ability to transcend any particular good" arises from the its "living relationship to the comprehensive good." This relationship requires that the will "invalidate the claim of any particular good" to be the good in common.[14]

To see the advantages of construing freedom as superdetermination, one might ponder the difference between a virtuous and nonvirtuous, though not necessarily vicious, agent. Someone, for example, who lacks the virtue of courage or possesses it imperfectly is, in a situation that calls for the exercise of courage, likely to lack determination, to be torn between the options of courage and cowardice. The virtuous person by contrast will readily and with delight conform to what courage demands. Indeed, a perfectly virtuous person is incapable of knowingly acting otherwise. The question is, Who is more free in this circumstance? The one who lacks virtue and thus has an indeterminate will? Or the virtuous one whose will is superdetermined? We are who we are, ordered to goods appropriate to our nature, no matter what we may think or do. Aquinas is thus diametrically opposed to the popular view that our freedom consists in our capacity of radical self-creation. Of course nature does not dictate one way of life for all; a variety of ways of life are compatible with the ends consonant to our nature. We can certainly act against our nature and

---

[14]Yves Simon, *Freedom of Choice* (New York: Fordham University Press, 1969), pp. 97–106 and 152–158.

frustrate its telos. Or we can actively, consciously, and freely appropriate natural ends and in that sense "make" them our own. In its fullest sense, then, freedom would consist in self-appropriation, in embracing in a concrete and personal way the hierarchy of goods appropriate to our nature.

Throughout his reflections on human nature, Aquinas highlights the marvelous union of soul and body. The implications of that union are clear from his discussions of the human body and the passions. In response to the query whether God gave the human body an apt disposition (ST, I, 91, 3), Aquinas focuses on the "upright stature" of human beings.[15] The consequences for our relationship to the world are telling. In animals, the senses reside primarily in the face; since our face is not turned toward the ground, our senses are not confined to performing biological functions necessary for survival: pursuing food and fending off attackers. Our senses provide avenues for higher-level interaction with nature and other human beings. We are open to and receptive of the whole: "The subtlety of sight surveys the truth of all things." Our mouths do not protrude and are not primarily suited for self-defense and procuring food. If our mouths and tongues were like those of other animals, they would "hinder speech which is the proper work of reason."

It has sometimes been suggested that Western philosophical reflection about mind is wedded to an abstract and detached model of objectivity, which crystallizes in a penchant for comparing mind exclusively with sight. Aquinas's emphasis on the embodiment of reason in speech and on touch as the most human of the senses undercuts such a model. In response to the question whether the rational soul is united to an appropriate body, he highlights the importance of the sense of touch (ST, I, 76, 5).[16] By comparison with the bodies of other animals, the human body seems infirmed, that is, less immediately equipped with powers serving the maintenance of life. Instead of a "fixed" set of bodily powers, it has reason and the hand, the organ of organs, able to craft limitless tools. Moreover, the human body is ordered to activities eclipsing that of mere survival: knowledge-seeking, communication, and love. For these, it requires an "equable complexion, a mean between contraries," giving it the ability to receive and discriminate an array of sensible qualities. Such

---

[15]See Erwin Strauss, "The Upright Posture," in his *Phenomenological Psychology* (New York: Basic Books, 1996), pp. 137–165.   [16]See Stanley Rosen, "Thought and Touch: A Note on *Aristotle's De Anima*," *Phronesis* 6 (1961), pp. 127–137.

a complexion is prominent in the sense of touch, especially in the hand, which "actually grasps and takes on the form of the thing held."[17]

The participation of the lower, sensitive powers in reason is prominent in Aquinas's examination of the passions.[18] Since the passions reside in the sensitive rather than the intellectual appetite, it might seem they could not be subject to moral appraisal. The faulty assumption here is that of an unbridgable gap between intellect and will, on the one hand, and the sensitive appetite, on the other. Aquinas counters with Aristotle's teaching that, although the lower appetites are not intrinsically rational, they are amenable to rational persuasion and thus may participate in reason (ST, I-II, 24, 1, ad 2). Aquinas divides the passions into concupiscible and irascible. The former (which includes love and hatred, joy and sorrow) pertains to sensible good and evil absolutely, whereas the latter (which encompasses hope and despair, daring and fear) has a more narrow scope: the difficult good or evil (ST I-II 23, 1). The restricted scope of the irascible passions indicates their auxiliary and subordinate role; they are called into action when we encounter arduous goods or onerous evils. Since they concern a restricted good, they pertain to movement alone, as in struggle or flight, not to repose. Thus, the concupiscible powers are prior to the irascible; and among the concupiscible, the first is love, whose inclination to the good is the cause of all the passions (ST, I-II, 25, 2). We can see here an important consequence of Aquinas's view of desire and natural inclination as ordered to appropriate ends, as fulfilled in joyful repose.

Aquinas's conception of the dignity of the human body and of the participation of the sensitive powers in reason underscores the mysterious unity of body and soul, what the poet John Donne calls the "subtile knot, which makes us man."[19] His poem "The Extasie" begins with a seemingly Platonic scene: two lovers lying next to one another while their souls ascend above their bodies and become one. The immateriality of the souls does not preclude their union with their bodies; in fact, that union is nat-

---

[17]Leon Kass writes: "Thinking about the body is . . . constraining and liberating for the thinker: constraining because it shows him the limits on the power of thought to free him from embodiment, setting limits on thought understood as a tool for mastery; liberating because it therefore frees him to wonder about the irreducibly mysterious union and concretion of mind and body that we both are and live," in *Toward a More Natural Science* (New York: Free Press, 1985), p. 295.
[18]See Mark Jordan, "Aquinas's Construction of a Moral Account of the Passions," *Freiburger Zeitschrift fur Philosophie unde Theologie* 33 (1986). [19]"The Extasie," in *The Complete Poetry and Selected Prose of John Donne* (New York: Modern Library, 1952), pp. 39–41.

ural and appropriate, providing suitable vehicles for the communication of love. In Thomistic fashion, Donne proceeds to reverse the Platonic thesis of the soul trapped in the body:

> So must pure lovers soules descend
> T'affections, and to faculties,
> Which sense may reach and apprehend.
> Else a great Prince in prison lies.
> To' our bodies turn we then, that so
> Weake men on love reveal'd may looke;
> Loves mysteries in soules doe grow,
> But yet the body is his booke.

I would like to thank Stephen Brown, Alfred Freddoso, and Brian Rak for their comments on this Introduction.

Thomas S. Hibbs
Boston College

1

THE IMPORTANCE OF THE STUDY OF
THE SOUL AND ITS METHOD

Aristotle's *De Anima*
(402ª1–403ª2)

BOOK I, CHAPTER 1

Introduction. The Importance and
Difficulty of the Study of the Soul

Holding as we do that knowledge is a good and honorable thing, yet that some kinds of knowledge are more so than others, either because they are more certain or because they deal with subjects more excellent and wonderful, we naturally give a primary place, for both these reasons, to an enquiry about the soul. §§ 1–6

Indeed an acquaintance with the soul would seem to help much in acquiring all truth, especially about the natural world; for it is, as it were, the principle of living things. § 7

We seek then to consider and understand, first, its nature and essence, then whatever qualities belong to it. Of these, some seem to be proper to the soul alone, others to be shared in common and to exist in animate beings on account of it. § 8

To ascertain, however, anything reliable about it is one of the most difficult of undertakings. Such an enquiry being common to many topics—I mean, an enquiry into the essence, and what each thing *is*—it might seem to some that one definite procedure were available for all things of which we wished to know the essence; as there is demonstration for the acciden-

Selections on pp. 1–59 reprinted from Thomas Aquinas, *Commentary on Aristotle's De Anima*, translated by Kenelm Foster, O.P., and Silvester Humphries, O.P. (1954; rp:. South Bend, Ind.: Dumb Ox Books). Used with permission. Headings are those of the translators.

tal properties of things. So we should have to discover what is this one method. But if there is no one method for determining what an essence is, our enquiry becomes decidedly more difficult, and we shall have to find a procedure for each case in particular. If, on the other hand, it is clear that either demonstration, or division, or some such process is to be employed, there are still many queries and uncertainties to which answers must be found. For the *principles* in different subject-matters are different, for instance in the case of numbers and surfaces. Perhaps the first thing needed is to divide off the genus of the subject and to say what sort of thing it is,—I mean, whether it be a particular thing or substance, or a quality, or quantity, or any other of the different categories. Further, whether it is among things in potency or is an actuality—no insignificant distinction. Again, whether it is divisible or indivisible, and whether every soul is of the same sort or no: and if not, whether they differ specifically or generically. Indeed those who at present talk of and discuss the soul seem to deal only with the human soul. One must be careful not to leave unexplored the question whether there is a single definition of it, as of "animal" in general, or a different one for each [of its kinds]: as, say, for horse, dog, man or god. Now "animal" as a universal is nothing re   al, or is secondary; and we must say the same of any other general predicate.

§§ 9–13

Further, if there are not many souls, but only many parts of a single one, we must ask whether one ought to look first at the whole or the parts. It is difficult to see what parts are by nature diverse from one another, and whether one ought to look first at the parts or their functions, for instance at the act of understanding or at the intellective power, at the act of sensing or at the sensitive faculty; and likewise in other instances. But if one is to examine first the operations, it might be asked whether one should not first enquire about their objects, as, in the sensitive function, the thing sensed; and in the intellectual, the thing intelligible.   § 14

Now, it seems that not only does knowledge of the essence help one to understand the causes of the accidents of any substance (as in Mathematics to know what is the straight and the curved and what is a line and what a plane enables one to discover the number of right angles to which those of a triangle are equal) but, conversely, accidental qualities contribute much to knowing what a thing essentially is. When we can give an account of such qualities (some or all) according to appearances, then we shall have material for dealing as well as possible with the essence. The principle of every demonstration is *what* a thing is. Hence, whatsoever definitions do not afford us a knowledge of accidents, or even a fair conjecture about them, are obviously vain and sophistical.   § 15

Aquinas's Commentary
Lecture 1

§ 1. In studying any class of things, it is first of all necessary, as the Philosopher says in the *De Animalibus*, to consider separately what is common to the class as a whole, and afterwards what is proper to particular members of the class. Such is Aristotle's method in First Philosophy; for at the beginning of the *Metaphysics* he investigates the common properties of being as such, and only then does he go on to the particular kinds of being. The reason for this procedure is that it saves frequent repetition.

Now living beings taken all together form a certain class of being; hence in studying them the first thing to do is to consider what living things have in common, and afterwards what each has peculiar to itself. What they have in common is a life-principle or soul;[1] in this they are all alike. In conveying knowledge, therefore, about living things one must first convey it about the soul as that which is common to them all. Thus when Aristotle sets out to treat of living things, he begins with the soul; after which, in subsequent books, he defines the properties of particular living beings.

§ 2. In the present treatise on the soul we find, first, an Introduction: in which the author does the three things that should be done in any Introduction. For in writing an Introduction one has three objects in view: first, to gain the reader's good will; secondly, to dispose him to learn; thirdly, to win his attention. The first object one achieves by showing the reader the value of the knowledge in question; the second by explaining the plan and divisions of the treatise; the third by warning him of its difficulties. And all this Aristotle does here. First, he points out the high value of the science he is introducing. Secondly, at "We seek then . . ."he explains the plan of the treatise. Thirdly, at "To ascertain anything reliable . . ." he warns of its difficulty. Under the first point he explains, first the dignity of this science, and then, at "Indeed, an acquaintance . . ." its utility.

§ 3. As regards, then, the said dignity we should note that, while all knowledge is good and even honourable, one science can surpass another

---

[1] *Anima*: henceforth rendered "soul."

in this respect. All knowledge is obviously good because the good of anything is that which belongs to the fulness of being which all things seek after and desire; and man as man reaches fulness of being through knowledge. Now of good things some are just valuable, namely, those which are useful in view of some end—as we value a good horse because it runs well; whilst other good things are also honourable: namely, those that exist for their own sake; for we give honour to ends, not means. Of the sciences some are practical, others speculative; the difference being that the former are for the sake of some work to be done, while the latter are for their own sake. The speculative sciences are therefore honourable as well as good, but the practical are only valuable. Every speculative science is both good and honourable.

§ 4. Yet even among the speculative sciences there are degrees of goodness and honourableness. Every science is valued first of all as a kind of activity, and the worth of any activity is reckoned in two ways: from its object and from its mode or quality. Thus building is a better activity than bed-making because its object is better. But where the activities are the same in kind, and result in the same thing, the quality alone makes a difference; if a building is better built it will be a better building. Considering then science, or its activity, from the point of view of the object, that science is nobler which is concerned with better and nobler things; but from the point of view of mode or quality, the nobler science is that which is more certain. One science, then, is reckoned nobler than another, either because it concerns better and nobler objects or because it is more certain.

§ 5. Now there is this difference between sciences, that some excel in certainty and yet are concerned with inferior objects, while others with higher and better objects are nevertheless less certain. All the same, that science is the better which is about better and nobler things; because, as the Philosopher observes in Book XI of the *De Animalibus*, we have a greater desire for even a little knowledge of noble and exalted things—even for a conjectural and probable sort of knowledge—than for a great and certain knowledge of inferior things. For the former is noble in itself and essentially, but the latter only through its quality or mode.

§ 6. Now this science of the soul has both merits. It has certainty; for everyone knows by experience that he has a soul which is his life-principle. Also it has a high degree of nobility; for among lower things the soul has a special nobility. This is what Aristotle means here when he says, "Holding as we do that knowledge," i.e. speculative science, "is good and honourable." And one science is better and nobler than another in two ways: either, as we have seen, because it is more certain—hence he says "more certain,"—or because it is about "more excellent" things, i.e. things that are good in themselves, and "more wonderful things," i.e. things whose cause is unknown. "For both these reasons," he goes on to say, "we give a primary place to an enquiry about the soul." He uses the term "enquiry" because he is going to discuss the soul in a general way, without attempting, in this treatise, a thorough examination of all its properties. As to the words "a primary place," if they are taken as applying to the whole of Natural Science, then they refer to superiority in dignity and not to priority in order; but if they refer to the science of living things only, they mean priority of order.

§ 7. Then, with "Indeed an acquaintance etc." he gains the reader's good will by showing the utility of this science. Some knowledge of the soul, he says, would seem to be very useful in all the other sciences. It can be of considerable service to philosophy in general. In First Philosophy it is impossible to attain knowledge of the divine and highest causes except through what we can acquire by actualising our intellectual power; and if we knew nothing about the nature of this power we should know nothing about the immaterial substances, as the Commentator remarks *à propos* of Book XI of the *Metaphysics*. Again, as regards Moral Philosophy. We cannot master the science of morals unless we know the powers of the soul; thus in the Ethics[2] the Philosopher assigns the virtues to the different powers. So, too, it is useful for the Natural Scientist, because many of the things he studies are animate things, all of whose movements originate in the soul: "for it is," says Aristotle, "as it were, the principle of living things": The phrase "as it were" does not express a comparison; it is descriptive.

§ 8. Next, at "We seek then," he states the plan of his treatise, saying that we are "to consider," i.e. by way of outward symptoms, and "to understand," i.e. by way of demonstration, what the soul really is in its nature and essence; "and then whatever qualities belong to it" or affect it. But in the latter a diversity appears: for while some of the soul's modifications, such as understanding and speculative knowledge, seem to belong to the soul of and in itself, others, such as pleasure and pain, the senses and imagination, though they depend on some soul or other, seem to be common to all animals.

§ 9. Then at "To ascertain," he introduces the difficulty of this study; and this from two points of view. It is hard, first, to know the essence of the soul, and secondly to know its accidents or characteristic qualities. As

---

[2]E.N., I, 13, 1102a 5ss.

to the essence, there is a double difficulty: first, as to how it ought to be defined, and then as to the elements of the definition (this point comes at "Perhaps the first thing needed").

He remarks, therefore, that while knowledge of the soul would be valuable, it is not easy to know just what the soul is. Now this is a difficulty in studying anything; for the question about substance and essence is common to the study of soul and of many other things; the first difficulty being that we do not know what method to use; for some say we should use deductive demonstration, others the method of elimination, others one of comparison. Aristotle himself preferred the method of comparison.

§ 10. The second difficulty concerns the elements of the definition. A definition manifests a thing's essence; and this cannot be grasped apart from the principles on which it depends. But different things have different principles, and it is hard to see which principle is involved in any particular thing. Hence, in formulating or seeking for a definition of soul we encounter three main difficulties: (*a*) concerning its essence; (*b*) concerning its parts; (*c*) concerning that necessary contribution to a definition which comes from knowing the soul's accidental qualities.

§ 11. As regards the essence of soul there is a doubt about that which is the first thing to be looked for in defining anything, i.e. the genus to which it belongs. What is the genus of soul? Is it a substance or a quantity or a quality? And not only must we decide upon the ultimate genus, but also on the proximate one; thus we do not define man as a substance, but as an animal. And if soul is found to belong to the genus of substance we shall still have to decide whether it is actual or potential substance, since every genus can be regarded both as potential and as actual. Also, since substances are either composite or simple, we shall have to ask whether soul is one or the other, and whether it is divisible or indivisible. There is also the question whether all souls are of the same species or not; and if they are not, whether they are generically different or not. Again there is uncertainty as to what is to be included in the definition, some things being defined in terms of genus, some as species; hence the question whether we should define soul in terms of genus or as the specification of a species.

§ 12. For some enquirers seem to have in view only the human soul. Among the earlier philosophers there were two opinions about soul. The Platonists, holding that universals existed separately as the Forms or Ideas that caused knowledge and being in individual things, maintained that there was a Soul-in-Itself which was the cause and "idea" of particular souls and from which all that we find in these drew its origin. On the other hand were the Natural Philosophers who maintained that no universal substances existed in the real world, that the only real things were individuals. And this raises the question for us, whether we, like the Platonists, ought to look for one common idea of Soul; or rather, as the Natural Philosophers said, study this or that particular soul, e.g. of horse or man, or god. He says "or god" because at that time men believed that the heavenly bodies were gods, and that they were alive.

§ 13. However, Aristotle chose to seek a definition of both—of Soul in general and of each kind of soul. But when he says, on this point, that "animal as universal is nothing real, or is secondary," we must understand that one can speak of a "universal animal" in two ways: either as *universal*, i.e. as one nature existing in, or predicated of, many individuals; or as *animal*. And both these aspects can be regarded either in relation to existence in the real world or as existing in the mind. As regards existence in the real world, Plato held that the universal animal did so exist and existed prior to particular animals; because, as has been said, he thought that there were universals and ideas with an independent existence. Aristotle, however, said that the universal as such had no real existence, and that if it was anything at all it came after the individual thing. But if we regard the nature of animals from a different point of view, i.e. not as a universal, then it is indeed something real, and it precedes the individual animal as the potential precedes the actual.

§ 14. Then, at "Further, if there are not many," Aristotle touches on the difficulties that arise concerning the soul's potentialities. For in the soul are "parts" that exist as potencies: the intellectual and sensitive and vegetative "parts." The question is whether these are different souls, as the Platonists liked to think (and even maintained), or are only potencies in the soul. And if they are potencies, we must further decide whether to enquire first into the potencies themselves, and then into their acts, or into the acts first and then the potencies—e.g. into the act of understanding before the intellect. And if we take the acts first, there is still the question whether the *objects* of these acts should be studied before the faculties, e.g. the sense-object before the sense-faculty or the thing understood before the understanding.

§ 15. Next, at "Now it seems," he states the difficulties that arise with regard to those accidental qualities which contribute to a definition of the soul. These are relevant here because a definition ought to reveal a thing's accidental qualities, as well as its essential principles. If indeed the latter could be known and correctly defined there would be no need to define the former; but since the essential principles of things are hidden from us we are compelled to make use of accidental differences as indications of what is essential. Thus to be two-footed is not of the essence of anything, yet it helps to indicate an essence. By such accidental differences we are led towards knowledge of the essential ones. It would indeed be easier to grasp even what is accidental to the soul if we could only first understand its essence, just, as in mathematics, it is a great help towards understanding that the angles of a triangle are equal to (two) right angles to know first what is meant by straight, curved and plane. Hence the difficulty of our present position. On the other hand a prior examination of the accidental factors is a considerable help towards knowing the essence, as has been said. If, therefore, one were to propose a definition from which no knowledge of the accidental attributes of the defined thing could be derived, such a definition would not be real, but abstract and hypothetical. But one from which a knowledge of the accidents flows is a real definition, based on what is proper and essential to the thing.

BOOK I, CHAPTER 1, CONTINUED

Introduction Continued
Questions of Method

The modifications of the soul present a problem: are they all shared by
what has soul, or are some proper to the soul alone?   § 16

It is necessary indeed, but not easy, to deal with this problem. For in
most cases there is, apparently, no action or being acted on without the
body; as in anger, desire, confidence, and sensation in general. Understanding however would seem especially proper to the soul. Yet if this too
is a sort of imagination, or never occurs without it, not even this exists, in
fact, apart from the body.   §§ 17–20

But if the soul has some operation or affection exclusive to itself, then
it could exist as a separate entity. If, however, there is nothing thus proper
to it, then it is not separable, but is like a straight line, which has, as such,
many properties—such as being able to touch a bronze sphere at a given
point; but straightness separated does not touch it; not being in fact separable, since it is always with a bodily subject.   § 21

Now all the soul's modifications do seem to involve the body—anger,
meekness, fear, compassion, and joy and love and hate. For along with
these the body also is to some degree affected. An indication of this is that
sometimes violent and unmistakable occurrences arouse no excitement or
alarm; while at other times one is moved by slight and trifling matters,
when the physical system is stimulated to the condition appropriate to
anger. This is still more evident when, nothing fearful being present, feel-
ings occur as in one who is frightened. If this is the case, it is evident that
the passions are material principles; hence such terms as "becoming
angry" mean a motion of such and such a body, or of a part or power proceeding from and existing for the body.   § 22

For this reason, therefore, the natural scientist ought to examine the
soul, either all kinds, or this kind.   § 23

The natural scientist and the dialectician will define each of those modifications differently. Take the question, what is anger? The latter will say, a desire for retaliation, or something similar; the former, an effervescence of blood or heat about the heart. Of these, the natural scientist designates the matter, the dialectician, the form or idea. For this "idea" is the thing's form. This however must have existence in material of the sort in question; if it is a house, one formula will be, "a covering to prevent destruction from wind and rain and excessive heat;" the other, "stones and beams and timber;" another, "the form; in these materials; for those reasons." Which is the physical definition? That which states the matter and ignores the idea? Or that which states the idea only? Or rather, the compound of both? What then of the other two? Now there is no one who deals with inseparable qualities of matter, precisely as inseparable from it; but he who is concerned with the affections and activities of the special matter of this or that body is the natural scientist; whereas whatever things are not specifically such, another considers; in certain matters it may perchance be a technical expert, a carpenter or physician. Concerning however what is inseparable from matter, and yet as *not* involved in the specific qualities of this or that body, but abstracted from any, the mathematician; and concerning what is separable, the "first philosopher."

§§ 24–9

To return from our digression. We were saying that the passions of the soul are not separable from the physical material of animals (anger and fear having this kind of existence), and yet also that they differ, in this, from the line and the surface.

Aquinas's Commentary
Lecture 2

§ 16. Having stated the difficulty of this science in respect of the problem of the soul's substance and essence, the Philosopher proceeds to the problem of its modifications and accidental qualities. And here he does two things: he states, first, and solves a difficulty concerning the soul's modifications; and then, using this solution, he shows that knowledge of the soul pertains to natural science or "physics," where he says, "For this reason, therefore, the natural scientist. . . ." As to the first point, he says it is a problem whether the soul's modifications and activities belong to it independently of the body, as Plato thought, or are none of them peculiar to the soul, being all shared by soul and body together.

§ 17. Going on at "It is necessary," he again does two things. First he shows the difficulty of the question, and then, at "But if the soul. . . ." the necessity of putting it. He begins then by observing that we cannot avoid the question whether the soul's modes and activities are proper to it or shared by the body, and that this is not an easy question but a very difficult one. The difficulty, as he explains, arises from the fact that many activities *seem* to be common to soul and body and to require the body, for instance, getting angry and having sensations and so on; which all involve body as well as soul. If there is anything peculiar to the soul it would appear to be the intellectual activity or understanding; this seems to belong to the soul in a special way.

§ 18. And yet, on closer consideration, even understanding would not seem to pertain to the soul alone. For either it is the same as imagination, as the Platonists thought, or it does not occur without the use of imagination (for there used to be men, such as the early natural philosophers, who said that intellect in no way differed from the senses, which would imply that it does not differ from the imagination; as indeed the Platonists were led to say). As, then, imagination presupposes the body and depends on it they said that understanding was common to soul and body together, rather than the work of the soul alone. And even granted that intellect and imagination are not identical, still the one cannot function without the other. It would follow that understanding is not of the soul alone, since imagining presupposes the body. Understanding then, it seems, does not occur where there is no body.

§ 19. Now although Aristotle clears up this problem in Book III, we shall say something about it here. Understanding, then, is in one sense, proper to the soul alone, and in another sense common to both soul and body. For it should be realised that certain activities or modifications of the soul depend on the body both as an instrument and as an object. Sight, for instance, needs a body as object—because its object is colour, which is only found in bodies;—and also as an instrument—because, while the act of seeing involves the soul, it cannot occur except through the instrumentality of a visual organ, the pupil of the eye. Sight then is the act of the organ as well as of the soul. But there is one activity which only depends on the body to provide its object, not its instrument; for understanding is not accomplished with a bodily organ, though it does bear on a bodily object; because, as will be shown later, in Book III, the phantasms in the imagination are to the intellect as colours to sight: as colours provide sight with its object, so do the phantasms serve the intellect. Since then there cannot be phantasms without a body, it seems that understanding presupposes a body—not, however, as its instrument, but simply as its object.

§ 20. Two things follow from this. (1) Understanding is an act proper to the soul alone, needing the body, as was said above, only to provide its object; whereas seeing and various other functions involve the compound of soul and body together. (2) Whatever operates of itself independently, has also an independent being and subsistence of its own; which is not the case where the operation is not independent. Intellect then is a self-subsistent actuality, whereas the other faculties are actualities existing in matter. And the difficulty in dealing with this type of question arises simply from the fact that all functions of the soul seem at first sight to be also functions of the body.

§ 21. After this, when Aristotle says "But if the soul" he states a reason for putting this question, namely, that on its answer depends the answer to a question that everyone asks very eagerly about the soul: whether it can be separated from the body. So he says that if the soul has any function proper to itself it can certainly be separated, because, as was pointed out above, whatever can operate on its own can exist on its own. Conversely, if the soul had no such proper function it would not be separable from the body; it would be in the same case as a straight line—for though many things can happen to a straight line *qua* straight line, such as touching a brass sphere at a certain point, still they can only come about in a material way: a straight line cannot touch a brass sphere at any point except materially. So also with the soul; if it has no activity proper to itself, then, however many things affect it, they will do so only in a material way.

§ 22. Next, when he says "Now all the soul's" he draws out what had been presupposed above, namely that certain modifications affect soul and body together, not the soul alone. And this he shows by one argument in two parts; which runs as follows. Whenever the physical constitution of the body contributes to a vital activity, the latter pertains to the body as well as the soul; but this happens in the case of all the "modifications" of the soul, such as anger, meekness, fear, confidence, pity and so on; hence all these "modifications" would seem to belong partly to the body. And to show that the physical constitution plays a part in them he uses two arguments. (1) We sometimes see a man beset by obvious and severe afflictions without being provoked or frightened, whereas when he is already excited by violent passions arising from his bodily disposition, he is disturbed by mere trifles and behaves as though he were really angry. (2) At "This is still more evident": what makes this point even clearer is that we see in some people, even when there is no danger present, passions arising that resemble one such "modification" of the soul; for instance melancholy people, simply as a result of their physical state, are often timid when there is no real cause to be. Obviously then, if the bodily constitution has this effect on the passions, the latter must be "material principles," i.e. must exist in matter. This is why "such terms," i.e. the definitions of these passions, are not to be predicated without reference to matter; so that if anger is being defined, let it be called a movement "of some body" such as the heart, or "of some part or power" of the body. Saying this he refers to the subject or material cause of the passion; whereas "proceeding from" refers to the efficient cause; and "existing for" to the final cause.

§ 23. Then at "For this reason," he concludes from the foregoing that the study of the soul pertains to natural science—a conclusion following from the way the soul is defined. So he does two things here: (1) he proves his statement; (2) he pursues his discussion of definitions, where he says "the natural scientist and the dialectician." The proof of his statement runs thus. Activities and dispositions of the soul are also activities and dispositions of the body, as has been shown. But the definition of any disposition must include that which is disposed; for its subject always falls within the definition of a disposition. If, then, dispositions of this kind are in the body as well as in the soul, the former must be included in their definition. And since everything bodily or material falls within the scope of natural science, so also must the dispositions of which we speak. Moreover, since the subject of any dispositions enters into the study of them, it must be the task of the natural scientist to study the soul,—either absolutely "all" souls, or "of this kind," i.e. the soul that is joined to a body. He adds this because he has left it uncertain whether intellect is joined to the body.

§ 24. Where he says "The natural scientist and the dialectician" he continues his discussion of definitions. Explaining that, while some definitions of the dispositions of the soul include matter and the body, others exclude matter and refer only to the form, he shows that the latter kind of definition is inadequate. This leads him to go into the difference between these types of definition. Sometimes the body is omitted, as when anger is defined as a desire of revenge; and sometimes the bodily or material factor is included, as when anger is called a heating of blood round the heart. The former is a logical definition, but the latter is physical, since it includes a material factor, and so pertains to the natural scientist. The natural scientist points to the material factor when he says that anger is a heating of blood round the heart; whereas the dialectician points to the species or formal principle; since to call anger a desire of revenge is to state its formal principle.

§ 25. Now the first type of definition is obviously inadequate. The definition of any form existing in a particular matter must take account of the matter. This form, "the desire for retaliation," exists in a definite matter, and if the matter is not included, the definition is clearly inadequate. The definition, then, must state that this thing, i.e. the form, has being in this particular sort of matter.

§ 26. Thus we have three kinds of definition. The first states the species and specific principle of a thing, and is purely formal,—as if one were to define a house as a shelter from wind, rain and heat. The second kind indicates the matter, as when a house is called a shelter made of stones and beams and wood. But the third kind includes in the definition "both," namely matter and form, calling a house a particular kind of shelter, built of particular material, for a particular purpose—to keep out the wind, etc. So he says that "another" definition has three elements: the material, "in these," i.e. beams and stones; the formal, "the form"; and the final, "for those reasons," i.e. to keep out the wind. So matter is included when he says "in these," form when he says "form," and the final cause when he says "for those reasons." All three are needed for a perfect definition.

§ 27. To the question which of these types of definition pertains to the natural scientist, I answer that the purely formal one is not physical but logical. That which includes matter but omits the form pertains to no one but the natural scientist, because only he is concerned with matter. Yet that which includes both factors is also in a special way the natural scientist's. Thus two of these definitions pertain to natural science, but of the two the merely material one is imperfect, while the other, that includes the form also, is perfect. For only the natural scientist studies the *inseparable* dispositions of matter.

§ 28. But there are various ways of studying the dispositions of matter, as Aristotle now proceeds to show. He divides the students of these dispositions into three classes. One class consists of those who, while they study material dispositions, differ from the natural scientist in their point of view; thus the craftsman differs from the scientist in that he starts from the point of view of art, but the natural scientist from that of real nature. Another class consists of those who, though they consider forms that exist in sense-perceptible matter, do not include such matter in their definitions. The forms referred to are such as curved, straight, and so on, which, though they exist in matter and are, in fact, inseparable from it, are not, by the mathematician, regarded under their sense-perceptible aspect.

The reason is that if it is through its *quality* that a thing is sense-percepti-ble, quality *presupposes* quantity; hence the mathematician abstracts from this or that particular material factor in order to attend exclusively to the purely quantitative. Finally, the third class studies things whose existence is either completely independent of matter or can be found without mat-ter. This is First Philosophy.

§ 29. Note that this division of Philosophy is entirely based on defini-tion and the method of defining. The reason is that definition is the prin-ciple of demonstration. Since things are defined by their essential principles, diverse definitions reveal a diversity of essential principles; and this implies a diversity of sciences. . . .

2

DEFINING SOUL

Aristotle's *De Anima*
(412ª1–412ᵇ9)

BOOK II, CHAPTER 1
The Definition of the Soul

Hitherto we have spoken of what our predecessors handed down to us about the soul. But let us now re-open the enquiry from the beginning and endeavour to determine what the soul is and what is its most comprehensive definition.   § 211

Now, we say that one of the kinds of things that are is substance. Of this, there is one element, matter, which of itself is no particular thing; another, the form or species according to which it is called "this particular thing"; and a third, that which is from both of these. Matter is, indeed, potency, and the form, act; and this latter has two modes of being, one, like knowledge possessed, the other, like the act of knowing.   §§ 212–16

Bodies especially seem to be substances; and, among these, natural bodies, for these are the principles of the others. Of natural bodies, some possess vitality, others do not. We mean by "possessing vitality," that a thing can nourish itself and grow and decay.   §§ 217–19

Therefore every natural body sharing in life will be a substance, and this substance will be in some way composite. Since, however, it is a body of such and such a nature, i.e. having vitality, the soul will not itself be the body. For the body is not one of the factors existing in the subject; rather, it *is* as the subject and the matter. It is necessary, then, that the soul be a substance in the sense of the specifying principle of a physical body potentially alive. Now, substance [in this sense] is act; it will therefore be the act of a body of this sort.   §§ 220–6

16

[handwritten note] ↑ not an artificial or non-living body.
* Soul is the actuality of a living body *

Now this can mean one of two things: one, as is the possession of knowledge; another, as is the act of knowing. It is plain that it is like knowledge possessed. For the soul remains in the body whether one is asleep or awake. Being awake is comparable to the act of knowing, sleep to possession without use. Now knowledge possessed is prior in the order of generation, in one and the same thing. The soul, therefore, is the primary act of a physical body capable of life.   §§ 227–9

Such a body will be organic. Parts of plants, indeed, are organs, though very elementary—the leaf is the covering of the pericarp and the pericarp of the fruit: roots, too, are like mouths, for both draw in nourishment.

§§ 230–2

If, then, there is any one generalisation to be made for any and every soul, the soul will be the primary act of a physical bodily organism.

§ 233

Hence it is unnecessary to enquire whether the soul and body be *one*, any more than whether the wax and an impression made in it are one; or in general, the matter of anything whatever, and that of which it is the matter. For while *one* and *being* are predicated in many ways, that which is properly so is actuality.   § 234

Aquinas's Commentary

Lecture 1

§ 211. Having reviewed, in Book One, other men's opinions on the soul, Aristotle now begins Book Two of his Treatise, in which he sets out what he himself holds on the matter. First, then, linking up with what has gone before, he states his general aim; and secondly, at "Now we say that one," he starts to carry it out. He begins by saying that despite all the previous accounts of the soul it is necessary to go into the whole matter again from the beginning. The subject is so difficult that it is wiser to assume that the truth about it has not yet been discovered. And in answer to the question raised in the Introduction to Book One, whether one should first define the soul, and afterwards its parts, he decides now to define the essence of the soul before coming to conclusions about its parts. As though explaining this decision, he adds that we shall thus have acquired the most comprehensive idea of soul. For the definition of the soul itself comprises what is most common or general, whereas that of each of its parts or potencies comprises only some special aspect of it. And as he explains at the beginning of the *Physics*, the right way to teach is to begin with what is most general and end with precisions in detail.

§ 212. Beginning then at "Now we say," his treatment divides into two parts, in the first of which he shows what soul in general is, and in the second, starting at "Of the soul's powers," what are its parts or powers. The first part subdivides into (*a*) a definition that concludes, and (*b*) one that introduces, a demonstrative argument;—this latter part comes at "Since it is from the less clear." Note in passing that any definition, as he says in Book I of the *Posterior Analytics*, is either the conclusion of a demonstration, e.g. "Thunder is a continuous noise in the clouds," or it is the demonstration's starting point, e.g. "Thunder is the extinction of fire in the clouds," or it is the demonstration itself, but thrown into a different order, e.g. "Thunder is a continuous noise etc., caused by the extinction of fire etc." in which the conclusion and the starting point both appear, though not in syllogistic order.

As to (*a*), it includes first a definition of the soul, and then, at "It has been stated then," an explanation of the definition. And to clear the ground before the defining proper begins (at "Therefore every natural body") he makes some preliminary distinctions.

§ 213. It should be noted here that, according to the teaching of Book VII of the *Metaphysics*, there is this difference between defining substance and defining accidents that in the former case nothing *extrinsic* is included: every substance is defined in terms merely of its material and formal principles; but in the latter case something extrinsic to the thing defined is referred to, i.e. the subject of the accidents in question—as when one defines snubness as "curvature of the nose." The reason is that a definition must express what a thing is, and while substance is something complete in its being and kind, accidents have being only in relation to a substance. In the same way no *form* as such is complete in kind; completeness in this sense belongs only to the substance composed of form and matter; so that the latter's definition is complete without reference to anything else, whilst that of the form has to include a reference to its proper subject which is matter. Hence, if the soul is a form its definition will not be complete without reference to its subject or matter.

§ 214. So, in the first part of this section, he makes certain distinctions, first in view of the work of defining the soul's *essence*, and then, at "Bodies especially seem to be substances . . ." in view of defining its *subject*. As regards the former point he alludes to three distinctions, of which the first is that of being into the ten categories; this he hints at when he says that substance is reckoned to be "one of the kinds of things that are."

§ 215. The second distinction alluded to is that of substance into matter, form and the compound of both. Matter is that which is not as such a "particular thing," but is in mere potency to become a "particular thing." Form is that by which a "particular thing" actually exists. And the compound is, the "particular thing" itself; for that is said to be a "particular thing" (i.e. something you can point to) which is complete in being and in kind; and among material things only the compound is such. For although immaterial substances are not compounds of matter and form, still they are particular things, having actual existence in themselves, and being complete in their own nature. Not so the rational soul; for though it has the existence in itself which belongs to a "particular thing," it is not a complete nature by itself; it is rather a *part* of a specific nature. Hence it is not in all respects a "particular thing."

Matter, then, differs from form in this, that it is potential being; form is the "entelechy" or actuality that renders matter actual; and the compound is the resulting actual being.

§ 216. Thirdly, he distinguishes two senses of the term "act." In one sense knowledge is an act, in the other thinking is an act; and the difference can be understood by relating these acts to their potencies. Before one acquires the grammatical habit and becomes a grammarian, whether self-taught or led by another, one is only potentially so; and this potency is actualised by the *habit*. But once the habit is acquired one is still in potency to the *use* of it, so long as one is not actually thinking about grammar; and this thinking is a further actualisation. In this sense, then, knowledge is one act and thinking another.

§ 217. Then at "Bodies especially" he alludes to three distinctions which are presupposed by his enquiry into the meaning of the definition of the soul, so far as the *subject* endowed with soul is concerned. The first is the distinction between corporeal and incorporeal substances. Now the former are the most evident to us: for, whatever the latter may be in themselves, they do not impinge on our senses, but are only discoverable by an exercise of the reason. Hence he says that "bodies especially seem to be substances."

§ 218. The next distinction is between physical or natural bodies and artificial bodies. Man and wood and stone are natural bodies, but a house or a saw is artificial. And of these the natural bodies seem to be the more properly called substances, since artificial bodies are made out of them. Art works upon materials furnished by nature, giving these, moreover, a merely accidental form, such as a new shape and so forth; so that it is only in virtue of their matter, not their form, that artificial bodies are substances at all; they are substances because natural bodies are such. Natural bodies therefore are the more properly called substances, being such through their form as well as through their matter.

§ 219. Thirdly, he distinguishes between living and non-living natural bodies; and the living are those which of themselves take nutriment and grow and decay. Note here that this is said by way of example rather than definition. For, besides growth and decay, living things may exhibit sensation and intellectual knowledge and other vital activities. Immaterial substances, as is proved in the *Metaphysics*, Book XI, have the life of intellect and volition, though they cannot grow and do not take food. But because, in the sphere of things that are born and die, the plant-soul (the principle of nutrition and growth) marks the point where life begins, this soul is here taken as the type of all living things. However, life is essentially that by which anything has power to move itself, taking movement in its wide sense so as to include the "movement" or activity of the intellect. For we call those things inanimate which are moved only from outside.

§ 220. After this, at "Therefore every natural body," he begins to define the soul, presupposing the distinctions already made. And his enquiry here has three parts: (*a*) he enquires into the elements of the definition taken separately; (*b*) at, "If, then, there is any one generalisation," he states his definition; and (*c*) at "Hence it is unnecessary," he uses it to refute an objection. As to (*a*) he first deals with the elements that refer to the soul's *essence*, and then to those that refer to its *subject*, at "Such a body will be organic," and in the part that concerns the essence he considers first the statement that the soul is an "act," and then, at "Now this can mean one of two things," that it is "primary act."

Aristotle's first conclusion, then, in line with what has been said already, is that if physical bodies are substances in the fullest sense, all living bodies are substances too, for they are physical bodies. And as each living body is an actual being, it must be a compound substance. But just because to say "living body" is to imply two things, the body itself and that modification of body by which it is alive, it cannot be said that the element in the composition referred to by the term body is itself the principle of life or the "soul." By "soul" we understand that by which a living thing is alive; it is understood, therefore, as existing *in* a subject, taking "subject" in a broad sense to include not only those *actual* beings which are subjects of their accidental modifications, but also bare matter or potential being. On the other hand the body that receives life is more like a subject and a matter than a modification existing in a subject.

§ 221. Since, then, there are three sorts of substance: the compound; matter; and form; and since the soul is neither the compound—the living body itself; nor its matter—the body as the subject that receives life; we have no choice but to say that the soul is a substance in the manner of a form that determines or characterises a particular sort of body, i.e. a physical body potentially alive.

§ 222. Note that he does not say simply "alive," but "potentially alive." For by a body actually alive is understood a living compound; and no compound as such can enter into the definition of a form. On the other hand the matter of a living body stands to the body's life as a potency to its act; and the soul is precisely the actuality whereby the body has life. It is as though we were to say that shape is an actuality; it is not exactly the actuality of an actually shaped body—i.e. the compound of body and shape—but rather of the body as able to receive a shape, of the body as in potency to an actual shape.

§ 223. But lest it be thought that soul is an actuality in the manner of any merely accidental form, he adds that it is a substantial actuality or form. And since every form has the matter proper to it, the soul must actualise just this special sort of body.

§ 224. The difference between accidental form and substantial form is that whereas the former does not make a thing simply be, but only makes it be in this or that mode—e.g. as quantified, or white—the substantial form gives it simple being. Hence the accidental form presupposes an already existing subject; but the substantial form presupposes only potentiality to existence, i.e. bare matter. That is why there cannot be more than one substantial form in any one thing; the first makes the thing an actual being; and if others are added, they confer only accidental modifications, since they presuppose the subject already in act of being.

§ 225. We can therefore reject the view of Avicebron (in the Book called *Fons Vitae*) that according to the way in which any given thing can be divided into genera and species so it can be divided into substantial forms. Thus an individual man would have one form that made him a substance, another that gave him a body, another that gave him life, and so on. But what our premises compel us to say is that it is one and the same substantial form that makes a man a particular thing or substance, and a bodily thing, and a living thing, and so on. For the higher form can give to its matter all that a lower form gives, and more; the soul gives not only substance and body (as a stone's form does) but life also. We must not think, therefore, of the soul and body as though the body had its own form making it a body, to which a soul is super-added, making it a living body; but rather that the body gets both its being and its life from the soul. This is not to deny, however, that bodily being as such is, in its imperfection, material with respect to life.

§ 226. Therefore, when life departs the body is not left specifically the same; the eyes and flesh of a dead man, as is shown in the *Metaphysics*, Book VII, are only improperly called eyes and flesh. When the soul leaves the body another substantial form takes its place; for a passing-away always involves a concomitant coming-to-be.

§ 227. Then, at "Now this can mean," he examines the second term in the definition. He observes that there are two kinds of actuality, as we explained above, the kind that is like knowledge and the kind like thinking. And clearly the soul is of the former kind; for it is due to the soul that an animal is able to be both awake and asleep; and while waking is similar to thinking (for it is a use of the exterior senses just as thinking is a use of knowledge already possessed), sleep is more like the knowledge which lies dormant in the mind so long as it is not actually being used; for in sleep an animal's faculties are quiescent.

§ 228. Now, of these two actualities, knowledge comes first in the order of coming-to-be in the same person; for it stands to thinking as potency to act. But in the order of nature or essence act is prior to potency (see the *Metaphysics*, Book IX) as the end and complete perfection of potency. And even in the temporal order of coming-to-be, act, in a quite general sense, is prior; for the potential is actualised only by something already in act. But in this or that particular thing considered in itself potentiality may come first; the thing may be actualised by degrees. Hence his remark that "knowledge . . . is prior (i.e. to thinking) in the order of generation in one and the same thing."

§ 229. So he concludes that soul is the primary act of a physical body potentially alive, where act means the same sort of actuality as knowledge. He says *primary* act, not only to distinguish soul from its subsequent activities, but also to distinguish it from the forms of the elements; for these retain their own proper activities, unless impeded.

§ 230. Next, at "Such a body," he examines that part of the definition which has to do with the soul's *subject*, observing that the "physical body" referred to is any organic body, i.e. any body equipped with the various organs required by a living body in consequence of the life-principle's various vital activities. For from this principle (the soul) which is the richest of embodied forms, spring many different activities, so that it requires, in the matter informed by it, a full equipment of different organs. Not so the less perfect forms of inanimate things.

§ 231. Now plants, the least perfect of animate things, exhibit less organic diversity than animals. That is why Aristotle chooses plants to illustrate his assertion that every animate body is organic, saying that even plants have organically diversified parts. But these parts are very simple, i.e. like to one another; they lack the differentiation that we find in animals. Thus the foot of an animal is made up of different parts, flesh, nerves, bones and so forth, but the organs of plants are composed of less diverse sets of parts.

§ 232. The organic character of the parts of plants is displayed in their diverse functions. Thus a leaf functions as a covering for the pericarp or fruit-bearing part, i.e. for the part in which the fruit is born. The pericarp, again, protects the fruit itself. So too the roots have a function in a plant similar to that of the mouth in an animal; they draw in nourishment.

§ 233. Next, at "If then," he gathers all these observations into one definition, saying that if any definition covers all types of "soul" it will be this: *the soul is the primary actuality of a physical bodily organism.* He does not need to add "having life potentially"; for this is implied in "organism."

§ 234. Then at "Hence it is" he applies this definition to solve a difficulty. There had been much uncertainty about the way the soul and body are conjoined. Some had supposed a sort of medium connecting the two together by a sort of bond. But the difficulty can be set aside now that it has been shown that the soul is the *form* of the body. As he says, there is no more reason to ask whether soul and body together make one thing than to ask the same about wax and the impression sealed on it, or about any other matter and its form. For, as is shown in the *Metaphysics*, Book VIII, form is directly related to matter as the actuality of matter; once matter actually *is* it is *informed.* Moreover, although, as he goes on to say, being and unity are variously predicated (in one way of potential, and in another way of actual, being), that is primarily and properly a being and a unity which has actuality. Just as potential being is only a being under a certain aspect, so it is only a unity under a certain aspect; for unity follows being. Therefore, just as the body gets its being from the soul, as from its form, so too it makes a unity with this soul to which it is immediately related. If, on the other hand, we regard the soul in its function as the *mover* of the body, then there is no reason why it should not move by means of a medium, moving one part of the body by means of another.

Aristotle's *De Anima*
(412ᵇ10–413ᵃ10)

BOOK II, CHAPTER 1, CONTINUED
The Definition Explained
Soul and Body

It has been stated, then, what the soul in general is. It is "substance" as definable form; and this means what is the essence of such a kind of body. If some utensil, for example an axe, were a natural body, then "being-an-axe" [axeishness] would be its substance, and this would be its soul. Apart from this, it would no longer be an axe, save equivocally. As it is, it is really an axe. And the soul is not the essence or "what-it-is" of such a body as this, but of a *natural* body, such as has in itself the principle of motion and rest.   § 235–8

Now what has been said should be considered with respect to parts. For if the eye were an animal, sight would be its soul. For this is the substance, in the sense of the definable form, of the eye. The eye is the matter of sight, and apart from this it is an eye no longer save equivocally, as with a painted or stone eye. What, therefore, holds of a part, we ought to apply to the whole living body: for the relation of a part [of the soul] to part [of the body] corresponds to that of sensitivity as a whole to the whole sensitive body, considered as such.   § 239

Not that which has cast off its soul is "capable of life," but that which possesses it. But seed and fruit are only in potency such a body. As cutting or seeing is act, so is consciousness. The soul is like sight and the capacity of a tool; the body, like the thing in potency. But as an eye is a pupil together with the power of sight, so is there a living thing where there are both body and soul.   §§ 240–1

Therefore it is evident enough that the soul is inseparable from the body—or certain parts of it, if it naturally has parts; for it is of certain bodily parts themselves that it is the act. But with respect to certain of its parts there is nothing to prevent its being separated, because these are acts of nothing bodily. Furthermore, it is not clear that the soul is not the "act" of the body in the way that a sailor is of his ship. Let these remarks serve to describe and define the soul, in outline.   §§ 242–4

Aquinas's Commentary
Lecture 2

§ 235. The Philosopher now begins to explain the definition of the soul given in Lectio 1; after which, at "Therefore it is evident," he draws a conclusion from it. The explanation has two parts, in the first of which he is concerned directly with the soul itself, while in the second, where he says "Not that which has cast off," he explains that part of the definition which refers to the subject which has a soul. With regard to the soul itself, he begins by illustrating the definition by a comparison with artificial things; and then goes on, at "Now what has . . ." to explain it by considering the parts of the soul separately.

In artificial things, made by human skill, the forms imposed on the material are accidental forms; and since these are easier for us to perceive than is substantial form, as being more accessible to the senses, it is obviously reasonable to approach the soul, which is a substantial form, through a comparison with accidental forms. And again, the soul's parts or potencies are more readily perceptible to us than its essence; for all our enquiry into the soul has to start from the objective terms of its activities and then proceed from these activities to their potencies, and thence to an understanding of the soul in its essence; that is why a study of the soul's parts can throw light on the definition of it.

§ 236. First then, he observes that the definition given above is "general," i.e. it applies to any soul. It posits the soul as a substance which is a form; and this means that it presents to us the idea of the essence of something. For there is this difference between a form that is substance and one that is not, that the latter sort are not strictly of the essence or "whatness" of a thing: whiteness is not of the essence of a white body; whereas substantial form is essential and quidditative. To call the soul a substantial form, therefore, is to imply that it is of the essence and "whatness" of the body it animates. Hence he says "this," i.e. this quidditative substance, "is the essence of this body," i.e. of the body that is what it is precisely through having this particular form. For this form is essential to the thing, and is denoted by the definition of what the thing is.

§ 237. And because substantial forms, including the forms of natural bodies, are not evident to us, Aristotle makes his meaning clear with an example taken from the forms (accidental) of artificial things. "If," he says, "some utensil (i.e. an artificial instrument) for example an axe, were a physical (i.e. a natural) body," it would possess a form in the manner already explained. So he continues: "Then being-an-axe would be its substance," i.e. would be the substantial form of the axe, which is that to which we refer our idea of axe as such. This idea of axe as such he identifies with the essence of the axe, with what causes it to *be* an axe; and this essential form he identifies with the substance of the axe. He says "substance" because the forms of natural bodies are substantial forms. Furthermore, if the axe were not merely a natural, but also an animate, body, its form would be a *soul*; and if it lost this soul it would no longer be an axe, except in name; just as when the soul leaves the body there is no longer an eye or flesh, except in name. Of course the axe, not being in fact a natural body, has no axe-form which is of the essence of the body that it is; so that if it lost the form of axe, the axe would still exist *substantially*, because the substance of artificial things is their matter which remains when the artificial form and, with this artificial form, the actuality of the artificial body as such, is removed.

§ 238. Then he explains why he has distinguished between the axe as it actually is and as it would be were it a physical (that is, a natural) living body: for the soul is not the essence and idea, i.e. the form, of an artificial body like an axe, but "of such a physical body," i.e. of a body that is alive. To make this clearer he adds "as has in itself the principle of movement and rest"—which is characteristic of *natural* things. For Nature is this sort of principle, as he says in the *Physics*, Book II.

§ 239. Then at "Now what has been said," he applies what has been concluded about the soul as a whole, and the animate body as a whole, to the parts of each. If, he says, the eye were a whole animal, its soul would be sight; for sight is the essential form of the eye; which in itself is the material condition of sight, in the same way as an organic body is the material condition of a soul. Once sight is lost, the eye is no longer an eye, except in the sense that a stone or painted eye may be *called* an eye equivocally (this term is used when the same name is given to essentially different things). Remove, then, what makes an eye really an eye, and there is left only the name. And the same argument applies to the animate body as a whole: what makes it an animate body is its form, the soul. This removed, you have a living body only equivocally. For as one part of the sensitive soul is to one part of the sensitive body, so the faculty of sense as a whole is to the whole sensitive body as such.

§ 240. Next, at "Not that which has cast off," he explains what was meant by defining the soul as the "act of a potentially animate body." Now "potentially" may be said about a thing in either of two senses: (*a*) as lacking the power to act; (*b*) as possessed of this power but not acting by it. And the body, whose act is the soul, is potentially animate in the second sense only. So, when he calls the body a thing potentially alive he does not mean that it has *lost* the soul it had and now lacks a life-principle altogether; he is speaking of what still has such a principle. On the other hand, seeds and the fruits that contain them are only potentially living bodies with souls; for a seed as yet lacks a soul. It is "potential" therefore like that which has lost its soul.

§ 241. And to show just how the body is potential to the actuality that comes from its soul he adds that being awake is the actuality of the sensitive soul in the same way as cutting is the actuality of a knife and seeing is that of an eye; for each of these acts is the activity and use of a principle already there. But the soul is the first and underlying actuality; like the faculty of sight itself or the capacity of any tool; for each of these is the operative principle itself. So the body, complete with its soul, is potentially animate in the sense that, though it has its first actuality, it may lack the second. And as the eye is a thing composed of a pupil as its matter and the faculty of sight as its form, so an animal is a thing composed of soul as its form and body as its matter.

§ 242. Then, at "Therefore it is evident," he deduces a truth from the foregoing. Having shown that the soul is the whole body's actuality, its "parts" being the actualities of the body's parts, and granted that an actuality or form cannot be separated from that which is actual and has form, we can certainly conclude that no soul can be separated from its body,—at least certain parts of the soul cannot be separated, if the soul can be said to have parts. For obviously some "parts" of the soul are nothing but actualities of parts of the body; as we have seen in the case of sight, that it is the eye's actuality. On the other hand, certain parts of the soul may well be separable from the body, since they are not the actuality of any corporeal part, as will be proved when we come to treat of the intellect.

§ 243. As to Plato's opinion that the soul is the act of the body not as its *form* but as its *mover*, he adds that it is not yet clear whether the soul is the act of the body as a sailor of a ship, i.e. as its mover only.

§ 244. Finally, recapitulating, he says that the foregoing is an "outline" description of the soul, meaning that it is extrinsic, as it were, and superficial and incomplete. It will be completed when he comes to define the innermost nature of the soul and the nature of each of its parts.

Aristotle's *De Anima*
(413ᵃ11–413ᵇ13)

BOOK II, CHAPTER 2
The Definition Justified
Modes of Life

Since it is from the less clear, though more obvious, facts that what is certain and more evident to thought emerges, let us attempt to approach the matter afresh.   § 245

For it is not enough that a defining principle should merely show a fact, as do most formulae, but also there should be contained and made plain the causes involved. Usually the constituent terms are like conclusions: for instance, what is a square that is equal to an oblong? An equilateral orthogon. Such a term is of the nature of a conclusion. But to say that a square is the discovery of a mean line states the reason why.

§§ 246–52

Going back, then, to the beginning of our enquiry, let us say that the animate is distinguished from the inanimate by being alive.

To live, however, is predicated in several ways; and even if one only of these is present, we say there is life; as, for example, intellection, sensation, or movement and rest in place; as well as the movement and rest involved in nourishment, and growth and decay.   §§ 253–5

Hence all plants seem to live. They appear to have in themselves a power and principle of this kind, by which they increase or decay in various directions—that is to say, they do not grow up but not down, but alike either way; and in all their parts they are continually nourished, and they live so long as they can take nourishment.   §§ 256–7

It is possible for this power to exist apart from the others; but for the others to exist apart from it is impossible, at least in mortal beings. This is evident in plants; for there is in them no other soul-power. To live by this principle, then, is common to all living things.   § 258

But an animal is such primarily by sensation. For we also call animals things that do not move or change their place, provided they have sensation, and do not merely live.

28

There seem to be many of this sort: by nature they stay in one place, but they have one of the senses. § 259

Touch is in all, primarily. As the vegetative powers can be separated from touch and all sensation as a whole, so can touch from the other senses. (We give the name "vegetative" to that part of the soul in which plants participate). All animals are seen to possess the sense of touch. § 260

For what cause each of these facts is so we shall say later on. At present only this need be said: that soul is the principle of the qualities we have discussed, and is characterised by the vegetative, sensitive, intellective and motive powers. § 261

Aquinas's Commentary

Lecture 3

§ 245. Having defined the soul the Philosopher now sets out to prove his definition. First he says what he intends to do, and then, at "Going back, then," proceeds to do it. As to the former point, he first determines the method of demonstration that he intends to use; after which, at "For it is not enough," he explains how certain types of definition can be proved. With regard to the method to be used we should note that, since we can only come to know the unknown if we start from what we know, and since the purpose of demonstration is precisely to cause knowledge, it follows that every demonstration must begin from something more knowable to us than the thing to be made known by it. Now in certain subjects, such as mathematics, which abstract from matter, what is the more knowable is such both in itself and relatively to us; hence in these subjects, demonstration can start from what is absolutely and of its nature more knowable, and therefore can deduce effects from their causes; whence the name given it of *a priori* demonstration. But in the quite different sphere of the natural sciences, what is more knowable is not the same thing in itself and relatively to us; for sensible effects are generally more evident than their causes. Hence in these sciences we generally have to begin from what is, indeed, absolutely speaking less knowable, but is more evident relatively to us (see the *Physics*, Book I).

§ 246. And this is the kind of demonstration which will be used here. So he says that what is of its nature more certain, and is more evident to thought, becomes certain to us by means of things less certain in nature but more certain to us; and that this shows us the method to use in enquiring once more into the soul and showing the grounds of the definition given above.

§ 247. Then, at "For it is not enough," he tells us why the question must be taken up again. Certain definitions can, he says, be demonstrated, and in these cases it is not enough for the defining formula to express, as most "formulae," i.e. definitions, do, the mere fact; it should also give the cause of the fact; and this being given, one can then proceed to deduce the definition which states the mere fact. At present many definitions are given in the form of conclusions; and he gives an example from geometry.

§ 248. To understand which we must note that there are two kinds of four-sided figure: those whose angles are all right angles, and these are called rectangles; and the kind with no right angles, and these are called rhomboids. Of the rectangles, again, there is one with four equal sides— the square or tetragon; and another which, without having all four sides equal, has two pairs of equal, and opposite sides—the oblong. Thus:

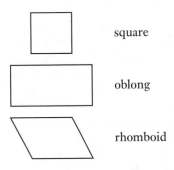

square

oblong

rhomboid

§ 249. Note further, that in any rectangular surface the two straight lines enclosing the right angle are said to contain the whole figure; because, the other two sides being equal to these two, each equal to its opposite, it follows that one of the enclosing lines measures the length of the whole figure, and the other its breadth: so that the whole figure is given in the contact of the two lines. If we imagine one of these lines moving along the other we see the whole figure form itself.

§ 250. Note also that if, between the two unequal sides that contain the oblong, one takes the proportional mean and squares it, one gets a quadrilateral equal to the oblong. This would take too long to prove geometrically, so let a numerical argument do for the present. Let our oblong then have its longer side 9 feet and its shorter side 4 feet. Then the proportional mean line will be 6 feet; for as 6 is to 9; so 4 is to 6. Now the square of this line must equal the oblong; which is obvious numerically: $4 \times 9 = 36$, $6 \times 6 = 36$.

§ 251. Now it is thus, he says, that the question, What is a square (i.e. the quadrilateral equal to an oblong)? is answered; it is said "to be an orthogon," i.e. a right-angled plane figure, which is "equilateral," i.e. having all its sides equal, and so on. "Such a term," i.e. a definition of this sort, is really "of the nature of a conclusion," namely of a presupposed demonstration; whereas if one were to say that a square is "the discovery of a mean line," i.e. of the proportional mean between the two unequal sides of the oblong, meaning that a square is what is constructed from this line, then at last the definition would disclose the "reason why" of the thing defined.

§ 252. Note, however, that this example is only relevant to the definition of the soul in so far as this definition is simply to be demonstrated; it must not be taken to imply that our demonstration can proceed *a priori* from causes to effects.

§ 253. Next, at "Going back then," he begins to prove the definition of the soul given above; and this in the way indicated, i.e. from effects to causes. This is how he sets about it: the first principle of life in things is the actuality and form of living bodies; but soul is the first principle of life in living things; therefore it is actuality and form of living bodies. Now this argument is clearly *a posteriori*; for *in reality* the soul is the source of vital activities because it is the form of a living body, not *e converso*. So he has to do two things here; first, to show that soul is the source or principle of vitality, and secondly, to show that the first principle of vitality is the form of living bodies (this comes at "Since that whereby etc."). With regard to the first point he does three things: (*a*) he distinguishes modes of life, (*b*) he shows that the soul is the principle of living activities—at "Hence all plants"; and (*c*) he explains how these parts of the soul are interrelated, by means of which it originates vital activities. This is at "We now ask whether each of these."

§ 254. He starts then by saying that to carry out our intention of proving the definition of the soul, we must assume as a kind of principle that things with souls differ from those without souls in being alive. Life is the test; and as life shows itself in several ways, if a thing has life in only one of these ways it is still said to be alive and to possess a soul.

§ 255. Life, he says, shows itself in four modes: (1) as intellectual; (2) as sensitive; (3) as the cause of motion or rest in space; (4) as cause of the motions of taking nourishment, decay and growth. He distinguishes only these four modes, although he has already distinguished five main types of vital activity, and this because he is thinking here and now of the degrees of animate being. There are four such degrees, distinguished in the same way as the four modes in which life is manifested: for some living things, i.e. plants, only take nourishment and grow and decay; some have also sensation, but are always fixed to one place—such are the inferior animals like shell-fish; some again, i.e. the complete animals like oxen and horses, have, along with sensation, the power to move from place to place; and finally some, i.e. men, have, in addition, mind. The appetitive power, which makes a fifth type of vitality, does not, however, imply a distinct degree of living being; for it always accompanies sensation.

§ 256. Next, at "Hence all plants," he shows that a soul is involved in all these modes of life. He does this with regard (1) to plants, and (2) to animals, at "But an animal is such, primarily." Then (3), he summarises, at "For what cause," what has been said and remains to be said. As to (1) he does two things. First he shows that the life-principle in plants is a soul. We have remarked, he says, that whatever evinces one of the four modes of life mentioned above can be said to live. Therefore plants are alive; for they all possess some intrinsic power or principle of growth and decay.

§ 257. Now this principle is not mere nature. Nature does not move in opposite directions, but growth and decay are in opposite directions; for all plants grow not only upwards or downwards, but in both directions. Hence a soul, not nature, is clearly at work in them. Nor do plants live only when actually growing or decaying, but, as things that take nourishment, they live so long as they can assimilate the food that induces growth.

§ 258. Next, at "It is possible," he shows that this principle of feeding and growing can exist apart from other life-principles, but these cannot exist apart from it, at least in things subject to death. He adds this last clause because of immortal beings like immaterial substances or heavenly bodies; because, if these have a soul, it is intellectual; it is not a capacity to take nourishment. And the separability of this life principle from others is clearly evident in plants which have, in fact, no other one but this. It follows that what first of all causes life in mortal things is this principle of growth and nourishment, the so-called vegetative soul.

§ 259. Then, at "But an animal is such primarily," he shows that a soul is the source of living in animals. And here he does two things. First he observes that what primarily distinguishes animals is sensation, though there are animals which have local movement as well; for we call those things *animals* (not just living beings) which have sensation, even if they are fixed to one place. For there are many such animals whose nature restricts them to one place, but which have the power of sense, e.g. shell-fish, which cannot move from place to place.

§ 260. Then, at "Touch is," he shows that touch is the primary sense in animals. For just as the vegetative soul, he says, is separable from all the senses including touch, so touch is separable from all the other senses. For many inferior animals have only the sense of touch; but there are no animals without this sense. Now that degree of soul in which even plants participate we call the vegetative. Hence we can distinguish three degrees of living beings: first, plants; secondly, the inferior animals fixed to one place and with no sense but touch; and, thirdly, the higher, complete animals which have the other senses and also the power to move from place to place. And a fourth degree consists, evidently, of beings which have all this and mind as well.

§ 261. Finally, at "For what cause," summarising what has been said and remains to be said, he remarks that the cause of both these phenomena, namely the separability of the vegetative principle from sensation and of touch from the other senses, will be given later on. He does this at the end of the whole Treatise. For the present it suffices to say that "soul" is the one principle underlying the four distinct modes in which life is manifested, namely the vegetative mode which belongs to plants and to all living things; the sensitive mode in all animals; the intellectual mode in all men; and fourthly, the mode that is a power to move from place to place, which exists in all the higher animals, both those with senses only and those with intellect as well.

3

THE NATURE OF THE INTELLECT, ITS ACTIVITY, AND ITS SEPARABILITY

Aristotle's *De Anima*
(429ª10–429ᵇ4)

BOOK III, CHAPTER 4
The Intellect in General

As to the part of the soul by which it knows and is wise (whether separate spatially or only in idea) we must consider how it is differentiated and, further, how the operation of understanding arises. §§ 671–4

For if understanding is like sensing, it will be some kind of reception from an intelligible object, or some thing of that nature. It must then be impassible and yet receptive of a species, which it must already be potentially but not actually: and as the sense faculty stands to the sense-object, so will the intellective to the intelligible. §§ 675–6

immaterial: not compounded w/ a body

It is also necessary, since its understanding extends to everything, that, as Anaxagoras says, it be uncompounded with anything so that it may command, i.e. know. *understand.* For what appeared inwardly would prevent and impede what was without. Hence it has no nature and is not one, except in being potential. What then is called the "intellect" of the soul (I mean that mind by which the soul forms opinions and understands) is not, before it understands, in act of any reality. §§ 677–83

Hence, it is a reasonable inference that it is not involved in the body. Were it so, it would also have some quality either hot or cold, and it would have an organ, like the sensitive faculties; but there is in fact none such. §§ 684–5

And they spoke to the point who said that the soul was the place of forms—yet not the whole soul, but the intellectual part; nor actually, but only potentially, is it any form. § 686

That the impassibility of the sensitive faculty is not like that of the intellective faculty, is evident from the organs and from sensation itself. For the sense cannot receive an impression from too violent a sense-object—e.g. a sound from very great sounds, whilst from over-powerful odours there comes no smell, nor from over-strong colour any seeing. But when the intellect understands something highly intelligible, it does not understand what is inferior to these less than before, but more so. For whereas the sensitive faculty is not found apart from the body, the intellect is separate. §§ 687–99

Aquinas's Commentary
Lecture 7

§ 671. Having treated of the sensitive part of the soul, and shown that to sense and to understand are quite distinct operations, the Philosopher now turns to the intellectual part. His treatment falls into two main divisions. First, he comes to certain conclusions on the intellectual part in general; after which, from what has been concluded about sense and intellect he deduces, at "And now recapitulating," some necessary consequences with regard to the soul as a whole. The former division falls into two sections: one on the intellect as such, and one comparing intellect with the senses. The latter begins at "And it seems that the sense-object." The intellect as such is first treated in itself, and then, at "Intelligence etc.," in its activity. The former part then subdivides again into three parts: (*a*) on the potential intellect; (*b*) on the agent intellect; and (*c*) on intellect as in act. After defining the potential intellect, he determines its object, and then adduces an objection. The definition of potential intellect involves explanations (i) of its nature, and (ii) of the way it proceeds into act. And as to its nature, he first states the problems he is attempting to solve; after which, at "For if understanding is like sensing," he propounds his own view.

§ 672. So he says that, having dealt with the sensitive part of the soul, and shown that judgement and understanding differ from sensation, it is now time to discuss that part of the soul "by which it knows," i.e. understands, and "is wise." We have already distinguished between being wise and understanding; to be wise pertains to intellectual *judgement*, to understand pertains to intellectual *apprehension*.

§ 673. At this point an old problem emerges (which Aristotle for the time being sets aside), namely whether this part of the soul is a really separate being, distinct from the other parts, or is merely separable in thought. He refers to the former alternative when he speaks of being "spatially" separable, and he uses this expression because Plato, who thought of the soul's parts as really distinct entities, associated the latter with different organs of the body. This problem Aristotle sets aside.

§ 674. And he keeps two ends in view. One is to examine how this part of the soul differs from the others, if it can be separated from them in thought. And, as potencies are known from their acts, his second aim is to examine the act of understanding itself, i.e. how intellectual activity is completed.

§ 675. Next, at "For if understanding," he sets down his own view in three stages: (1) he suggests a similarity between intellect and sense; (2) whence he argues, at "It is also necessary," to a conclusion touching the nature of the potential intellect; (3) whence in turn he deduces a difference between intellect and sense, at "That the impassibility."

First of all then, as a preliminary to the statement of his own theory, he suggests that the acts of understanding and of sensing are similar, in that, just as sensing is a kind of knowing, and as it may be either potential or actual, so understanding is a kind of knowing which may be either potential or actual. Whence it follows that, as sensing is a certain state of being passive to a sensible object (something like a passion in the strict sense of the term) so understanding is either a being passive to an intelligible object, or something else that resembles passion, in the strict sense.

§ 676. Of these alternatives the second is the more likely to be true. For even sensing, as we have seen, is not strictly a being passive to anything—for this, strictly, involves an object of a nature contrary to the passive subject. Yet sensing resembles a passion inasmuch as the sense is potential with respect to its object; for it receives sensible impressions. So far then as understanding resembles sensation the intellect too will be impassible (taking passivity in the strict sense), yet will it show some likeness to what is passive, in its receptivity to intelligible ideas; for these it possesses only potentially, not actually. Thus, as sensitive life is to sensible objects, so is the intellect to intelligible objects, each being potential with respect to its object and able to receive that object.

§ 677. Then at "It is also necessary" he proceeds to deduce the nature of the potential intellect. First he shows that this intellect is not a bodily thing nor compounded of bodily things; and then, at "Hence it is a reasonable," that it has no bodily organ. As to the first point, we should note that there used to be two opinions about the intellect. Some—and this, as we have seen, was the view of Empedocles—thought that intellect was a composition of all the principles of things, and that this explained its universal knowledge. On the other hand Anaxagoras thought it was simple and pure and detached from all bodily things. And therefore, precisely because the intellect, as he has just said, is not in act of understanding, but in potency only, and in potency to know everything, Aristotle argues that it cannot be compounded of bodily things, as Empedocles thought, but must be separate from such things, as Anaxagoras thought.

§ 678. Now the reason why Anaxagoras thought this was that he regarded intellect as the principle that dominated and initiated all movement; which it could not be if it were either a composition of bodily things or identified with any one of such things; for in these cases it would be restricted to one course of action only. Hence Aristotle's observation that, in Anaxagoras' view, the intellect was detached "so that it might command" and, commanding, initiate all movement.

§ 679. But, since we are not concerned at present with the all-moving Mind, but with the mind by which the soul understands, we require a different middle term to prove that the intellect is unmixed with bodily things; and this we find in its universal knowledge. That is why Aristotle adds "That it might know," as if to say: as Anaxagoras maintained that intellect was unmixed because it commands, so we have to maintain that it is unmixed because it knows.

§ 680. The following argument may make this point clear. Anything that is in potency with respect to an object, and able to receive it into itself, is, as such, without that object; thus the pupil of the eye, being potential to colours and able to receive them, is itself colourless. But our intellect is so related to the objects it understands that it is in potency with respect to them, and capable of being affected by them (as sense is related to sensible objects). Therefore it must itself lack all those things which of its nature it understands. Since then it naturally understands all sensible and bodily things, it must be lacking in every bodily nature; just as the sense of sight, being able to know colour, lacks all colour. If sight itself had any particular colour, this colour would prevent it from seeing other colours, just as the tongue of a feverish man, being coated with a bitter moisture, cannot taste anything sweet. In the same way then, if the intellect were restricted to any particular nature, this connatural restriction would prevent it from knowing other natures. Hence he says: "What appeared inwardly would prevent and impede" (its knowledge of) "what was without"; i.e. it would get in the way of the intellect, and veil it so to say, and prevent it from inspecting other things. He calls "the inwardly appearing" whatever might be supposed to be intrinsic and co-natural to the intellect and which, so long as it "appeared" therein would necessarily prevent the understanding of anything else; rather as we might say that the bitter moisture was an "inwardly appearing" factor in a fevered tongue.

§ 681. From this he concludes, not that in fact the nature of the intellect is "not one," i.e. that it has no definite nature at all; but that its nature is simply to be open to all things; and that it is so inasmuch as it is capable of knowing, not (like sight or hearing) merely one particular class of sensible objects, nor even all sensible accidents and qualities (whether these be common or proper sense-objects) but quite generally the *whole* of sensible nature. Therefore, just as the faculty of sight is by nature free from *one* class of sensible objects, so must the intellect be entirely free from *all* sensible natures.

§ 682. He concludes further that what we call our intellect is not in act with respect to real beings until it actually understands. This is contrary to the early philosophers' principle that intellect must be compounded of all things if it can know all things. But if it knew all things, as containing them all in itself already, it would be an ever-actual intellect, and never merely in potency. In the same way he has remarked already of the senses, that if they were intrinsically made up of the objects they perceive, their perceptions would not presuppose any exterior sensible objects.

§ 683. And lest anyone should suppose this to be true of any and every intellect, that it is in potency to its objects before it knows them, he adds that he is speaking here of the intellect by which the soul understands and forms opinions. Thus he excludes from this context the Mind of God, which, far from being potential, is a certain actual understanding of all things, and of which Anaxagoras said that it could command all because it was perfectly unmixed.

§ 684. Next, at "Hence it is a reasonable," he shows that the intellect has no bodily organ; and then, at "They spoke to the point," approves a saying of the early philosophers. First, then, he concludes from what has been said, that if the mind's universal capacity for knowledge implies its intrinsic distinction from all the corporeal natures that it knows, for the same reason it can be argued that the mind is not "involved in the body," i.e. that it has no bodily organ, as the sensitive part of the soul has. For if the intellect had, like the sensitive part, a bodily organ, it would necessarily be just one particular sensible nature among many. Therefore he says "some quality" etc., meaning that a nature of this kind would have some particular sensible quality such as actual heat or cold; for it is obvious that, if the soul acts through a bodily organ, the soul itself must correspond to that organ as being in potency to its act.

§ 685. It makes no difference to the act of the potency whether it is the potency itself that has a particular sensible quality or the organ, since the act is not of the potency alone but of potency and organ together. In the same way sight would be impeded if it were the visual potency, not the pupil of the eye, that was coloured. So he says that it comes to the same to maintain that intellect has no bodily organ and that it has no particular bodily nature; and concludes that the intellectual part of the soul, unlike the sensitive, has no bodily organ.

§ 686. Next, where he says "And they spoke to the point," he relates his view to an opinion of the early philosophers, saying that, granted intellect's lack of a bodily organ, we can see the point of the old saying that the soul is the "place" of forms—meaning that it receives these into itself. Now this saying would be false if every part of the soul had its bodily organ, for then the forms would be received into the composition of soul and body, not into the soul alone; for it is not *sight* that receives visible forms, but the eye. It follows that the soul as a whole is not the "place" of forms, but only that part of it which lacks a bodily organ, i.e. the intellect; and even this part does not, as such, possess them actually, but potentially only.

§ 687. Then, at "That the impassibility," he shows how the intellect and the senses differ with respect to impassibility. He has already observed that neither sensation nor understanding is a passion in the precise sense of a state of being passively affected; whence he had inferred that the intellect was impassible. But, lest it be supposed that sense and intellect were impassible in the same degree, he now distinguishes them in this respect. Though the senses as such are not, strictly speaking, passively affected by their objects, they are *indirectly* so affected, inasmuch as the equilibrium of the sense-organ is disturbed by any excess in its object. But the same is not true of the intellect, since it has no organ; it is therefore neither directly nor indirectly passible.

§ 688. This is what he means when he proceeds to say that the dissimilarity between sense and intellect in point of passibility appears "from the organs and from sensation." For a very strong sense-object can stun the faculty of sense. One can be deafened by great sounds, blinded by strong colours, made powerless to smell anything by over-powering odours; and this because the organ in each case is injured. But since the intellect has no organ that could be injured by an excess of its appropriate object, its activity is not, in fact, weakened by a great intelligibility in its object; indeed it is rather strengthened thereby; and the same would be true of the senses, if they could exist without bodily organs. All the same, an injury to an organ of the body may indirectly weaken the intellect, in so far as the latter's activity presupposes sensation. The cause, then, of the difference is that sensitivity acts in the body, but the intellect acts on its own.

§ 689. All this goes to show the falsity of the opinion that intellect is the same as imagination, or as anything else in our nature that depends on the body's constitution. On the other hand, this same text has been, for some, an occasion of falling into the error of regarding the intellectual power as quite separated from the body, as a substance that *exists* on its own. Which is an utterly indefensible position.

§ 690. For it is clear that the actually intelligent being is this particular man. Whoever denies this implies that he himself understands nothing; and therefore that one need pay no attention to what he says. But if he *does* understand anything he must do so in virtue of some principle in him of this particular activity of understanding; which is the intellectual power (as potential) to which the Philosopher refers when he says: "I mean that mind by which the soul understands and forms opinions." The potential intellect then is precisely that by which this particular man understands. Now that in virtue of which, as a principle of activity, an agent acts may certainly exist in separation from the agent; as e.g. a king and his bailiff have separate existence, though the latter acts only as moved by the king. But it is quite impossible for the agent to exist separately from that by which, formally and immediately, he is an agent; and this because action only proceeds from an agent in so far as the latter is in a state of actuality. It follows that the agent and the proper and immediate principle of his activity must exist together in one act; which could not be if they were separate beings. Hence the impossibility of a separation in being of an agent from its formal principle of activity.

§ 691. With this truth in mind, those who maintained the opinion to which I refer tried to think out some way of so linking up and uniting the separated substance, which for them was the intellectual potency, with ourselves, as to identify its act of understanding with our own. They said then that the form of the potential intellect, that by which it is brought into act, was the intelligible idea; and that the *subject* possessed of this idea was a kind of phantasm produced by ourselves. In this way, they said, the potential intellect is linked with us through its form.

§ 692. But this theory entirely fails to prove any continuity between the intellect and ourselves. For the intellectual power is only united with an intelligible object in the degree that it is in act; just as we have seen that the senses cannot unite with their appropriate objects so long as these remain in potency. Therefore the intelligible idea cannot be the form of the intellectual power until it is actually understood; and this cannot happen until it is disengaged from phantasms by abstraction. Hence, precisely in the degree that it is joined to the intellect it is removed from phantasms. Not in this way therefore could an intellectual power be united with us.

§ 693. And obviously the upholder of this view was led astray by a *fallacia accidentis*. For his argument comes to this: phantasms are somehow united to intelligible ideas, and these to the potential intellect; and therefore the latter is united to the phantasms. But, as I say, it is clear that, in the degree that the intelligible idea is one with the intellectual power, it is abstracted from phantasms.

§ 694. But even granted that between the intellectual power and ourselves there existed some such union as this view supposes, it would not in fact cause us to understand, but rather to be understood. If the eye contains a likeness of a coloured wall, this does not cause the colour to see, but, on the contrary, to be seen. Therefore if the intelligible idea in the intellect is a sort of likeness of our phantasms, it does not follow that we perceive anything intellectually, but rather that we—or more precisely our phantasms—are understood by that separated intellectual substance.

§ 695. Many other criticisms might be urged, such as I have set out in more detail elsewhere. Enough to note for the present that the theory in question is an implicit denial of the existence of thinking in the human individual.

§ 696. Furthermore, it is also clearly contrary to the teaching of Aristotle. First, because he has explicitly said (at the beginning of the treatise) that the subject matter of his enquiry is a *part of the soul*, not any separated substance.

§ 697. Moreover, he has set out to examine the intellect leaving aside the question whether it is a being distinct from the rest of the soul; so that even if it be not distinct in this way, that does not affect his argument.

§ 698. Again, Aristotle calls the intellect that *by which* the soul understands.

All these indications show that he did not assert that the intellect was a separate substance.

§ 699. Indeed it is astonishing how easily some have let themselves be deceived by his calling the intellect "separate"; for the text itself makes it perfectly clear what he means,—namely that, unlike the senses, the intellect has no bodily organ. For the nobility of the human soul transcends the scope and limits of bodily matter. Hence it enjoys a certain activity in which bodily matter has no share; the potentiality to which activity is without a bodily organ; and in this sense only is it a "separate" intellect.

Aristotle's *De Anima*
(429^b5–429^b22)

BOOK III, CHAPTER 4, CONTINUED
Intellectual Abstraction

But when it becomes particular objects, as in a man of science, the intellect is said to be in act. (This comes about as soon as such a one is able to operate of himself.) It is, then, in a way still in potency, but not in the way it was before it learned or discovered. And then, too, it is able to think itself. §§ 700–704

Now, as *dimension* is one thing and the *being of dimension* another, and as *water* is one thing and the *being water* another, and so with many other things (but not all things, for in certain things "flesh" is the same as "being flesh") accordingly it discriminates either by some other [faculty] or by the same faculty differently disposed. For flesh is not separable from matter; it is like the snub of a nose, one [thing] existing in the other. There is discerned therefore by the sensitive faculty what is hot, what is cold, and anything else of which the flesh is a certain ratio. But either by another and separate faculty, or as if it were bent back upon itself (whereas it was previously straight), does it perceive the being of flesh. §§ 705–13

Again, in the abstract sphere the straight line is as the snub-nose; for it goes with the continuum. But its essence, if being [straight] is other than a straight line, is different. Let it be, for instance, Duality. Then [the mind] discerns either by another faculty or by the same differently disposed. In general, then, as things are separable from matter, so are intellectual operations. § 714–19

Aquinas's Commentary
Lecture 8

§ 700. Having reached certain conclusions about the intellect as potential with respect to intelligible objects, the Philosopher now goes on to show how it is actualised. And first he shows that it is actualised *intermittently*; and then, at "Now as dimension," what is the precise *object* of its actualisation.

He explains how the intellect is actualised thus. The intellectual soul is, we have said, only in potency to its ideas at first. "But when it becomes particular objects," i.e. when the mind reaches the degree of actual apprehension of intelligibles that is found in the knowledge habitually possessed by a man of science, then it can already be called an intellect in act; and that degree is reached as soon as one is capable of producing, on one's own initiative, the intellectual activity called understanding. For the actual possession of any form is coincident with the ability to act accordingly.

§ 701. Yet though a mind is already, in a way, in act when it has intelligible notions in the manner of one who possesses a science habitually, none the less the mind then is still, in a way, in potency; though not in the same way as it was before it acquired the science, either by being taught it or by its own unaided efforts. Before it acquired the habit of a science—which is its first state of actuality—it could not actualise itself at will, it needed to be brought into act by the mind of another; but once such a habit is acquired, the intellect has the power to bring itself into action at will.

§ 702. What is said here disproves the un-aristotelian position of Avicenna touching intelligible ideas. Avicenna maintained that ideas are not *retained* by the potential intellect, but exist in it only so long as it is actually understanding. Whence it follows that, for this intellect to come to the act of understanding anything, it must have recourse to a *separated* active intellect, the source of intelligible ideas in the intellectual potency.

§ 703. But against this Aristotle is clearly saying that the manner in which the mind becomes actually possessed of ideas is that of one who, possessing a science habitually, is still in potency to a given act of understanding. Thus the mind actually understanding possesses its ideas in fullest actuality; and so long as it has the habit of a science, it possesses them in a manner half-way between mere potency and complete actuality.

§ 704. And having asserted that, once the mind has become partly actual with respect to certain ideas hitherto potentially apprehended, it is capable of understanding, whereas simply regarded in itself it lacks the capacity, because this might lead one to suppose that even as in act the mind never thinks of itself, Aristotle adds that, once in act, the mind is able to think not only of other things, but also of itself.

§ 705. Next at "Now, as dimension is one," Aristotle elucidates the object of the intellect. To understand him here we must recall the problem stated in Book VII of the *Metaphysics*, namely whether the "whatness" or quiddity or essence of a thing—whatever is signified by its definition—whether this is the same as the thing itself. And whilst Plato had separated the quiddities (called by him "ideas" or "species") of things from things in their singularity, Aristotle was concerned to show that quiddities are only accidentally distinct from singular things. For example, a white man and his essence are distinct just in so far as the essence of man includes *only* what is specifically human, whereas the thing called one white man includes something else as well.

§ 706. And the same is true of anything whose form exists in matter; there is something in it besides its specific principle. The specific nature is individualised through matter; hence the individualising principles and individual accidents are not included in the essence as such. That is why there can be many individuals of the same specific nature—having this nature in common, whilst they differ in virtue of their individuating principles. Hence, in all such things, the thing and its essence are not quite identical. Socrates is not his humanity. But where the form does not exist in matter, where it exists simply in itself, there can be nothing except the essence; for then the form is the entire essence. And in such cases, of course, there cannot be a number of individuals sharing the same nature; nor can the individual and its nature be distinguished.

§ 707. This also should be considered, that things existing concretely in Nature—*physical* things—are not alone in having their essences in matter; the same is also true of *mathematical* entities. For there are two kinds of matter: sensible matter, which is intrinsic to physical things and from which the mathematician abstracts; and intelligible matter, intrinsic to mathematical entities. For it is clear that, whereas quantity pertains to a substance immediately, sensible qualities, like white and black or heat and cold, *presuppose* quantity. Now given two things of which one is prior to the other, if you remove the second, the first remains; hence if only its sensible qualities are removed from a substance by a mental abstraction, continuous quantity still remains, in the mind, after the abstraction.

§ 708. For there are some forms which can only exist in a matter which is possessed of certain definite sensible qualities; and such are the forms of physical things; and such things therefore always involve sensible matter. But there are other forms which do not call for matter possessed of definite sensible qualities, yet do require matter existing as quantity. These are the so-called mathematical objects such as triangles, squares and the like; they are abstracted from sensible matter, but not from intelligible matter; for the mind retains the notion of a quantitative continuum after abstracting from sensible quality. Clearly then, both physical and mathematical objects have their forms in matter, and in both there is a difference between a thing and its essence; which is why in both cases many individual things are found to share the same nature: e.g. men and triangles.

§ 709. If these points are understood, the text of Aristotle should present no difficulties. For he says "dimension" and the being of "dimension" differ, meaning a dimension and its essence—for by "the being of dimension" he means its essence. So also "water" and its "being" are distinct; and similarly in the case of "many other things;" i.e. in all physical and mathematical objects. Hence his choice of these two examples: for dimension is a mathematical object and water a physical one.

§ 710. But this distinction is not verified in "all things"; for in perfectly immaterial substances the thing is identical with its essence. And as such substances are beyond the reach of the human mind, Aristotle could not assign proper names to them, as he could to physical and mathematical objects; so he describes them in terms drawn from physical objects. That is why he says that "in certain things flesh" and "its being" are identical. He does not mean this literally, else he would not have said "in certain things," but would have absolutely identified flesh and its being. He means that "in certain things," i.e. immaterial substances, the two factors which we distinguish as the concrete thing and what is predicated of it—for instance flesh and its being—are identical.

§ 711. And since diversity in objects known implies diversity in the knowing faculties, he concludes by saying that either the soul knows a thing with one faculty and its essence with another, or both with the same faculty functioning in different ways. For it is obvious that flesh can only exist in matter; its form being in a certain definite and particular sensible matter. The being, too, which has flesh is a definite sensible thing, e.g. a nose. Now this sensitive nature the soul knows through the senses; that is why he adds that it is by the sense-faculty that the soul discerns the hot and the cold and so forth, of which flesh is a certain "ratio," i.e. proportion. For the form of flesh requires a certain definite proportion of heat and cold and so forth.

§ 712. But the "being of flesh," i.e. its essence, must be "discerned" by some other faculty. But the functioning of two distinct "faculties" takes place in two ways. In one way flesh and its essence can be discerned by powers in the soul which are completely distinct; the essence discerned by the intellect, the flesh by the senses; and this happens when we know the individual in itself and the specific nature in itself. But in another way the flesh and its essence may be discerned, not by two distinct faculties, but by one faculty knowing in two distinct ways—knowing in one way flesh, in another the essence of flesh; and this happens when the knowing soul correlates the universal and the individual. For, just as it would be impossible for us (as we have seen) to distinguish sweetness from whiteness if we had not a common sense faculty which knew both at once, so also we could not make any comparison between the universal and the individual if we had not a faculty which perceived both at once. The intellect therefore knows both at once, but in different ways.

§ 713. It knows the specific nature or essence of an object by going out directly to that object; but it knows the individual thing indirectly or reflexively, by a return to the phantasms from which it abstracted what is intelligible. This Aristotle expresses by saying that the intellectual soul either knows flesh sensitively and discerns the "being of flesh" with "another" and "separate" potency,—i.e. other than sensitivity, in the sense that intellect is a power distinct from the senses; or it knows flesh and the "being of flesh" by one and the same intellectual power functioning diversely; in so far as it can "bend back," so to say, "upon itself." As "stretched out straight," and apprehending directly, it "discerns" the "being" or essence of flesh; but by reflection it knows the flesh itself.

§ 714. Next, at "Again, in the abstract sphere," he applies what he had said of physical objects to mathematical objects, saying that "in the abstract sphere," i.e. in mathematics, where we abstract from sensible matter, the straight line is like the snub-nosed in the sphere of sensible matter. For line is a mathematical object, as a snub-nose is a physical one; and line essentially involves a continuum, as what is snub-nosed a nose. But the continuum is intelligible matter, as what is snub-nosed is sensible matter. Therefore in mathematics also the thing and its essence, e.g. the straight line and its straightness, are different; hence too, even in mathematics, things and essences must be objects of different kinds of knowing.

§ 715. As an instance of this let us suppose for a moment, with Plato, that the essence of straight line is duality (for Plato identified the essences of mathematical objects with numbers, so that a line was unity, a straight line duality, and so on). The soul then must know mathematical objects and their essences in different ways. Hence, just as it can be shown, in the case of physical objects, that the intellect knowing their essences is other than the senses which know them in their individuality, so too, in the case of mathematics, it can be shown that what knows the essences, i.e. the intellect, is distinct from what apprehends mathematical objects themselves, i.e. the imagination.

§ 716. And lest it be said that the mind works in the same way in mathematics and in natural science, he adds that the relation of things to the intellect corresponds to their separability from matter. What is separate *in being* from sensible matter can be discerned only by the intellect. What is not separate from sensible matter in being, but only *in thought*, can be perceived in abstraction from sensible matter, but not from *intelligible* matter. Physical objects, however, though they are intellectually discerned in abstraction from *individual* matter, cannot be completely abstracted from sensible matter; for "man" is understood as *including* flesh and bones; though in abstraction from *this* flesh and *these* bones. But the singular individual is not directly known by the intellect, but by the senses or imagination.

§ 717. From this text of Aristotle one can go on to show that the intellect's proper object is indeed the essence of things; but not the essence by itself, in separation from things, as the Platonists thought. Hence this "proper object" of our intellect is not, as the Platonists held, something existing outside sensible things; it is something intrinsic to sensible things; and this, even though the mode in which essences are grasped by the mind differs from their mode of existence in sensible things; for the mind discerns them apart from the individuating conditions which belong to them in the order of sensible reality. Nor need this involve the mind in any falsehood; for there is no reason why, of two conjoined things, it should not discern one without discerning the other; just as sight perceives colour without perceiving odour, though not without perceiving colour's necessary ground which is spatial magnitude. In like manner, the intellect can perceive a form apart from its individuating principles, though not apart from the matter required by the nature of the form in question; thus it cannot understand the snub-nosed without thinking of nose, but it can understand a curve without thinking of nose. And it was just because the Platonists failed to draw this distinction that they thought that mathematical objects and the essences of things were as separate from matter in reality as they are in the mind.

§ 718. Furthermore, it is clear that the intelligible ideas by which the potential intellect is actualised are not in themselves the intellect's object: for they are not that which, but that *by* which it understands. For, as with sight the image in the eye is not what is seen, but what gives rise to the act of sight (for what is seen is colour which exists in an exterior body), so also what the intellect understands is the essence existing in things; it is not its own intelligible idea, except in so far as the intellect reflects upon itself. Because, obviously, it is what the mind understands that makes up the subject-matter of the sciences; and all these, apart from rational science, have realities for their subject-matter, not ideas. Clearly then, the intellect's object is not the intelligible idea, but the essence of intelligible realities.

§ 719. From which we can infer the futility of an argument used by some to prove that all men have only one potential intellect in common.

They argue from the fact that all men can understand one and the same object; and say that if there were really many human intellects they would necessarily have many intelligible ideas. But these intelligible ideas are not precisely *what* the mind understands; they are only the latter's likeness present in the soul; hence it is quite possible for many intellects to possess likenesses of one and the same object, so that one thing is understood by all. Besides, the separated substances must know the essences of the physical things which we know; and clearly their intellects are distinct. Hence, if the above argument were valid, its conclusion—that all men have only one intellect—would still involve a difficulty; for one cannot reduce *all* intellects to one.

Aristotle's *De Anima*
(429^{b}23–430^{a}9)

BOOK III, CHAPTER 4, CONTINUED
Problems Arising Intellect as Intelligible

One might well enquire (if the intellect is simple and impassible, having nothing in common with anything else, as Anaxagoras said) how it understands, if understanding is a receiving. For it seems that one thing acts and another is acted on, only in so far as there is a factor common to the two. § 720

Again, if it is itself an intelligible: then either there is intellect in other intelligible things—(unless it is intelligible by virtue of some extrinsic principle) the intelligible being specifically one; or it will have, mixed with itself, something that makes it intelligible, as other things have. §§ 721–2

Or what about the receptivity in a general sense, already alluded to in making distinctions on this point? Before it makes an act of understanding, the intellect is its intelligible objects potentially, but not actually. It must be as with a tablet on which there is nothing actually written; and so indeed it is in the case of intellect. §§ 722–3

And it is itself an intelligible like other intelligible objects. For in things separated from the material, intellect and what is understood by it are identical. Speculative knowledge is the same as what is knowable in this way. §§ 724–6

The reason why there is not always understanding must be considered. In material things, each intelligible object exists only potentially. Hence in them is no intellect, for the mind that understands such things is an immaterial potency. The intelligible exists, however [in them]. § 727

Aquinas's Commentary
Lecture 9

§ 720. Having outlined the nature and object of the potential intellect, Aristotle now goes on to discuss some relevant difficulties; and this in two stages: first stating two problems and then, at "Or what about the receptivity," answering them. The first of the two problems might be stated thus: if intellect is, as Anaxagoras said, something simple and impassible and removed from all else, how can it actually understand? For to understand is a kind of receiving, and every receiver, as such, would seem to be affected by an agent; and it is precisely through having something in common that two things are related as agent and patient, this mutual relationship implying a material factor in common, as is shown in Book I of the *De Generatione.*

§ 721. The second difficulty he states at "Again, if it is." This difficulty is occasioned by his earlier statement that once the mind is in act it can understand itself. Now if intellect itself is intelligible, it is so in either of two ways: either merely of itself, or by way of something else conjoined with it. If the first alternative be true, then, since the intelligible as such forms one species, and since *this* intelligible is an intellect, it seems to follow that other intelligibles are also intellects, and thus everything intelligible is also intelligent. Should we take the second alternative, however, it would follow that the mind was like other things that are understood in being conjoined with something which makes it intelligible,—with the result, it might seem, here also, that that which is understood is always possessed of understanding.

§ 722. Then at "Or what about the receptivity," he removes these difficulties. As to the first, relying on his earlier analysis of passivity, he reminds us that one can speak of passivity in a general sense which is common to two different kinds of change: to the mutual alteration of things which have their material factor in common and mutually exclusive, alternating formal determinations; and also to the change which implies nothing more than a reception of forms from outside the changed thing. The mind, then, is called passive just in so far as it is in potency, somehow, to intelligible objects which are not actual in it until understood by it. It is like a sheet of paper on which no word is yet written, but many can be written. Such is the condition of the intellect as a potency, so long as it lacks actual knowledge of intelligible objects.

§ 723. This is against, not only the early natural philosophers' view that the soul knows all things because it is composed of all things, but also Plato's opinion that the human soul is by nature in possession of a universal knowledge which only its union with the body has caused it to forget. (This theory is implicit in Plato's reduction of learning to remembering.)

§ 724. After this, at "And it is itself," he answers the second difficulty; and then, at "The reason why there is not," a fresh objection. First, then, he says that the potential intellect is itself intelligible, not indeed immediately, but like other intelligible things, through a concept. To prove this he has recourse to the principle that the actually understood object and the actually understanding subject are one being—just as he said earlier in this book, that the actually sensed object and the actually sensing subject are one being. Now the actually understood is so in virtue of an abstraction from matter; for, as we have seen, things become objects of the understanding just in the degree that they can be separated from matter. So he says "in things separated from the material." So the understanding and the understood are one being, provided the latter is actually understood; and the same is true of the object and subject of sensation. Speculative knowledge and what is knowable "in this way" (i.e. in act) are identical. Therefore the concept of the actually understood thing is also a concept of the understanding, through which the latter can understand itself. That is why all the foregoing discussion of the potential intellect has been carried on in terms of the latter's act and object. For we only know the intellect through our knowledge that we are using it.

§ 725. The reason why the potential intellect cannot be known immediately, but only through a concept, is the fact that it is potential also as an intelligible object; for, as it is proved in Book IX of the *Metaphysics*, intelligibility depends upon actuality. And there is a like dependence in the field of sensible realities too. In this field what is purely potential, i.e. bare matter, cannot act of itself, but only through some form conjoined with it; whereas sensible substances, being compositions of potency and act, can act, to some extent, of themselves. So, too, the potential intellect, being purely potential in the order of intelligible things, neither understands nor is understood except through its own concepts.

§ 726. But God who, among intelligible objects, is the one that is perfect actuality, and also the other immaterial substances midway between potency and act, know and are known simply of and in themselves.

§ 727. Next, at "The reason why," he answers an objection to the above solution. For if our mind, like other things, is rendered intelligible by union with some principle of intelligibility which is not precisely itself, why should not any intelligible object be itself a subject which understands;—or, as he says, we still have to enquire into "the reason" for "not always understanding." Now the reason is that in any material thing the form is not actually intelligible; it is only potentially so; and only what is actually intelligible, not the merely potentially so, is identical with intellect; so that things whose form exists in matter are not themselves possessed of an intellect with which to understand. The "mind that understands such things" (i.e. intelligible objects) a certain immaterial potency. The material thing is indeed intelligible but only potentially; whereas what exists in an intellect is an actually intelligible form.

BOOK III, CHAPTER 5
The Agent Intellect

Now since in all nature there is a factor that is as matter in the genus, and is potentially all that is in the genus, and something else which is as cause and agent as making everything in it (thus art is related to its material): so there must be these differences in the soul. There is that intellect, which is such as being able to become everything; and there is that which acts upon everything, as a sort of state, like light; for light too, in a way, makes potential colours actual.   §§ 728–31

And this is intellect separable, uncompounded and incapable of being acted on, a thing essentially in act. For the agent is always more excellent than the recipient, and the principle than its material.   §§ 732–9

Knowledge in act is the same as the thing itself. But what is potential has temporal priority in the individual; yet this is not true universally, even with respect to time. Mind does not know at one time and not know at another time.   §§ 740–1

Only separated, however, is it what it really is. And this alone is immortal and perpetual.   §§ 742–3

It does not remember, because it is impassible; the passive intellect is corruptible, and the soul understands nothing apart from this latter.[1]
                                                             §§ 744–5

---

[1]A much-disputed passage. A safe rendering of the Greek is: "This alone is immortal and perpetual. We have however no memory of it because it is impassible, whereas the passive intellect (or, the mind that can be affected) is perishable; and without it nothing thinks"—taking "it" to refer to the agent intellect. The Latin translation, however, followed by St. Thomas, takes this "it" to mean the "passive intellect" and inserts *anima*, "the soul," as subject of "thinks." Hence St. Thomas takes the whole section to refer to the state of the intellect after death: it "does not remember," etc., once the passive intellect has perished; the latter is only "called" intellect and is really a *pars animae corporalis*. . . .

Aquinas's Commentary
Lecture 10

§ 728. Having examined the potential intellect, the Philosopher now turns his attention to the agent intellect. He first shows by argument and illustration that there is such a thing as the agent intellect; and then, at "And this is intellect," he explains its nature. The argument he uses is this. In any nature which alternates between potency and actuality we must posit (1) a factor akin to the matter which, in any given class of things, is potentially all the particulars included in the class; and (2) another factor which operates as an active and productive cause, like art with respect to its material. Since then the intellectual part of the soul alternates between potency and act, it must include these two distinct principles: first, a potentiality within which all intelligible concepts can be actualised (this is the potential intellect already discussed); and then, also, a principle whose function it is to actualise those concepts. And this latter is the agent intellect,— being "a sort of state."

§ 729. This last phrase has led some to suppose that the agent intellect is one with the "intellect" which is a habitual apprehension of first principles. But it is not so; for the latter "intellect" *presupposes* the actual presence in the mind of certain intelligible and understood objects, which are the terms in understanding which we apprehend the truth of first principles. So the view in question would imply that the agent intellect was not, as Aristotle here maintains, the primary source, for us, of the actual intelligibility of anything. Therefore I hold that the term "state" is used here in the sense in which Aristotle often calls any form or nature a "state," to distinguish it from a privation or a potency. In this case the agent intellect is called a state to distinguish it from that intellect in potency.

§ 730. So he calls it a state, and compares it to light which "in a way" brings colours from potency to act;—"in a way" because, as we have seen, colour is visible of itself; all that light does is to actualise a transparent medium which can then be modified by colour so that colour is seen. The agent intellect, on the other hand, actualises the intelligible notions themselves, abstracting them from matter, i.e. bringing them from potential to actual intelligibility.

§ 731. The reason why Aristotle came to postulate an agent intellect was his rejection of Plato's theory that the essences of sensible things existed apart from matter, in a state of actual intelligibility. For Plato there was clearly no need to posit an agent intellect. But Aristotle, who regarded the essences of sensible things as existing in matter with only a potential intelligibility, had to invoke some abstractive principle in the mind itself to render these essences actually intelligible.

§ 732. Next, at "And this etc.," he states four qualities or conditions of the agent intellect: first, its separation from matter; second, its impassibility; third, its purity, by which he means that it is neither made up of bodily natures nor conjoined with a bodily organ. Now these three qualities are also found in the potential intellect; but the fourth is proper to the agent intellect, and consists in its being essentially in act; whereas the potential intellect is essentially potential and comes to act only by receiving an intelligible object.

§ 733. To demonstrate these qualities he argues as follows. What acts is nobler than what is acted on, an active principle is nobler than its material. Now the agent intellect, as we have said, is to the potential intellect as an active principle to its material; therefore it is the nobler of the two. If, then, the potential intellect be (as has been shown) free from matter and impassible and pure, *a fortiori* the agent intellect. Consequently the agent intellect is also essentially actual, for only in virtue of its actuality is an active principle nobler than a passive one.

§ 734. Now what is said here has led some to conceive of the agent intellect as a separated substance, subsisting apart from the potential intellect. But this does not seem to be true; for human nature would be a deficient nature if it lacked any one of the principles that it needs for its naturally appropriate activity of understanding; and this requires both the potential and the agent intellects. Hence, complete human nature requires that both of these be intrinsic to man. Moreover, just as the potential intellect's function of receiving intelligible objects is attributed to the individual man as its subject, so also is the work of the agent intellect, the abstracting of such objects from matter. And this is only possible in so far as the formal principle of the latter activity is one in being with the individual man.

§ 735. Nor is it enough to say that the intelligible notions formed by the agent intellect subsist somehow in phantasms, which are certainly intrinsic to us; for as we have already observed in treating of the potential intellect, objects only become actually intelligible when abstracted from phantasms; so that, merely by way of the phantasms, we cannot attribute the work of the agent intellect to ourselves. Besides, the agent intellect is to ideas in act in the mind as art is to the ideas it works by; and obviously the things on which art impresses such ideas do not themselves produce the art; hence, even granted that we were the subjects of ideas made actually intelligible in us, it would not follow that it is we who produce them by means of an agent intellect in ourselves.

§ 736. Nor does the above theory agree with Aristotle who expressly states that these two distinct powers, the agent and the potential intellects, are in the soul; thus making it quite clear that he takes them to be parts or potencies of the soul, not distinct substances.

§ 737. The chief difficulty arises from the fact that, while the potential intellect is in potency to intelligible objects, the agent intellect stands to the latter as a being already in act. And it would seem impossible that one and the same thing should be at once in act and in potency to the same object; and therefore that these two intellects should belong to the one substance of the soul.

§ 738. But there is really no difficulty in this if we understand aright how the potential intellect is potential with respect to intelligible objects, and how the latter are potential with respect to the agent intellect. In the former case the potentiality is that of the indefinite to the definite; for the potential intellect is not, as such, endowed with any definite and particular sensible thing's nature. Yet only definite particular natures are, as such, intelligible—hence Aristotle's earlier comparison of the intellectual power's relation to intelligible objects with that of a sheet of paper to particular definite pictures. And from this point of view the agent intellect is not in act.

§ 739. For if the agent intellect as such included the definite forms of all intelligible objects, the potential intellect would not depend upon phantasms; it would be actualised simply and solely by the agent intellect; and the latter's relation to intelligible objects would not be that of a maker to something made, as the Philosopher here says; for it would simply be identical with them. What makes it therefore in act with respect to intelligible objects is the fact that it is an active immaterial force able to assimilate other things to itself, i.e. to immaterialise them. In this way it renders the potentially intelligible actually so (like light which, without containing particular colours, actually brings colours into act). And because this active force is a certain participation in the intellectual light of separated substances, the Philosopher compares it to a state and to light; which would not be an appropriate way of describing it if it were itself a separate substance.

§ 740. Next, at "Knowledge in act," he states his conclusions concerning intellect as in act; and first he states its properties; and then, at "Only separated," how the intellectual part of the soul in general differs from the rest of the soul. Regarding the former point, he states three properties of intellect in act. First, its actual knowledge is identical with the thing known; which is not true of intellect as potential. Secondly, though in one and the same thing potential knowledge is prior *in time* to actual knowledge, yet, speaking universally, potential knowledge is not prior either *in nature* or *in time*. In Book IX of the *Metaphysics* Aristotle had said that act is by nature prior to potency, but not in time in one and the same thing; for a thing is first in potency and afterwards in act. But universally speaking act takes priority even in time; because no potency would ever be actualised unless something were already in act. So, even in the case of potential knowledge, no one ever comes to know anything actually, whether through his own effort or another's teaching, except in virtue of some pre-existing actual knowledge, as it is said in Book I of the *Posterior Analytics*.

§ 741. The third property of intellect as in act, differentiating it from the potential intellect and from intellect in habitual possession of knowledge, is that it is always in act; for it simply is the act of understanding. In the other cases intellect is sometimes in act and sometimes in potency.

§ 742. Next, at "Only separated," he states the properties of the intellect as a whole; first stating the truth, and then refuting an objection. He says, then, that only the mind separated from matter is that which really is mind; and he speaks here, not of the agent or passive intellect in isolation, but of both together, since both have been described as separated from matter. And the whole intellect is so described because it operates without a bodily organ.

§ 743. And in line with what he said at the beginning of this book, that the soul might be separable from the body if any of its activities were proper to itself, he now concludes that the soul's intellectual part alone is immortal and perpetual. This is what he has said in Book II, namely that this "kind" of soul was separable from others as the perpetual from the mortal,—perpetual in the sense that it survives for ever, not in the sense that it always *has* existed; for as he shows in Book XII of the *Metaphysics*, forms cannot exist before their matter. The soul, then (not all of it, but only its intellectual part) will survive its matter.

§ 744. Next, at "It does not remember," he meets an objection. For we might suppose that knowledge would remain unchanged in the intellectual part of the soul which survives. But already in Book I he has disallowed this, where he observed that the act of the intellect must cease when something else dies; and that after death the soul remembers and loves no more.

§ 745. So now he adds that what we have known in life is not recalled after death; because "it is impassible," i.e. that part of the intellectual soul of which he speaks; which, therefore, is unaffected by passions such as love and hatred and reminiscence and so forth, which all depend on modifications of the body. For the "passive intellect"—a part of the soul which depends on the aforesaid passions—is certainly mortal; for it belongs to our sensitive nature. Nevertheless, it is called "intellect" and "rational" because it has a certain share in reason: it obeys and is governed by reason (see Book I of the *Ethics*). And without the co-operation of this embodied part of the soul there is no understanding anything; for the intellect always requires phantasms, as we shall see. Hence, after the body's death the soul no longer knows anything in the same way as before. But how it does know anything then is not part of our present enquiry.

4

SOUL AND BODY

Summa Theologica

PART ONE
QUESTION 75

On Man Who Is Composed of a Spiritual and a Corporeal Substance: And First, Concerning What Belongs to the Essence of the Soul.

Having treated of the spiritual and of the corporeal creature, we now proceed to treat of man, who is composed of a spiritual and of a corporeal substance. We shall treat first of the nature of man, and secondly of his origin.[1] Now the theologian considers the nature of man in relation to the soul, but not in relation to the body, except in so far as the body has relation to the soul. Hence the first object of our consideration will be the soul. And since Dionysius says that three things are to be found in spiritual substances—essence, power and operation[2]—we shall treat first of what belongs to the essence of the soul; secondly, of what belongs to its power[3]; thirdly, of what belongs to its operation.[4]

Concerning the first, two points have to be considered; the first is the nature of the soul considered in itself; the second is the union of the soul with the body[5]. . . .

FIRST ARTICLE
Whether the Soul Is a Body?

We proceed thus to the First Article:—

Selections on pp. 60–208 reprinted from *Basic Writings of Saint Thomas Aquinas*, edited and annotated by Anton C. Pegis (Indianapolis: Hackett Publishing Company, 1997). Reprinted by permission of the publisher.
[1]Q. 90.   [2]*De Cael. Hier.*, XI, 2 (PG 3, 284).   [3]Q. 77.   [4]Q. 84.
[5]Q. 76.

Objection 1. It would seem that the soul is a body. For the soul is the mover of the body. Nor does it move unless moved. First, because apparently nothing can move unless it is itself moved, since nothing gives what it has not. For instance, what is not hot does not give heat. Secondly, because if there be anything that moves and is itself not moved, it must be the cause of eternal and uniform movement, as we find proved *Physics* viii.[6] Now this does not appear to be the case in the movement of an animal, which is caused by the soul. Therefore the soul is a moved mover. But every moved mover is a body. Therefore the soul is a body.

Obj. 2. Further, all knowledge is caused by means of a likeness. But there can be no likeness of a body to an incorporeal thing. If, therefore, the soul were not a body, it could not have knowledge of corporeal things.

Obj. 3. Further, between the mover and the moved there must be contact. But contact is only between bodies. Since, therefore, the soul moves the body, it seems that the soul must be a body.

On the contrary, Augustine says that the soul *is simple in comparison with the body, inasmuch as it does not occupy space by any bulk.* [7]

I answer that, To seek the nature of the soul, we must premise that the soul is defined as the first principle of life in those things in our world which live; for we call living things *animate*, and those things which have no life, *inanimate*. Now life is shown principally by two activities, knowledge and movement. The philosophers of old, not being able to rise above their imagination, supposed that the principle of these actions was something corporeal[8]; for they asserted that only bodies were real things, and that what is not corporeal is nothing.[9] Hence they maintained that the soul is some sort of body.[10] This opinion can be proved in many ways to be false; but we shall make use of only one proof, which shows quite universally and certainly that the soul is not a body.

It is manifest that not every principle of vital action is a soul, for then the eye would be a soul, as it is a principle of vision; and the same might be applied to the other instruments of the soul. But it is the *first* principle of life which we call the soul. Now, though a body may be a principle of life, as the heart is a principle of life in an animal, yet no body can be the first principle of life. For it is clear that to be a principle of life, or to be a

---

[6]Aristotle, *Phys.*, VIII, 10 (267b 3).   [7]*De Trin.*, VI, 6 (PL 42, 929).
[8]Democritus and Empedocles, according to Aristotle, *De An.*, I, 2 (404a 1; b 11).
[9]Cf. q. 50, a. 1.   [10]Cf. Macrobius, *In Somn. Scipion.*, I, 14 (p. 543); Nemesius, *De Nat. Hom.*, II (PG 40, 536); St. Augustine, *De Civit. Dei*, VIII, 5 (PL 41, 230).

living thing, does not belong to a body as a body, since, if that were the case, every body would be a living thing, or a principle of life. Therefore a body is competent to be a living thing, or even a principle of life, as *such* a body. Now that it is actually such a body it owes to some principle which is called its act. Therefore the soul, which is the first principle of life, is not a body, but the act of a body; just as heat, which is the principle of calefaction, is not a body, but an act of a body.

Reply Obj. 1. Since everything which is moved must be moved by something else, a process which cannot be prolonged indefinitely, we must allow that not every mover is moved. For, since to be moved is to pass from potentiality to actuality, the mover gives what it has to the thing moved, inasmuch as it causes it to be in act. But, as is shown in *Physics* viii., there is a mover which is altogether immovable, and which is not moved either essentially or accidentally; and such a mover can cause an eternally uniform movement.[11] There is, however, another kind of mover, which, though not moved essentially, is moved accidentally; and for this reason it does not cause a uniform movement. Such a mover is the soul. There is, again, another mover, which is moved essentially—namely, the body. And because the philosophers of old believed that nothing existed but bodies, they maintained that every mover is moved, and that the soul is moved essentially, and is a body.[12]

Reply Obj. 2. It is not necessary that the likeness of the thing known be actually in the nature of the knower. But given a being which knows potentially, and afterwards knows actually, the likeness of the thing known must be in the nature of the knower, not actually, but only potentially; and thus color is not actually in the pupil of the eye, but only potentially. Hence it is necessary, not that the likeness of corporeal things be actually in the nature of the soul, but that there be a potentiality in the soul for such a likeness. But the ancient naturalists did not know how to distinguish between actuality and potentiality[13]; and so they held that the soul must be a body in order to have knowledge of a body, and that it must be composed of the principles of which all bodies are formed.

Reply Obj. 3. There are two kinds of contact, that of *quantity*, and that of *power*. By the former a body can be touched only by a body; by the latter a body can be touched by an incorporeal reality, which moves that body.

---

[11]Aristotle, *Phys.*, VIII, 5 (258b 4); 6 (258b I5); 10 (267b 3).   [12]Cf. Aristotle, *De An.*, I, 2 (403b 29).   [13]Cf. Aristotle, *De Gener.*, I, 10 (327b 23).

SECOND ARTICLE
Whether the Human Soul Is Something Subsistent?

We proceed thus to the Second Article:—

Objection 1. It would seem that the human soul is not something subsistent. For that which subsists is said to be *this particular thing*. Now *this particular thing* is said not of the soul, but of that which is composed of soul and body. Therefore the soul is not something subsistent.

Obj. 2. Further, everything subsistent operates. But the soul does not operate, for, as the Philosopher says, *to say that the soul feels or understands is like saying that the soul weaves or builds.*[14] Therefore the soul is not subsistent.

Obj. 3. Further, if the soul were something subsistent, it would have some operation apart from the body. But it has no operation apart from the body, not even that of understanding; for the act of understanding does not take place without a phantasm, which cannot exist apart from the body. Therefore the human soul is not something subsistent.

On the contrary, Augustine says: *Whoever understands that the nature of the mind is that of a substance and not that of a body, will see that those who maintain the corporeal nature of the mind are led astray because they associate with the mind those things without which they are unable to think of any nature*—i.e., imaginary pictures of corporeal things.[15] Therefore the nature of the human mind is not only incorporeal, but it is also a substance, that is, something subsistent.

I answer that, It must necessarily be allowed that the principle of intellectual operation, which we call the soul of man, is a principle both incorporeal and subsistent. For it is clear that by means of the intellect man can know all corporeal things. Now whatever knows certain things cannot have any of them in its own nature, because that which is in it naturally would impede the knowledge of anything else. Thus we observe that a sick man's tongue, being unbalanced by a feverish and bitter humor, is insensible to anything sweet, and everything seems bitter to it. Therefore, if the intellectual principle contained within itself the nature of any body, it would be unable to know all bodies. Now every body has its own determinate nature. Therefore it is impossible for the intellectual principle to be a body. It is also impossible for it to understand by means of a bodily organ, since the determinate nature of that organ would likewise impede knowledge of all bodies; as when a certain determinate color is not only in the

---

[14]*De An.*, I, 4 (408b 11).   [15]*De Trin.*, X, 7 (PL 42, 979).

pupil of the eye, but also in a glass vase, the liquid in the vase seems to be of that same color.

Therefore the intellectual principle, which we call the mind or the intellect, has essentially an operation in which the body does not share. Now only that which subsists in itself can have an operation in itself. For nothing can operate but what is actual, and so a thing operates according as it is; for which reason we do not say that heat imparts heat, but that what is hot gives heat. We must conclude, therefore, that the human soul, which is called intellect or mind, is something incorporeal and subsistent.

Reply Obj. 1. *This particular thing* can be taken in two senses. Firstly, for anything subsistent; secondly, for that which subsists and is complete in a specific nature. The former sense excludes the inherence of an accident or of a material form; the latter excludes also the imperfection of the part, so that a hand can be called *this particular thing* in the first sense, but not in the second. Therefore, since the human soul is a part of human nature, it can be called *this particular thing* in the first sense, as being something subsistent; but not in the second, for in this sense the composite of body and soul is said to be *this particular thing*.

Reply Obj. 2. Aristotle wrote those words as expressing, not his own opinion, but the opinion of those who said that to understand is to be moved, as is clear from the context.[16] Or we may reply that to operate through itself belongs to what exists through itself. But for a thing to exist through itself, it suffices sometimes that it be not inherent, as an accident or a material form; even though it be part of something. Nevertheless, that is rightly said to subsist through itself which is neither inherent in the above sense, nor part of anything else. In this sense, the eye or the hand cannot be said to subsist through itself; nor can it for that reason be said to operate through itself. Hence the operation of the parts is through each part attributed to the whole. For we say that man sees with the eye, and feels with the hand, and not in the same sense as when we say that what is hot gives heat by its heat; for heat, strictly speaking, does not give heat. We may therefore say that the soul understands just as the eye sees; but it is more correct to say that man understands through the soul.

Reply Obj. 3. The body is necessary for the action of the intellect, not as its organ of action, but on the part of the object; for the phantasm is to the intellect what color is to the sight. Neither does such a dependence on

---

[16]*De An.*, I, 4 (408a 34).

the body prove the intellect to be non-subsistent, or otherwise it would follow that an animal is non-subsistent simply because it requires external sensibles for sensation.

THIRD ARTICLE

Whether the Souls of Brute Animals Are Subsistent?

We proceed thus to the Third Article:—

Objection 1. It would seem that the souls of brute animals are subsistent. For man is of the same genus as other animals, and, as we have shown, the soul of man is subsistent. Therefore the souls of other animals are subsistent.

Obj. 2. Further, the relation of the sensitive power to sensible objects is like the relation of the intellectual power to intelligible objects. But the intellect, without the body, apprehends intelligible objects. Therefore the sensitive power, without the body, perceives sensible objects. Therefore, since the souls of brute animals are sensitive, they are subsistent, for the same reason that the human soul, which is intellectual, is subsistent.

Obj. 3. Further, the soul of brute animals moves the body. But the body is not a mover, but is moved. Therefore the soul of brute animals has an operation apart from the body.

On the contrary, Is what is written in the book *De Ecclesiasticis Dogmatibus: Man alone we believe to have a subsistent soul; whereas the souls of animals are not subsistent.*[17]

I answer that, The early philosophers[18] made no distinction between sense and intellect, and referred both to a corporeal principle, as has been said. Plato, however, drew a distinction between intellect and sense, but he referred both to an incorporeal principle, maintaining that sensing, like understanding, belongs to the soul as such.[19] From this it follows that even the souls of brute animals are subsistent.[20] But Aristotle held that, of the operations of the soul, understanding alone is performed without a corporeal organ.[21] On the other hand, sensation and the attendant operations of the sensitive soul are evidently accompanied with change in the body; and thus, in the act of vision, the pupil of the eye is affected by the likeness of color. So with the other senses. Hence it is clear that the sensi-

---

[17]Gennadius, *De Eccles. Dogm.*, XVI (PL 58, 984).   [18]Empedocles, according to Aristotle, *De An.*, III, 3 (427a 21).   [19]Cf. Nemesius, *De Nat. Hom.*, VI (PG 40, 637); Plato, *Theaetet.* (p. 184c).—Cf. also St. Augustine, *De Musica*, VI, 5 (PL 32, 1168).   [20]Cf. Nemesius, *De Nat. Hom.*, II (PL 40, 582).   [21]*De An.*, III, 4 (429a 24).

tive soul has no *per se* operation of its own, and that every operation of the sensitive soul belongs to the composite. Therefore we conclude that as the souls of brute animals have no *per se* operations they are not subsistent. For the operation of anything follows the mode of its being.

Reply Obj. 1. Although man is of the same *genus* as other animals, he is of a different *species*. Now, specific difference is derived from the difference of form; nor does every difference of form necessarily imply a diversity of *genus*.

Reply Obj. 2. The relation of the sensitive power to the sensible object is in one way the same as that of the intellectual power to the intelligible object, in so far as each is in potentiality to its object. But in another way their relations differ, inasmuch as the impression of the sensible on the sense is accompanied with change in the body; so that when the intensity of the sensible is excessive, the sense is corrupted. This is a thing that never occurs in the case of the intellect. For an intellect that understands the highest of intelligible objects is more able afterwards to understand those that are lower.—If, however, in the process of intellectual operation the body is weary, this result is accidental, inasmuch as the intellect requires the operation of the sensitive powers in the production of the phantasms.

Reply Obj. 3. A motive power is of two kinds. One, the appetitive power, which commands motion. The operation of this power in the sensitive soul is not without the body; for anger, joy and passions of a like nature are accompanied by some change in the body. The other motive power is that which executes motion in adapting the members for obeying the appetite; and the act of this power does not consist in moving, but in being moved. Whence it is clear that to move is not an act of the sensitive soul without the body.

FOURTH ARTICLE
Whether the Soul Is Man?

We proceed thus to the Fourth Article:—

Objection 1. It would seem that the soul is man. For it is written (*2 Cor.* iv. 16): *Though our outward man is corrupted, yet the inward man is renewed day by day.* But that which is within man is the soul. Therefore the soul is the inward man.

Obj. 2. Further, the human soul is a substance. But it is not a universal substance. Therefore it is a particular substance. Therefore it is a *hypostasis* or a person; and it can be only a human person. Therefore the soul is a man, for a human person is a man.

On the contrary, Augustine commends Varro as holding *that man is not the soul alone, nor the body alone, but both soul and body.*[22]

I answer that, The assertion, *the soul is a man,* can be taken in two senses. First, that man is a soul, though this particular man (Socrates, for instance) is not a soul, but composed of soul and body. I say this, because some held that the form alone belongs to the species,[23] while matter is part of the individual, and not of the species. This cannot be true, for to the nature of the species belongs what the definition signifies, and in natural things the definition does not signify the form only, but the form and the matter. Hence, in natural things the matter is part of the species; not, indeed, signate matter, which is the principle of individuation, but common matter. For just as it belongs to the nature of this particular man to be composed of this soul, of this flesh, and of these bones, so it belongs to the nature of man to be composed of soul, flesh, and bones; for whatever belongs in common to the substance of all the individuals contained under a given species must belong also to the substance of the species.

That *the soul is a man* may also be understood in this sense, namely, that this soul is this man. Now this could be held if it were supposed that the operation of the sensitive soul were proper to it without the body; because in that case all the operations which are attributed to man would belong only to the soul. But each thing is that which performs its own operations, and consequently that is man which performs the operations of a man. But it has been shown above that sensation is not the operation of the soul alone. Since, then, sensation is an operation of man, but not proper to the soul, it is clear that man is not only a soul, but something composed of soul and body.—Plato, through supposing that sensation was proper to the soul, could maintain man to be *a soul making use of a body.*[24]

Reply Obj. 1. According to the Philosopher, each thing seems to be chiefly what is most important in it.[25] Thus, what the governor of a state does, the state is said to do. In this way sometimes what is most important in man is said to be man: sometimes it is the intellectual part which, in accordance with truth, is called the *inward* man; and sometimes the sensitive part with the body is called man in the opinion of those who remain the slaves of sensible things. And this is called the *outward* man.

---

[22]*De Civit. Dei,* XIX, 3 (PL 41, 626).   [23]Averroes, *In Metaph.,* VII, comm. 21; comm. 24 (VIII, 80v; 82v).—Cf. St. Thomas, *In Metaph.,* VII, lect. 9. [24]Cf. Nemesius, *De Nat. Hom.,* I (PG 40, 505).—Plato, *Alcib.* (p. 130c). [25]*Eth.,* IX, 8 (1168b 31).

Reply Obj. 2. Not every particular substance is a hypostasis or a person, but that which has the complete nature of its species. Hence a hand, or a foot, is not called a hypostasis, or a person; nor, likewise, is the soul alone so called, since it is a part of the human species.

FIFTH ARTICLE
Whether the Soul Is Composed of Matter and Form?

We proceed thus to the Fifth Article:—

Objection 1. It would seem that the soul is composed of matter and form. For potentiality is opposed to actuality. Now, whatsoever things are in actuality participate in the First Act, which is God. It is by participation in God that all things are good, beings, and living things, as is clear from the teachings of Dionysius.[26] Therefore, whatsoever things are in potentiality participate in the first potentiality. But the first potentiality is primary matter. Therefore, since the human soul is, after a manner, in potentiality (which appears from the fact that sometimes a man is potentially understanding), it seems that the human soul must participate in primary matter, as a part of itself.

Obj. 2. Further, wherever the properties of matter are found, there matter is. But the properties of matter are found in the soul—namely, to be a subject, and to be changed. For the soul is subject to science, and virtue; and it changes from ignorance to knowledge and from vice to virtue. Therefore there is matter in the soul.[27]

Obj. 3. Further, things which have no matter have no cause of their being, as the Philosopher says in *Metaph.* viii.[28] But the soul has a cause of its being, since it is created by God. Therefore the soul has matter.

Obj. 4. Further, what has no matter, and is only a form, is a pure act, and is infinite. But this belongs to God alone. Therefore the soul has matter.[29]

On the contrary, Augustine proves that the soul was made neither of corporeal matter, nor of spiritual matter.[30]

I answer that, The soul has no matter. We may consider this question in two ways. First, from the notion of a soul in general, for it belongs to the notion of a soul to be the form of a body. Now, either it is a form in its entirety, or by virtue of some part of itself. If in its entirety, then it is

---

[26]*De Div. Nom.*, V, 5 (PG 3, 820).   [27]Cf. St. Bonaventure, *In II Sent.*, d. iii, pt. 1, a. I. q. I (II, 89).   [28]Aristotle, *Metaph.*, VII, 6 (1045b 4).   [29]Cf. q. 50, a 2; St. Bonaventure, *In I Sent.*, d. viii, pt. 2 a. 1. q. 2 (I, 167).   [30]*De Genesi ad Litt.*, VII, 7; 8; 9 (PL 34, 359; 360).

impossible that any part of it should be matter, if by matter we understand something purely potential; for a form, as such, is an act, and that which is purely potential cannot be part of an act, since potentiality is repugnant to actuality as being its opposite. If, however, it be a form by virtue of a part of itself, then we shall call that part the soul, and that matter, which it actualizes first, we shall call the *primary animate*.

Secondly, we may proceed from the specific notion of the human soul, inasmuch as it is intellectual. For it is clear that whatever is received into something is received according to the condition of the recipient. Now a thing is known in as far as its form is in the knower. But the intellectual soul knows a thing in its nature absolutely: for instance, it knows a stone absolutely as a stone; and therefore the form of a stone absolutely, as to its proper formal notion, is in the intellectual soul. Therefore the intellectual soul itself is an absolute form, and not something composed of matter and form. For if the intellectual soul were composed of matter and form, the forms of things would be received into it as individuals, and so it would only know the individual; just as it happens with the sensitive powers which receive forms in a corporeal organ. For matter is the principle by which forms are individuated. It follows, therefore, that the intellectual soul, and every intellectual substance which has knowledge of forms absolutely, is exempt from composition of matter and form.

Reply Obj. 1. The First Act is the universal principle of all acts, because It is infinite, *precontaining all things* in its power, as Dionysius says.[31] Therefore It is participated in by things, not as a part of themselves, but by diffusion of Its processions. Now as potentiality is receptive of act, it must be proportionate to act. But the acts received which proceed from the First Infinite Act, and are participations thereof, are diverse, so that there cannot be one potentiality which receives all acts, in the same way that there is one act from which all participated acts are derived; for then the receptive potentiality would equal the active potentiality of the First Act. Now the receptive potentiality in the intellectual soul is other than the receptive potentiality of primary matter, as appears from the diversity of the things received by each. For primary matter receives individual forms; whereas the intellect receives absolute forms. Hence the existence of such a potentiality in the intellectual soul does not prove that the soul is composed of matter and form.

Reply Obj. 2. To be a subject and to be changed belong to matter by reason of its being in potentiality. Just as, therefore, the potentiality of the

---

[31]*De Div. Nom.*, V, 9 (PG 3, 825).

intellect is one thing and the potentiality of primary matter another, so in each is there a different manner of subjection and change. For the intellect is subject to knowledge, and is changed from ignorance to knowledge, by reason of its being in potentiality with regard to the intelligible species.

Reply Obj. 3. The form causes matter to be, and so does the agent; and so, the agent causes matter to be in so far as it changes it to the actuality of the form. A subsistent form, however, does not owe its being to some formal principle, nor has it a cause changing it from potentiality to act. So after the words quoted above, the Philosopher concludes that in things composed of matter and form *there is no other cause but that which moves from potentiality to act; while whatsoever things have no matter are truly beings in themselves.*[32]

Reply Obj. 4. Everything participated is compared to the participator as its act. But whatever created form be supposed to subsist *per se*, must have being by participation, for *even life*, or anything of that sort, *is a participator of being*, as Dionysius says.[33] Now participated being is limited by the capacity of the participator; so that God alone, Who is His own being, is pure act and infinite. But in intellectual substances, there is composition of actuality and potentiality, not, indeed, of matter and form, but of form and participated being. Therefore some say that they are composed of that *whereby they are* and that *which they are*[34], for being itself is that by which a thing is.

SIXTH ARTICLE
Whether the Human Soul Is Corruptible?

We proceed thus to the Sixth Article:—

Objection 1. It would seem that the human soul is corruptible. For those things that have a like beginning and process seemingly have a like end. But the beginning, by generation, of men is like that of animals, for they are made from the earth. And the process of life is alike in both; because *all things breathe alike, and man hath nothing more than the beast*, as it is written (*Eccles.* iii. 19). Therefore, as the same text concludes, *the death of man and beast is one, and the condition of both is equal.* But the souls of brute animals are corruptible. Therefore the human soul too is corruptible.

Obj. 2. Further, whatever is out of nothing can return to nothingness, because the end should correspond to the beginning. But as it is written

---

[32]*Metaph.*, VII, 6 (1045b 21).   [33]*De Div. Nom.*, V, 5 (PG 3, 820).   [34]Cf. q. 50. a. 2, ad 3.

(*Wis.* ii. 2), *We are born of nothing*; and this is true, not only of the body, but also of the soul. Therefore, as is concluded in the same passage, *After this we shall be as if we had not been*, even as to our soul.

Obj. 3. Further, nothing is without its own proper operation. But the operation proper to the soul, which is to understand through a phantasm, cannot be without the body. For the soul understands nothing without a phantasm, and *there is no phantasm without the body*, as the Philosopher says.[35] Therefore the soul cannot survive the dissolution of the body.

On the contrary, Dionysius says that human souls owe to divine goodness that they are *intellectual*, and that they have *an incorruptible substantial life*.[36]

I answer that, We must assert that the intellectual principle which we call the human soul is incorruptible. For a thing may be corrupted in two ways—in itself and accidentally. Now it is impossible for any subsistent being to be generated or corrupted accidentally, that is, by the generation or corruption of something else. For generation and corruption belong to a thing in the same way that being belongs to it, which is acquired by generation and lost by corruption. Therefore, whatever has being in itself cannot be generated or corrupted except in itself; while things which do not subsist, such as accidents and material forms, acquire being or lose it through the generation or corruption of composites. Now it was shown above that the souls of brutes are not self-subsistent, whereas the human soul is, so that the souls of brutes are corrupted, when their bodies are corrupted, while the human soul could not be corrupted unless it were corrupted in itself. This is impossible, not only as regards the human soul, but also as regards anything subsistent that is a form alone. For it is clear that what belongs to a thing by virtue of the thing itself is inseparable from it. But being belongs to a form, which is an act, by virtue of itself. And thus, matter acquires actual being according as it acquires form; while it is corrupted so far as the form is separated from it. But it is impossible for a form to be separated from itself; and therefore it is impossible for a subsistent form to cease to exist.

Granted even that the soul were composed of matter and form, as some pretend,[37] we should nevertheless have to maintain that it is incorruptible. For corruption is found only where there is contrariety, since generation and corruption are from contraries and into contraries. Therefore the heavenly bodies, since they have no matter subject to con-

---

[35] Aristotle, *De An.*, I, 1 (403a 9).   [36] *De Div. Nom.*, IV, 2 (PG 3, 696).
[37] Cf. above, a. 5 and q. 50, a. 2.

trariety, are incorruptible. Now there can be no contrariety in the intellectual soul; for it is a receiving subject according to the manner of its being, and those things which it receives are without contrariety. Thus, the notions even of contraries are not themselves contrary, since contraries belong to the same science. Therefore it is impossible for the intellectual soul to be corruptible.

Moreover we may take a sign of this from the fact that everything naturally aspires to being after its own manner. Now, in things that have knowledge, desire ensues upon knowledge. The senses indeed do not know being, except under the conditions of *here* and *now*, whereas the intellect apprehends being absolutely, and for all time; so that everything that has an intellect naturally desires always to exist. But a natural desire cannot be in vain. Therefore every intellectual substance is incorruptible.

Reply Obj. 1. Solomon reasons thus in the person of the foolish, as expressed in the words of *Wis.* ii. Therefore the saying that man and animals have a like beginning in generation is true of the body; for all animals alike are made of earth. But it is not true of the soul. For while the souls of brutes are produced by some power of the body, the human soul is produced by God. To signify this, it is written of other animals: *Let the earth bring forth the living soul* (*Gen.* i. 24); while of man it is written (*Gen.* ii. 7) that *He breathed into his face the breath of life.* And so in the last chapter of *Ecclesiastes* (xii. 7) it is concluded: *The dust returns into its earth from whence it was; and the spirit returns to God Who gave it.* Again, the process of life is alike as to the body, concerning which it is written (*Eccles.* iii. 19); *All things breathe alike*, and (*Wis.* ii. 2), *The breath in our nostrils is smoke.* But the process is not alike in the case of the soul, for man has understanding whereas animals do not. Hence it is false to say: *Man has nothing more than beasts.* Thus death comes to both alike as to the body, but not as to the soul.

Reply Obj. 2. As a thing can be created, not by reason of a passive potentiality but only by reason of the active potentiality of the Creator, Who can produce something out of nothing, so when we say that a thing can be reduced to nothing, we do not imply in the creature a potentiality to non-being, but in the Creator the power of ceasing to sustain being. But a thing is said to be corruptible because there is in it a potentiality to non-being.

Reply Obj. 3. To understand through a phantasm is the proper operation of the soul by virtue of its union with the body. After separation from the body, it will have another mode of understanding, similar to other substances separated from bodies, as will appear later on.[38]

SEVENTH ARTICLE
Whether the Soul Is of the Same Species as an Angel?

We proceed thus to the Seventh Article:—

Objection 1. It would seem that the soul is of the same species as an angel. For each thing is ordained to its proper end by the nature of its species, whence is derived its inclination for that end. But the end of the soul is the same as that of an angel—namely, eternal happiness. Therefore they are of the same species.

Obj. 2. Further, the ultimate specific difference is the noblest, because it completes the nature of the species. But there is nothing nobler either in an angel or in the soul than their intellectual being. Therefore the soul and the angel agree in the ultimate specific difference. Therefore they belong to the same species.

Obj. 3. Further, it seems that the soul does not differ from an angel except in its union with the body. But as the body is outside the essence of the soul, it does not seem to belong to its species. Therefore the soul and an angel are of the same species.

On the contrary, Things which have different natural operations are of different species. But the natural operations of the soul and of an angel are different, since, as Dionysius says, *Angelic minds have simple and blessed intellects, not gathering their knowledge of divine things from visible things.*[39] Subsequently he says the contrary of this about the soul. Therefore the soul and an angel are not of the same species.

I answer that, Origen held that human souls and angels are all of the same species,[40] and this because he supposed that in these substances the difference of degree was accidental, resulting from their free choice,[41] as we have seen above.[42] But this cannot be, for in incorporeal substances there cannot be diversity of number without diversity of species and inequality of nature; because, as they are not composed of matter and form, but are subsistent forms, it is clear that there is necessarily among them a diversity in species. For a separate form cannot be understood otherwise than as one of a single species. Thus, supposing a separate whiteness to exist, it could only be one, for one whiteness does not differ from another

---

[38]Q. 89, a. 1.   [39]*De Div. Nom.*, VII, 2 (PG 3, 868).   [40]*Peri Archon*, III, 5 (PG 11, 329).   [41]*Op. cit.*, I, 6; 8; II, 9; III, 5 (PG 11, 166; 178; 229; 329).   [42]Q. 47, a. 2.

except as in this or that subject. But diversity of species is always accompanied by diversity of nature. Thus, in the species of colors, one is more perfect than another; and the same applies to other species, because differences which divide a *genus* are contrary to one another. Contraries, however, are compared to one another as the perfect to the imperfect, since the *principle of contrariety is habit and privation*, as is written, *Metaph.* x.[43]

The same would follow if the aforesaid substances were composed of matter and form. For if the matter of one be distinct from the matter of another, it is required either that the form be the principle of the distinction of matter—that is to say, that the matter is distinct because of its relation to diverse forms, in which case there would still result a difference of species and an inequality of nature; or else that the matter is the principle of the distinction of forms. But one matter cannot be distinct from another, except by a distinction of quantity, which has no place in these incorporeal substances, such as an angel and the soul. Hence, it is not possible for the angel and the soul to be of the same species. How it is that there can be many souls of one species will be explained later.[44]

Reply Obj. 1. This argument is concerned with the proximate and natural end. Eternal happiness, however, is the ultimate and supernatural end.

Reply Obj. 2. The ultimate specific difference is the noblest because it is the most determinate, in the same way as actuality is nobler than potentiality. Thus, however, that which is intellectual is not the noblest, because it is indeterminate and common to many degrees of intellectuality; just as the sensible is common to many degrees of sensible being. Hence, just as all sensible things are not of one species, so neither are all intellectual beings of one species.

Reply Obj. 3. The body is not of the essence of the soul, but the soul, by nature of its essence, can be united to the body; so that, properly speaking, it is not even the soul, but rather the *composite*, which is in the species. And the very fact that the soul in a certain way requires the body for its operation proves that the soul is endowed with a grade of intellectuality inferior to that of an angel, who is not united to a body.

---

[43]Aristotle, *Metaph.*, IX, 4 (1055a 33).   [44]Q. 76, a. 2, ad 1.

PART ONE

QUESTION 76

The Union of Body and Soul

FIRST ARTICLE
Whether the Intellectual Principle
Is United to the Body as Its Form?

We proceed thus to the First Article:—

Objection 1. It seems that the intellectual principle is not united to the body as its form. For the Philosopher says that *the intellect is separate*, and that it is not the act of any body.[45] Therefore it is not united to the body as its form.

Obj. 2. Further, every form is determined according to the nature of the matter of which it is the form; otherwise no proportion would be required between matter and form. Therefore if the intellect were united to the body as its form, since every body has a determinate nature, it would follow that the intellect has a determinate nature; and thus, it would not be capable of knowing all things, as is clear from what has been said.[46] This is contrary to the nature of the intellect. Therefore the intellect is not united to the body as its form.

Obj. 3. Further, whatever receptive power is an act of a body, receives a form materially and individually; for what is received must be received according to the condition of the receiver. But the form of the thing understood is not received into the intellect materially and individually, but rather immaterially and universally. Otherwise, the intellect would not be capable of knowing immaterial and universal objects, but only individuals, like the senses. Therefore the intellect is not united to the body as its form.

Obj. 4. Further, power and action have the same subject, for the same subject is what can, and does, act. But intellectual action is not the action of a body, as appears from the above.[47] Therefore neither is the intellectual power a power of the body. But a virtue or a power cannot be more abstract or more simple than the essence from which the virtue or power is derived. Therefore, neither is the substance of the intellect the form of a body.

---

[45]*De An.*, III, 4 (429b 5).   [46]Q. 75, a. 2.   [47]*Ibid.*

Obj. 5. Further, whatever has being in itself is not united to the body as its form, because a form is that *by which* a thing exists; which means that the very being of a form does not belong to the form by itself. But the intellectual principle has being in itself and is subsistent, as was said above.[48] Therefore it is not united to the body as its form.

Obj. 6. Further, whatever exists in a thing by reason of its nature exists in it always. But to be united to matter belongs to the form by reason of its nature, because form is the act of matter, not by any accidental quality, but by its own essence; or otherwise matter and form would not make a thing substantially one, but only accidentally one. Therefore, a form cannot be without its own proper matter. But the intellectual principle, since it is incorruptible, as was shown above,[49] remains separate from the body, after the dissolution of the body. Therefore the intellectual principle is not united to the body as its form.

On the contrary, According to the Philosopher in *Metaph.* viii., difference is derived from the form.[50] But the difference which constitutes man is *rational*, which is said of man because of his intellectual principle. Therefore the intellectual principle is the form of man.

I answer that, We must assert that the intellect which is the principle of intellectual operation is the form of the human body. For that whereby primarily anything acts is a form of the thing to which the act is attributed. For instance, that whereby a body is primarily healed is health, and that whereby the soul knows primarily is knowledge; hence health is a form of the body, and knowledge is a form of the soul. The reason for this is that nothing acts except so far as it is in act; and so, a thing acts by that whereby it is in act. Now it is clear that the first thing by which the body lives is the soul. And as life appears through various operations in different degrees of living things, that whereby we primarily perform each of all these vital actions is the soul. For the soul is the primary principle of our nourishment, sensation, and local movement; and likewise of our understanding. Therefore this principle by which primarily we understand, whether it be called the intellect or the intellectual soul, is the form of the body. This is the demonstration used by Aristotle.[51]

But if anyone say that the intellectual soul is not the form of the body,[52] he must explain how it is that this action of understanding is the action of this particular man; for each one is conscious that it is he himself who

---

[48]*Ibid.*   [49]Q. 75, a. 6.   [50]*Metaph.*, VII, 2 (1042a 19).   [51]*De An.*, II, 2 (414a 12).   [52]Cf. St. Albert, *Summa de Creatur.*, II, q. 4, a. 1 (XXXV, 34).—Cf. also Avicenna, *De An.*, I, 1 (1rb); V, 4 (24va).

understands. Now an action may be attributed to anyone in three ways, as is clear from the Philosopher.[53] For a thing is said to move or act, either by virtue of its whole self, for instance, as a physician heals; or by virtue of a part, as a man sees by his eye; or through an accidental quality, as when we say that something that is white builds, because it is accidental to the builder to be white. So when we say that Socrates or Plato understands, it is clear that this is not attributed to him accidentally, since it is ascribed to him as man, which is predicated of him essentially. We must therefore say either that Socrates understands by virtue of his whole self, as Plato maintained, holding that man is an intellectual soul;[54] or that the intellect is a part of Socrates. The first cannot stand, as was shown above, because it is one and the same man who is conscious both that he understands and that he senses.[55] But one cannot sense without a body, and therefore the body must be some part of man. It follows therefore that the intellect by which Socrates understands is a part of Socrates, so that it is in some way united to the body of Socrates.

As to this union, the Commentator held that it is through the intelligible species,[56] as having a double subject, namely, the possible intellect and the phantasms which are in the corporeal organs. Thus, through the intelligible species, the possible intellect *is linked* to the body of this or that particular man. But this link or union does not sufficiently explain the fact that the act of the intellect is the act of Socrates. This can be clearly seen from comparison with the sensitive power, from which Aristotle proceeds to consider things relating to the intellect. For the relation of phantasms to the intellect is like the relation of colors to the sense of sight, as he says *De Anima* iii.[57] Therefore, just as the species of colors are in the sight, so the species of phantasms are in the possible intellect. Now it is clear that because the colors, the likenesses of which are in the sight, are on a wall, the action of seeing is not attributed to the wall; for we do not say that the wall sees, but rather that it is seen. Therefore, from the fact that the species of phantasms are in the possible intellect, it does not follow that Socrates, in whom are the phantasms, understands, but that he or his phantasms are understood.

Some,[58] however, have tried to maintain that the intellect is united to the body as its mover, and hence that the intellect and body form one

---

[53]*Phys.*, V, 1 (224a 31).   [54]Cf. above, q. 75, a. 4.   [55]*Ibid.*   [56]*In De An.*, III, comm. 5 (VI, 164v).   [57]Aristotle, *De An.*, III, 7 (431a 14).   [58]Cf. William of Auvergne, *De An.*, I, 7 (II Suppl., 72); VI, 35 (II, Suppl., 194).

thing in such a way that the act of the intellect could be attributed to the whole. This is, however, absurd for many reasons. First, because the intellect does not move the body except through the appetite, whose movement presupposes the operation of the intellect. The reason therefore why Socrates understands is not because he is moved by his intellect, but rather, contrariwise, he is moved by his intellect because he understands.—Secondly, because, since Socrates is an individual in a nature of one essence composed of matter and form, if the intellect be not the form, it follows that it must be outside the essence, and then the intellect is to the whole Socrates as a motor to the thing moved. But to understand is an action that remains in the agent, and does not pass into something else, as does the action of heating. Therefore the action of understanding cannot be attributed to Socrates for the reason that he is moved by his intellect.—Thirdly, because the action of a mover is never attributed to the thing moved, except as to an instrument, just as the action of a carpenter is attributed to a saw. Therefore, if understanding is attributed to Socrates as the action of his mover, it follows that it is attributed to him as to an instrument. This is contrary to the teaching of the Philosopher, who holds that understanding is not possible through a corporeal instrument.[59]—Fourthly, because, although the action of a part be attributed to the whole, as the action of the eye is attributed to a man, yet it is never attributed to another part, except perhaps accidentally; for we do not say that the hand sees because the eye sees. Therefore, if the intellect and Socrates are united in the above manner, the action of the intellect cannot be attributed to Socrates. If, however, Socrates be a whole composed of a union of the intellect with whatever else belongs to Socrates, but with the supposition that the intellect is united to the other parts of Socrates only as a mover, it follows that Socrates is not one absolutely, and consequently neither a being absolutely, for a thing is a being according as it is one.

There remains, therefore, no other explanation than that given by Aristotle—namely, that this particular man understands because the intellectual principle is his form.[60] Thus from the very operation of the intellect it is made clear that the intellectual principle is united to the body as its form.

The same can be clearly shown from the nature of the human species. For the nature of each thing is shown by its operation. Now the proper operation of man as man is to understand, for it is in this that he surpasses all animals. Whence Aristotle concludes that the ultimate happiness of

---

[59]*De An.*, III, 4 (429a 26).   [60]*Op. cit.*, II, 2 (414a 11).—Cf. *C. G.*, II, 59.

man must consist in this operation as properly belonging to him.[61] Man must therefore derive his species from that which is the principle of this operation. But the species of each thing is derived from its form. It follows therefore that the intellectual principle is the proper form of man.

But we must observe that the nobler a form is, the more it rises above corporeal matter, the less it is subject to matter, and the more it excels matter by its power and its operation. Hence we find that the form of a mixed body has an operation not caused by its elemental qualities. And the higher we advance in the nobility of forms, the more we find that the power of the form excels the elementary matter; as the vegetative soul excels the form of the metal, and the sensitive soul excels the vegetative soul. Now the human soul is the highest and noblest of forms. Therefore, in its power it excels corporeal matter by the fact that it has an operation and a power in which corporeal matter has no share whatever. This power is called the intellect.

It is well to remark, furthermore, that if anyone held that the soul is composed of matter and form,[62] it would follow that in no way could the soul be the form of the body. For since form is an act, and matter is being only in potentiality, that which is composed of matter and form cannot in its entirety be the form of another. But if it is a form by virtue of some part of itself, then that part which is the form we call the soul, and that of which it is the form we call the *primary animate*, as was said above.[63]

Reply Obj. 1. As the Philosopher says,[64] the highest natural form (namely, the human soul) to which the consideration of the natural philosopher is directed is indeed separate, but it exists in matter. He proves this from the fact that *man and the sun generate man from matter.* It is separate according to its intellectual power, because an intellectual power is not the power of a corporeal organ, as the power of seeing is the act of the eye; for understanding is an act which cannot be performed by a corporeal organ, as can the act of seeing. But it exists in matter in so far as the soul itself, to which this power belongs, is the form of the body, and the term of human generation. And so the Philosopher says that *the intellect is separate,*[65] because it is not the power of a corporeal organ.

From this it is clear how to answer the Second and Third objections. For in order that man may be able to understand all things by means of his intellect, and that his intellect may understand all things immaterial and

---

[61]*Eth.*, X, 7 (1177a 17).   [62]Cf. above, q. 75, a. 5; q. 50, a. 2.   [63]Q. 75, a. 5.   [64]*Phys.*, II, 2 (194b 12).   [65]*De An.*, III, 4 (429b 5).

universal, it is sufficient that the intellectual power be not the act of the body.

Reply Obj. 4. The human soul, by reason of its perfection, is not a form immersed in matter, or entirely embraced by matter. Therefore there is nothing to prevent some power of the soul from not being the act of the body, although the soul is essentially the form of the body.

Reply Obj. 5. The soul communicates that being in which it subsists to the corporeal matter, out of which and the intellectual soul there results one being, so that the being of the whole composite is also the being of the soul. This is not the case with other non-subsistent forms. For this reason the human soul retains its own being after dissolution of the body; whereas it is not so with other forms.

Reply Obj. 6. To be united to the body belongs to the soul by reason of itself, just as it belongs to a light body by reason of itself to be raised up. And just as a light body remains light, when removed from its proper place, retaining meanwhile an aptitude and an inclination for its proper place, so the human soul retains its proper being when separated from the body, having an aptitude and a natural inclination to be united to the body.

SECOND ARTICLE
Whether the Intellectual Principle is Multiplied According to the Number of Bodies?

We proceed thus to the Second Article:—

Objection 1. It would seem that the intellectual principle is not multiplied according to the number of bodies, but that there is one intellect in all men. For an immaterial substance is not multiplied numerically within one species. But the human soul is an immaterial substance, since it is not composed of matter and form, as was shown above.[66] Therefore there are not many human souls in one species. But all men are of one species. Therefore there is but one intellect in all men.

Obj. 2. Further, when the cause is removed, the effect is also removed. Therefore, if human souls were multiplied according to the number of bodies, it would follow that if the bodies were removed, the number of souls would not remain, but from all the souls there would be but a single remainder. This is heretical, for it would do away with the distinction of rewards and punishments.

Obj. 3. Further, if my intellect is distinct from your intellect, my intellect is an individual, and so is yours; for individuals are things which dif-

---

[66]Q. 75, a. 5.

fer in number but agree in one species.[67] Now whatever is received into anything must be received according to the condition of the receiver. Therefore the species of things would be received individually into my intellect, and also into yours; which is contrary to the nature of the intellect, which knows universals.

Obj. 4. Further, the thing understood is in the intellect which understands. If, therefore, my intellect is distinct from yours, what is understood by me must be distinct from what is understood by you; and consequently it will be reckoned *as something individual*, and be only *potentially something understood*.[68] Hence, the common intention will have to be abstracted from both, since from things which are diverse something intelligible and common to them may be abstracted. But this is contrary to the nature of the intellect, for then the intellect would not seem to be distinct from the imagination. It seems to follow, therefore, that there is one intellect in all men.

Obj. 5. Further, when the disciple receives knowledge from the teacher, it cannot be said that the teacher's knowledge begets knowledge in the disciple, because then knowledge too would be an active form, such as heat is; which is clearly false. It seems, therefore, that the same individual knowledge which is in the teacher is communicated to the disciple.[69] This cannot be, unless there is one intellect in both. Seemingly, therefore, the intellect of the disciple and teacher is but one; and, consequently, the same applies to all men.

Obj. 6. Further, Augustine says: *If I were to say that there are many human souls, I should laugh at myself.*[70] But the soul seems to be one chiefly because of the intellect. Therefore there is one intellect of all men.

On the contrary, The Philosopher says that the relation of universal causes to what is universal is like the relation of particular causes to individuals.[71] But it is impossible that a soul, one in species, should belong to animals of different species. Therefore it is impossible that one individual intellectual soul should belong to several individuals.

I answer that, It is absolutely impossible for one intellect to belong to all men. This is clear if, as Plato maintained, man is the intellect itself.[72] For if Socrates and Plato have one intellect, it would follow that Socrates and Plato are one man, and that they are not distinct from each other,

---

[67]Cf. Averroes, *In De An.*, III, Comm. 5 (VI, 166r). [68]*Ibid.* (VI, 163v– 164r). [69]Cf. Averroes, *In De An.*, III, comm. 5 (VI, 166rv). [70]*De Quant. An.*, XXXII (PL 32, 1073). [71]*Phys.*, II, 3 (195b 26). [72]Cf. above, q. 75, a. 4.

except by something outside the essence of each. The distinction between Socrates and Plato would then not be other than that of one man with a tunic and another with a cloak; which is quite absurd.

It is likewise clear that this is impossible if, according to the opinion of Aristotle, it is supposed that the intellect is a part or a power of the soul which is the form of man.[73] For it is impossible for many distinct individuals to have one form, just as it is impossible for them to have one being. For the form is the principle of being.

Again, this is clearly impossible, whatever one may hold as to the manner of the union of the intellect to this or that man. For it is manifest that, if there is one principal agent, and two instruments, we can say without qualification that there is one agent but several actions; as when one man touches several things with his two hands, there will be one who touches, but two contacts. If, on the contrary, we suppose one instrument and several principal agents, we can say that there are several agents, but one act; for example, if there be many pulling a ship by means of a rope, those who pull will be many, but the pulling will be one. If, however, there is one principal agent, and one instrument, we say that there is one agent and one action; as when the smith strikes with one hammer, there is one striker and one stroke. Now it is clear that no matter how the intellect is united or joined to this or that man, the intellect has the primacy among all the other things which pertain to man, for the sensitive powers obey the intellect, and are at its service. So if we suppose two men to have two intellects and one sense,—for instance, if two men had one eye,—there would be two seers, but one seeing. But if the intellect is held to be one, no matter how diverse may be all those things which the intellect uses as instruments, it is in no way possible to say that Socrates and Plato are more than one understanding man. And if to this we add that to understand, which is the act of the intellect, is not produced by any organ other than the intellect itself, it will further follow that there is but one agent and one action; in other words, all men are but one "understander," and have but one act of understanding,—I mean, of course, in relation to one and the same intelligible object.

Now, it would be possible to distinguish my intellectual action from yours by the distinction of the phantasms—because there is one phantasm of a stone in me, and another in you—if the phantasm itself, according as it is one thing in me and another in you, were a form of the possible intellect. For the same agent produces diverse actions through

---

[73]*De An.*, II, 2 (414a 13); 3 (414a 32).

diverse forms. Thus, through the diverse forms in things in relation to the same eye, there are diverse "seeings." But the phantasm itself is not the form of the possible intellect; the intelligible species abstracted from phantasms is such a form. Now in one intellect, from different phantasms of the same species, only one intelligible species is abstracted; as appears in one man, in whom there may be different phantasms of a stone, and yet from all of them only one intelligible species of a stone is abstracted, by which the intellect of that one man, by one operation, understands the nature of a stone, notwithstanding the diversity of phantasms. Therefore, if there were one intellect for all men, the diversity of phantasms in this man and in that would not cause a diversity of intellectual operation in this man and that man, as the Commentator imagines.[74] It follows, therefore, that it is altogether impossible and inappropriate to posit one intellect for all men.

Reply Obj. 1. Although the intellectual soul, like the angel, has no matter from which it is produced, yet it is the form of a certain matter; in which it is unlike an angel. Therefore, according to the division of matter, there are many souls of one species; while it is quite impossible for many angels to be of one species.

Reply Obj. 2. Everything has unity in the same way that it has being, and consequently we must judge of the multiplicity of a thing as we judge of its being. Now it is clear that the intellectual soul is according to its very being united to the body as its form. And yet, after the dissolution of the body, the intellectual soul retains its own being. In like manner, the multiplicity of souls is in proportion to the multiplicity of bodies; and yet, after the dissolution of the bodies, the souls remain multiplied in their being.

Reply Obj. 3. The individuality of the understanding being, or of the species whereby it understands, does not exclude the understanding of universals; or otherwise, since separate intellects are subsistent substances, and consequently individual, they could not understand universals. But it is the materiality of the knower, and of the species whereby he knows, that impedes the knowledge of the universal. For as every action is according to the mode of the form by which the agent acts, as heating is according to the mode of the heat, so knowledge is according to the mode of the species by which the knower knows. Now it is clear that the common nature becomes distinct and multiplied by reason of the individuating principles which come from the matter. Therefore if the form, which

---

[74]*In De An.*, III, comm. 5 (VI, 166v).

is the means of knowledge, is material—that is, not abstracted from material conditions—its likeness to the nature of a species or genus will be according to the distinction and multiplication of that nature by means of individuating principles; so that the knowledge of the nature in its community will be impossible. But if the species be abstracted from the conditions of individual matter, there will be a likeness of the nature without those things which make it distinct and multiplied. And thus there will be knowledge of the universal. Nor does it matter, as to this particular point, whether there be one intellect or many; because, even if there were but one, it would necessarily be an individual intellect, and the species whereby it understands, an individual species.

Reply Obj. 4. Whether the intellect be one or many, what is understood is one. For what is understood is in the intellect, not in itself, but according to its likeness; for *the stone is not in the soul, but its likeness is,* as is said *De Anima* iii.[75] Yet it is the stone which is understood, not the likeness of the stone, except by a reflection of the intellect on itself. Otherwise, the objects of sciences would not be things, but only intelligible species. Now it is possible for different things, according to different forms, to be likened to the same thing. And since knowledge is begotten according to the assimilation of the knower to the thing known, it follows that the same thing can be known by several knowers; as is apparent in regard to the senses, for several see the same color by means of diverse likenesses. In the same way several intellects understand one thing. But there is this difference, according to the opinion of Aristotle,[76] between the sense and the intellect—that a thing is perceived by the sense according to that disposition which it has outside the soul—that is, in its individuality; whereas, though the nature of the thing understood is outside the soul, yet its mode of being outside the soul is not the mode of being according to which it is known. For the common nature is understood as apart from the individuating principles; whereas such is not its mode of being outside the soul. (But according to the opinion of Plato, the thing understood exists outside the soul in the same way as it is understood.[77] For Plato supposed that the natures of things exist separate from matter.)

Reply Obj. 5. One knowledge exists in the disciple and another in the teacher. How it is caused will be shown later on.[78]

Reply Obj. 6. Augustine denies such a plurality of souls as would involve a denial of their communication in the one nature of the species.

---

[75]Aristotle, *De An.,* III, 8 (431b 29).   [76]*Ibid.* (432a 2).   [77]Cf. above, q. 6, a.4.   [78]Q. 117, a, 1.

THIRD ARTICLE
Whether Besides the Intellectual Soul There Are in Man Other Souls Essentially Different from One Another?

We proceed thus to the Third Article:—

Objection 1. It would seem that besides the intellectual soul there are in man other souls essentially different from one another; namely, the sensitive soul and the nutritive soul. For corruptible and incorruptible are not of the same substance. But the intellectual soul is incorruptible, whereas the other souls, namely, the sensitive and the nutritive, are corruptible, as was shown above.[79] Therefore in man the essence of the intellectual soul, the sensitive soul and the nutritive soul, cannot be the same.

Obj. 2. Further, if it be said that the sensitive soul in man is incorruptible, against this is the dictum that the *corruptible and the incorruptible differ generically*, according to the Philosopher in *Metaph.* x.[80] But the sensitive soul in the horse, the lion, and other brute animals, is corruptible. If, therefore, in man it be incorruptible, the sensitive soul in man and brute animals will not be of the same *genus*. Now, an animal is so called because it has a sensitive soul; and, therefore, *animal* will not be one genus common to man and other animals, which is absurd.

Obj. 3. Further, the Philosopher says that the embryo is an animal before it is a man.[81] But this would be impossible if the essence of the sensitive soul were the same as that of the intellectual soul; for an animal is such by its sensitive soul, while a man is a man by the intellectual soul. Therefore in man the essence of the sensitive soul is not the same as the essence of the intellectual soul.

Obj. 4. Further, the Philosopher says in *Metaph.* viii., that the genus is taken from the matter, and difference from the form.[82] But *rational*, which is the difference constituting man, is taken from the intellectual soul; while he is called *animal* by reason of his having a body animated by a sensitive soul. Therefore the intellectual soul is compared to the body animated by a sensitive soul as form to matter. Therefore in man the intellectual soul is essentially the same as the sensitive soul, but presupposes it as a material subject.

On the contrary, It is said in the book *De Ecclesiasticis Dogmatibus: Nor do we say that there are two souls in one man, as James and other Syrians*

---

[79]Q. 75, a. 6.　　[80]Aristotle, *Metaph.*, IX, 10 (1059a 10).　　[81]*De Gener. Anim.*, II, 3 (736a 35).　　[82]*Metaph.*, VII, 2 (1043a 5; a 19); cf. *Op. cit.*, VI, 12 (1038a 6).

write,—one, animal, by which the body is animated, and which is mingled with the blood; the other, spiritual, which obeys the reason; but we say that it is one and the same soul in man which both gives life to the body by being united to it, and orders itself by its own reason.[83]

I answer that, Plato held that there were several souls in one body, distinct even according to organs. To these souls he referred the different vital actions, saying that the nutritive power is in the liver, the concupiscible in the heart, and the knowing power in the brain.[84] Which opinion is rejected by Aristotle with reference to those parts of the soul which use corporeal organs.[85] His reason is that in those animals which continue to live when they have been divided, in each part are observed the operations of the soul, such as those of sense and appetite. Now this would not be the case if the various principles of the soul's operations were essentially diverse in their distribution through the various parts of the body. But with regard to the intellectual part, Aristotle seems to leave it in doubt whether it be *only logically* distinct from the other parts of the soul, *or also locally.*

The opinion of Plato could be maintained if, as he held, the soul were united to the body, not as its form, but as its mover. For nothing incongruous is involved if the same movable thing be moved by several movers; and still less if it be moved according to its various parts. If we suppose, however, that the soul is united to the body as its form, it is quite impossible for several essentially different souls to be in one body. This can be made clear by three reasons.

In the first place, an animal in which there were several souls would not be absolutely one. For nothing is absolutely one except by one form, by which a thing has being; because a thing has both being and unity from the same source, and therefore things which are denominated by various forms are not absolutely one; as, for instance, *a white man.* If, therefore, man were *living* by one form, the vegetative soul, and *animal* by another form, the sensitive soul, and *man* by another form, the intellectual soul, it would follow that man is not absolutely one. Thus Aristotle argues in *Metaph.* viii., against Plato, that if the Idea of an animal is distinct from the Idea of a biped, then a biped animal is not absolutely one.[86] For this reason, against those who hold that there are several souls in the body, he asks, *what contains them?*— that is, what makes them one?[87] It cannot be

---

[83]Gennadius, *De Eccles. Dogm.*, XV (PL 58, 984).—Cf. Pseudo-Augustine (Alcher of Clairvaux), *De Spir. et An.*, 48 (PL 40, 814).　　[84]Cf. Averroes, *In De An.*, I, comm. 90 (VI, 125v).—Cf. also Plato, *Timaeus* (p. 69e).　　[85]*De An.*, II, 2 (413b 13).　　[86]*Metaph.*, VII, 6 (1045a 14).　　[87]*De An.*, I, 5 (411b 6).

said that they are united by the unity of the body; because it is rather the soul that contains the body and makes it one, than the reverse.

Secondly, this is proved to be impossible by the mode in which one thing is predicated of another. Those things which are derived from various forms are predicated of one another either accidentally (if the forms are not ordered one to another, as when we say that something white is sweet), or essentially, in the second mode of essential predication (if the forms are ordered one to another, as when the subject enters into the definition of the predicate; and thus a surface is presupposed for color, so that if we say that a body with a surface is colored, we have the second mode of essential predication). Therefore, if we have one form by which a thing is an animal, and another form by which it is a man, it follows either that one of these two things could not be predicated of the other, except accidentally (supposing these two forms not to be ordered to one another), or that one would be predicated of the other according to the second mode of essential predication, if one soul be presupposed to the other. But both of these consequences are clearly false. For *animal* is predicated of man essentially and not accidentally, and man is not part of the definition of an animal, but the other way about. Therefore it is of necessity by the same form that a thing is animal and man. Otherwise man would not really be the being which is an animal, so that animal could be essentially predicated of man.

Thirdly, this is shown to be impossible by the fact that when one operation of the soul is intense it impedes another; which could never be the case unless the principle of such actions were essentially one.

We must therefore conclude that the sensitive soul, the intellectual soul and the nutritive soul are in man numerically one and the same soul. This can easily be explained, if we consider the differences of species and forms. For we observe that the species and forms of things differ from one another as the perfect and the less perfect; just as in the order of things, the animate are more perfect than the inanimate, animals more perfect than plants, and man more perfect than brute animals. Furthermore, in each of these genera there are various degrees. For this reason Aristotle compares the species of things to numbers, which differ in species by the addition or subtraction of unity.[88] He also compares the various souls to the species of figures, one of which contains another, as a pentagon contains and exceeds a tetragon.[89] Thus the intellectual soul contains virtually whatever belongs to the sensitive soul of brute animals, and to the

---

[88]*Metaph.*, VII, 3 (1043b 34). [89]*De An.*, II, 3 (414b 28).

nutritive soul of plants. Therefore, just as a surface which is of a pentagonal shape is not tetragonal by one shape, and pentagonal by another—
since a tetragonal shape would be superfluous, as being contained in the
pentagonal—so neither is Socrates a man by one soul, and an animal by
another; but by one and the same soul he is both animal and man.

Reply Obj. 1. The sensitive soul is incorruptible, not by reason of its
being sensitive, but by reason of its being intellectual. When, therefore, a
soul is sensitive only, it is corruptible; but when the intellectual is joined
to the sensitive, then the sensitive soul is incorruptible. For although the
sensitive does not give incorruptibility, yet it cannot deprive the intellectual of its incorruptibility.

Reply Obj. 2. Not forms, but composites, are classified either generically or specifically. Now man is corruptible like other animals. And so the
difference of corruptible and incorruptible which is on the part of the
forms does not involve a generic difference between man and the other
animals.

Reply Obj. 3. The embryo has first of all a soul which is merely sensitive, and when this is removed, it is supplanted by a more perfect soul,
which is both sensitive and intellectual, as will be shown farther on.[90]

Reply Obj. 4. We must not base the diversity of natural things on the
various logical notions or intentions which follow from our manner of
understanding; for reason can apprehend one and the same thing in various ways. Therefore since, as we have said, the intellectual soul contains
virtually what belongs to the sensitive soul, and something more, reason
can consider separately what belongs to the power of the sensitive soul, as
something imperfect and material. And because it observes that this is
something common to man and to other animals, it forms thence the
notion of the *genus*. On the other hand, that wherein the intellectual soul
exceeds the sensitive soul, the reason takes as formal and perfecting; and
thence it gathers the *difference* of man.

FOURTH ARTICLE
Whether in Man There Is Another
Form Besides the Intellectual Soul?

We proceed thus to the Fourth Article:—

Objection 1. It would seem that in man there is another form besides the
intellectual soul. For the Philosopher says that *the soul is the act of a physical body which has life potentially.*[91] Therefore the soul is to the body as a

---

[90]Q. 118, a. 2, ad 2.　　[91]*De An.*, II, 1 (412a 28).

form to matter. But the body has a substantial form by which it is a body. Therefore some other substantial form in the body precedes the soul.

Obj. 2. Further, man moves himself as every animal does. *Now everything that moves itself is divided into two parts, of which one moves, and the other is moved,* as the Philosopher proves.[92] But the part which moves is the soul. Therefore the other part must be such that it can be moved. But primary matter cannot be moved since it is a being only potentially,[93] while everything that is moved is a body. Therefore in man and in every animal there must be another substantial form, by which the body is constituted.

Obj. 3. Further, the order of forms depends on their relation to primary matter; for *before* and *after* apply by comparison to some beginning. Therefore, if there were not in man some other substantial form besides the rational soul, and if the rational soul inhered immediately to primary matter, it would follow that it ranks among the most imperfect forms which inhere to matter immediately.

Obj. 4. Further, the human body is a mixed body. Now mixture does not result from matter alone; for then we should have mere corruption. Therefore the forms of the elements must remain in a mixed body; and these are substantial forms. Therefore in the human body there are other substantial forms besides the intellectual soul.

On the contrary, Of one thing there is but one substantial being. But the substantial form gives substantial being. Therefore of one thing there is but one substantial form. But the soul is the substantial form of man. Therefore it is impossible that there be in man another substantial form besides the intellectual soul.

I answer that, If we supposed that the intellectual soul is not united to the body as its form, but only as its mover, as the Platonists maintain, it would necessarily follow that in man there is another substantial form by which the body is established in its being as movable by the soul.[94] If, however, the intellectual soul is united to the body as its substantial form, as we have said above, it is impossible for another substantial form besides the intellectual soul to be found in man.

In order to make this evident, we must consider that the substantial form differs from the accidental form in this, that the accidental form does not make a thing *to be absolutely,* but *to be such,* as heat does not make a thing to be absolutely, but only to be hot. Therefore by the coming of the accidental form a thing is not said to be made or generated absolutely, but to be made

---

[92]Aristotle, *Phys.,* VIII, 5 (257b 12).   [93]*Op. cit.,* V, 1 (225a 25).   [94]Cf. Alex. of Hales, *Summa Theol.,* II, I, no. 344 (II, 419).

such, or to be in some particular disposition; and in like manner, when an accidental form is removed, a thing is said to be corrupted, not absolutely, but relatively. But the substantial form gives being absolutely, and hence by its coming a thing is said to be generated absolutely, and by its removal to be corrupted absolutely. For this reason, the old natural philosophers, who held that primary matter was some actual being—for instance, fire or air, or something of that sort—maintained that nothing is generated absolutely, or corrupted absolutely; but that *every becoming is nothing but an alteration*, as we read *Physics* i.[95] Therefore, if besides the intellectual soul there pre-existed in matter another substantial form by which the subject of the soul were made an actual being, it would follow that the soul does not give being absolutely, and consequently that it is not the substantial form; and so at the advent of the soul there would not be absolute generation, nor at its removal absolute corruption. All of which is clearly false.

Whence we must conclude that there is no other substantial form in man besides the intellectual soul; and that just as the soul contains virtually the sensitive and nutritive souls, so does it contain virtually all inferior forms, and does alone whatever the imperfect forms do in other things. The same is to be said of the sensitive soul in brute animals, and of the nutritive soul in plants, and universally of all more perfect forms in relation to the imperfect.

Reply Obj. 1. Aristotle does not say that the soul is the act of a body only, but *the act of a physical organic body which has life potentially*; and that this potentiality *does not exclude the soul.*[96] Whence it is clear that in the being of which the soul is called the act, the soul itself is included; as when we say that heat is the act of what is hot, and light of what is lucid. And this means, not that the lucid is lucid in separation from light, but that it is lucid through light. In like manner, the soul is said to be the *act of a body*, etc., because it is by the soul that the body is a body, and is organic, and has life potentially. When the first act is said to be *in potentiality*, this is to be understood in relation to the second act, which is operation. Now such a potentiality *does not remove*—that is, does not exclude—the soul.

Reply Obj. 2. The soul does not move the body by its essence, as the form of the body, but by the motive power, whose act presupposes that the body is already actualized by the soul: so that the soul by its motive power is the part which moves; and the animate body is the part moved.

Reply Obj. 3. There are in matter various degrees of perfection, as *to be, to live, to sense, to understand*. Now what is added is always more perfect.

---

[95]Aristotle, *Phys.*, I, 4 (187a 30).   [96]*De An.*, II, 2 (412a 27; b 25).

Therefore that form which gives matter only the first degree of perfection is the most imperfect, while that form which gives the first, second, and third degree, and so on, is the most perfect: and yet it is present to matter immediately.

Reply Obj. 4. Avicenna held that the substantial forms of the elements remain entire in the mixed body, and that the mixture is made by the contrary qualities of the elements being reduced to an equilibrium.[97] But this is impossible. For the various forms of the elements must necessarily be in various parts of matter, and for the distinction of the parts we must suppose dimensions, without which matter cannot be divisible. Now matter subject to dimension is not to be found except in a body. But several distinct bodies cannot be in the same place. Whence it follows that the elements in the mixed body would be distinct as to position. Hence, there would not be a real mixture which affects the whole, but only a mixture that seems so to the sense because of the juxtaposition of very small particles.

Averroes[98] maintained that the forms of elements, by reason of their imperfection, are between accidental and substantial forms, and so can be *more* or *less*; and therefore in the mixture they are modified and reduced to an equilibrium, so that one form emerges among them. But this is even more impossible. For the substantial being of each thing consists in something indivisible, and every addition and subtraction varies the species, as in numbers, according to *Metaph.* viii.[99] Consequently, it is impossible for any substantial form to receive *more* or *less*. Nor is it less impossible for anything to be between substance and accident.

Therefore we must say, in accordance with the Philosopher,[100] that the forms of the elements remain in the mixed body, not actually, but virtually. For the proper qualities of the elements remain, though modified; and in these qualities is the power of the elementary forms. This quality of the mixture is the proper disposition for the substantial form of the mixed body; for instance, the form of a stone, or of any sort of soul.

FIFTH ARTICLE
Whether the Intellectual Soul Is Fittingly United to Such a Body?

We proceed thus to the Fifth Article:—

Objection 1. It would seem that the intellectual soul is not fittingly

---

[97]Cf. Averroes, *In De Gener.*, I, comm. 90 (V, 167r). [98]*In De Caelo*, III, comm. 67 (V, 105r). [99]Aristotle, *Metaph.*, VII, 3 (1044a 9). [100]*De Gener.*, I, 10 (327b 22).

united to such a body. For matter must be proportionate to the form. But the intellectual soul is an incorruptible form. Therefore it is not fittingly united to a corruptible body.

Obj. 2. Further, the intellectual soul is a perfectly immaterial form. A proof of this is its operation in which corporeal matter does not share. But the more subtle is the body, the less has it of matter. Therefore the soul should be united to a most subtle body, to fire, for instance, and not to a mixed body, still less to a terrestrial body.

Obj. 3. Further, since the form is the principle of the species, one form cannot produce a variety of species. But the intellectual soul is one form. Therefore, it should not be united to a body which is composed of parts belonging to various species.

Obj. 4. Further, a more perfect form should have a more perfect subject. But the intellectual soul is the most perfect of souls. Therefore since the bodies of other animals are naturally provided with a covering, for instance, with hair instead of clothes, and hoofs instead of shoes, and are, moreover, naturally provided with arms, as claws, teeth, and horns:—it seems that the intellectual soul should not have been united to a body which is imperfect, in being deprived of the above means of protection.

On the contrary, The Philosopher says that *the soul is the act of a physical organic body having life potentially.*[101]

I answer that, Since the form is not for the matter, but rather the matter for the form, we must gather from the form the reason why the matter is such as it is; and not conversely. Now the intellectual soul, as we have seen above,[102] holds in the order of nature the lowest place among intellectual substances. So much so, that it is not naturally endowed with the knowledge of truth, as the angels are, but has to gather knowledge from individual things by way of the senses, as Dionysius says.[103] But nature never fails anyone in what is necessary, and therefore the intellectual soul had to be endowed not only with the power of understanding, but also with the power of sensing. Now the action of the senses is not performed without a corporeal instrument. Therefore the intellectual soul had to be united to a body which could be the fitting organ of sense.

Now all the other senses are based on the sense of touch. But the organ of touch requires to be a medium between contraries, such as hot and cold, wet and dry, and the like, of which the sense of touch has the perception; and in this way it is in potentiality with regard to contraries, and is

---

[101]*De An.*, II, 1 (412a 27; b 5).   [102]Q. 55, a. 2.   [103]*De Div. Nom.*, VII, 2 (PG 3, 868).

able to perceive them. Therefore the more the organ of touch is reduced to an equable complexion, the more sensitive will be the touch. But the intellectual soul has the power of sense in all its completeness, because what belongs to the inferior nature pre-exists more perfectly in the superior, as Dionysius says.[104] Therefore the body to which the intellectual soul is united had to be a mixed body, above others reduced to the most equable complexion. For this reason, among animals man has the better sense of touch. And among men, those who have the better sense of touch have the better intellect. A sign of which is that we observe *those who are refined in body are well endowed in mind*, as is stated in *De Anima* ii.[105]

Reply Obj. 1. Perhaps someone might try to avoid this objection by saying that before sin the human body was incorruptible. But such an answer does not seem sufficient, because before sin the human body was immortal, not by nature, but by a gift of divine grace; or otherwise its immortality would not be forfeited through sin, as neither was the immortality of the devil.

Therefore we answer in another way. Now in matter two conditions are to be found: one which is chosen in order that the matter be suitable to the form; the other which follows necessarily as a result of a previous disposition. The artisan, for instance, chooses iron for the making of a saw, because it is suitable for cutting through hard material; but that the teeth of the saw may become blunt and rusted, follows from a necessity imposed by the matter itself. So the intellectual soul requires a body of equable complexion, which, however, is corruptible by necessity of its matter. If, however, it be said that God could avoid this necessity, we answer that in the establishment of natural things, the question is not what God can do, but what befits the natures of things, as Augustine says.[106] God, however, provided in this case by applying a remedy against death in the gift of grace.

Reply Obj. 2. A body is not necessary to the intellectual soul by reason of its intellectual operation considered as such, but because of the sensitive power, which requires an organ of equable temperament. Therefore the intellectual soul had to be united to such a body, and not to a simple element, or to a mixed body, in which fire was in excess; because otherwise there could not be an equability of temperament. And this body of an equable temperament has a dignity of its own in being remote from contraries. In this it resembles in a way a heavenly body.

---

[104]*Op. cit.*, V, 3 (PG 3, 817).   [105]Aristotle, *De An.*, II, 9 (412a 26).
[106]*De Genesi ad Litt.*, II, 1 (PL 34, 263).

Reply Obj. 3. The parts of an animal, for instance, the eye, hand, flesh, and bones, and so forth, do not make the species, but the whole does; and therefore, properly speaking, we cannot say that these have diverse species, but diverse dispositions. This is suitable to the intellectual soul, which, although it be one in its essence, yet because of its perfection, is manifold in its power. And so, for its various operations the soul requires various dispositions in the parts of the body to which it is united. For this reason we observe that there is a greater variety of parts in perfect than in imperfect animals; and in these a greater variety than in plants.

Reply Obj. 4. The intellectual soul, as comprehending universals, has a power that is open to infinite things. Therefore it cannot be limited by nature to certain fixed natural judgments or even to certain fixed means whether of defense or of clothing, as is the case with other animals, whose souls are endowed with a knowledge and a power for fixed particular things. Instead of all these, man has by nature his reason and his hands, which are *the organs of organs*,[107] since by their means man can make for himself instruments of an infinite variety, and for any number of purposes.

---

[107] Aristotle, *De An.*, III, 8 (432a 1-2).

PART ONE
QUESTION 91
The Production of the Body of the First Man

THIRD ARTICLE
Whether the Body of Man Was Given an Apt Disposition?

We proceed thus to the Third Article:—

Objection 1. It would seem that the body of man was not given an apt disposition. For since man is the noblest of animals, his body ought to be the best disposed in what is proper to an animal, that is, in sense and movement. But some animals have sharper senses and quicker movement than man; and thus dogs have a keener smell, and birds a swifter flight. Therefore man's body was not aptly disposed.

Obj. 2. Further, that is perfect which lacks nothing. But the human body lacks more than the bodies of other animals, for these are provided with covering and natural arms of defense, in which man is lacking. Therefore the human body is very imperfectly disposed.

Obj. 3. Further, man is more distant from plants than he is from the brutes. But plants are erect in stature, while brutes are prone in stature. Therefore man should not be of erect stature.

On the contrary, it is written (*Eccles.* vii. 30): *God made man right.*

I answer that, All natural things were produced by the divine art, and so may be called God's works of art. Now every artist intends to give to his work the best disposition; not absolutely the best, but the best as regards the proposed end. And even if this entails some defect, the artist cares not. Thus, for instance, when a man makes himself a saw for the purpose of cutting, he makes it of iron, which is suitable for the object in view; and he does not prefer to make it of glass, though this be a more beautiful material, because this very beauty would be an obstacle to the end he has in view. Therefore God gave to each natural being the best disposition; not absolutely so, but in view of its proper end. This is what the Philosopher says: *And because it is better so, not absolutely, but for each one's substance.*[108]

---

[108]*Op. cit.*, II, 7 (198b 8).

Now the proximate end of the human body is the rational soul and its operations; for matter is for the sake of the form, and instruments are for the actions of the agent. I say, therefore, that God fashioned the human body in that disposition which was best according as it was most suited to such a form and to such operations. If defect exists in the disposition of the human body, it is well to observe that such defect arises, as a necessary result of the matter, from the conditions required in the body in order to make it suitably proportioned to the soul and its operations.

Reply Obj. 1. The sense of touch, which is the foundation of the other senses, is more perfect in man than in any other animal; and for this reason man must have the most equable temperament of all animals. Moreover, man also excels all other animals in the interior sensitive powers, as is clear from what we have said above.[109] But by a kind of necessity, man falls short of the other animals in some of the exterior senses; and thus of all animals he has the weakest sense of smell. For of all animals man needs the largest brain as compared to the body; and this both for his greater freedom of action in the interior powers required for the intellectual operations, we as have seen above,[110] and in order that the low temperature of the brain may modify the heat of the heart, which has to be considerable in man for him to be able to stand up erect. So it happens that the size of the brain, by reason of its humidity, is an impediment to the smell, which requires dryness. In the same way, we may suggest a reason why some animals have a keener sight, and a more acute hearing then man, namely, because of a hindrance to his senses arising necessarily from the perfect equability of his temperament. The same reason suffices to explain why some animals are more rapid in movement than man, since this excellence of speed is inconsistent which the equability of the human temperament.

Reply Obj. 2. Horns and claws, which are the weapons of some animals, and toughness of hide and quantity of hair or feathers, which are the clothing of animals, are signs of an abundance of the earthly element; which does not agree with the equability and softness of the human temperament. Therefore such things do not suit the nature of man. Instead of these, he has reason and hands whereby he can make himself arms and clothes, and other necessaries of life, of infinite variety. And so the hand is called by Aristotle the *organ of organs*.[111] Moreover, it was more becoming to a rational nature, which is capable of conceiving an infinite number of things, to have the power of devising for itself an infinite number of instruments.

---

[109]Q. 78, a. 4.   [110]Q. 84, a. 7.   [111]Aristotle, *De An.*, III, 8 (432a 1).

Reply Obj. 3. An upright stature was becoming to man for four reasons. First, because the senses are given to man, not only for the purpose of procuring the necessaries of life, for which they are bestowed on other animals, but also for the purpose of knowledge. Hence, whereas the other animals take delight in the things of sense only as ordered to food and sex, man alone takes pleasure in the beauty of sensible things for its own sake, Therefore, as the senses are situated chiefly in the face, other animals have the face turned to the ground, as it were for the purpose of seeking food and procuring a livelihood; whereas man has his face erect, in order that by the senses, and chiefly by sight, which is more subtle and reveals many differences in things, he may freely survey the sensible things around him, both heavenly and earthly, so as to gather intelligible truth from all things. Secondly, for the greater freedom of the acts of the interior powers, which requires that the brain, wherein these actions are, in a way, performed, be not low down, but lifted up above other parts of the body. Thirdly, because if man's figure were prone to the ground, he would need to use his hands as fore-feet, and thus their utility for other purposes would cease. Fourthly, because if man's figure were prone to the ground, and he used his hands as fore-feet, he would be obliged to take hold of his food with his mouth. Thus he would have a protruding mouth, with thick and hard lips, and also a hard tongue, so as to keep if from being hurt by exterior things; as we see in other animals. Now such a disposition would completely hinder speech which is the proper work of the reason.

Nevertheless, though of erect stature, man is far above plants. For man's superior part, his head, is turned towards the superior part of the world, and his inferior part is turned towards the inferior world; and therefore he is perfectly disposed as to the general situation of his body. Plants have the superior part turned towards the lower world, since their roots correspond to the mouth; and their inferior part towards the upper world. But brute animals have a middle disposition, for the superior part of the animal is that by which it takes food, and the inferior part that by which it rids itself of the surplus.

5

THE POWERS OF THE SOUL

Summa Theologica

PART ONE
QUESTION 77
What Belongs to the Powers of the Soul in General

We proceed to consider those things which belong to the powers of the soul, first, in general, and secondly, in particular.[1]

FIRST ARTICLE
Whether the Essence of the Soul Is Its Power?

We proceed thus to the First Article:—

Objection 1. It would seem that the essence of the soul is its power. For Augustine says that *mind, knowledge and love are in the soul substantially, or, what is the same thing, essentially*[2]; *and that memory, understanding and will are one life, one mind, one essence.*[3]

Obj. 2. Further, the soul is nobler than primary matter. But primary matter is its own potentiality. Much more therefore is the soul its own power.

Obj. 3. Further, the substantial form is simpler than the accidental form; a sign of which is that the substantial form is not intensified or relaxed, but is indivisible. But the accidental form is its own power. Much more therefore is that substantial form which is the soul.

Obj. 4. Further, we sense by the sensitive power and we understand by the intellectual power. But *that by which we first sense and understand* is the soul, according to the Philosopher.[4] Therefore the soul is its power.

Obj. 5. Further, whatever does not belong to the essence is an accident. Therefore, if the power of the soul is something else beside the essence thereof, it is an accident; which is contrary to Augustine, who says that the foregoing [i.e., the trinities mentioned in objection 1] *are not in the soul as*

---

[1]Q. 78.　　[2]*De Trin.*, IX, 4 (PL 42, 963).　　[3]*Op. cit.*, X, 11 (PL 42, 984).
[4]*De An.*, II, 2 (414a 12).

98

*in a subject, as color or shape, or any other quality, or quantity, is in a body;
for such a thing does not exceed the subject in which it is, whereas the mind can
love and know other things.*[5]

Obj. 6. Further, *a simple form cannot be a subject.*[6] But the soul is a simple form, since it is not composed of matter and form, as we have said above.[7] Therefore the power of the soul cannot be in it as in a subject.

Obj. 7. Further, an accident is not the principle of a substantial difference. But *sensitive* and *rational* are substantial differences; and they are taken from sense and reason, which are powers of the soul. Therefore the powers of the soul are not accidents; and so it would seem that the power of the soul is its own essence.

On the contrary, Dionysius says that *heavenly spirits are divided into essence, power, and operation.*[8] Much more, then, in the soul is the essence distinct from the virtue or power.

I answer that, It is impossible to admit that the power of the soul is its essence, although some have maintained it.[9] For the present purpose this may be proved in two ways. First, because, since potency and act divide being and every kind of being, we must refer a potency and its act to the same genus. Therefore, if the act be not in the genus of substance, the potency which is said in relation to that act cannot be in the genus of substance. Now the operation of the soul is not in the genus of substance, for this belongs to God alone, whose operation is His own substance. Therefore the divine potency or power which is the principle of His operation is the divine essence itself. This cannot be true either of the soul or of any creature, as we have said above when speaking of the angels.[10] Secondly, this may be also shown to be impossible in the soul. For the soul by its very essence is an act. Therefore, if the very essence of the soul were the immediate principle of operation, whatever has a soul would always have actual vital actions, as that which has a soul is always an actually living thing. For, as a form, the soul is not an act ordained to a further act; it is rather the ultimate term of generation. Therefore, for it to be in potentiality to another act does not belong to it according to its essence as a form, but according to its power. So the soul itself, as the subject of its power, is called the first act, with a further relation to the second act.[11] Now we

---

[5]*De Trin.*, IX, 4 (PL 42, 963).   [6]Boethius, *De Trin.*, II (PL 64, 1250).
[7]Q. 75, a. 5.   [8]*De Cael. Hier.*, XI, 2 (PG 3, 284).   [9]William of Auvergne, *De An.*, III, 4 (II, Suppl., 89).— Cf. Peter Lombard, *Sent.*, I, iii, 2 (I, 35).   [10]Q. 54, a. 3.   [11]Aristotle, *De An.*, II, 1 (412a 27).

observe that what has a soul is not always actual with respect to its vital operations. Hence it is also said in the definition of the soul that it is *the act of a body having life potentially;* which potentiality, however, *does not exclude the soul.*[12] Therefore it follows that the essence of the soul is not its power. For nothing is in potentiality by reason of an act, as act.

Reply Obj. 1. Augustine is speaking of the mind as it knows and loves itself. Thus knowledge and love, as referred to the soul as known and loved, are substantially or essentially in the soul, for the very substance or essence of the soul is known and loved. In the same way are we to understand what he says in the other passage, that those things are *one life, one mind, one essence.* Or, as some say,[13] this passage is true in the sense in which the potential whole is predicated of its parts, being midway between the universal whole and the integral whole. For the universal whole is in each part according to its entire essence and power, as animal in a man and in a horse; and therefore it is properly predicated to each part. But the integral whole is not in each part, either according to its whole essence, or according to its whole power. Therefore in no way can it be predicated of each part. Yet in a way it is predicated, though improperly, of all the parts together; as if we were to say that the wall, roof and foundations are a house. But the potential whole is in each part according to its whole essence, not, however, according to its whole power. Therefore it can in a way be predicated of each part, but not so properly as the universal whole. In this sense, Augustine says that the memory, understanding and will are the one essence of the soul.

Reply Obj. 2. The act to which primary matter is in potentiality is the substantial form. Therefore the potentiality of matter is nothing else but its essence.

Reply Obj. 3. Action belongs to the composite, as does being; for to act belongs to what exists. Now the composite has being substantially through the substantial form; and it operates by the power which results from the substantial form. Hence an active accidental form is to the substantial form of the agent (for instance, heat compared to the form of fire) as the power of soul is to the soul.

Reply Obj. 4. That the accidental form is a principle of action is due to the substantial form. Therefore the substantial form is the first principle of action, but not the proximate principle. In this sense the Philosopher says that *the soul is that whereby we understand and sense.*

Reply Obj. 5. If we take accident as meaning what is divided against

---

[12]*Ibid.* (412a 25).   [13]St. Albert, *In I Sent.*, d. iii, a. 34 (XXV, 140).

substance, then there can be no medium between substance and accident; for they are divided by affirmation and negation, that is, according to being in a subject, and not being in a subject. In this sense, since the power of the soul is not its essence, it must be an accident. It belongs to the second species of accident, that of quality. But if we take accident as one of the five predicables, in this sense there is a medium between substance and accident. For the substance is all that belongs to the essence of a thing. But whatever is beyond the essence of a thing cannot be called accident in this sense; but only what is not caused by the essential principle of the species. For *property* does not belong to the essence of a thing, but is caused by essential principles of the species; and hence it is a medium between the essence and accident thus understood. In this sense the powers of the soul may be said to be a medium between substance and accident, as being natural properties of the soul. When Augustine says that knowledge and love are not in the soul as accidents in a subject, this must be understood in the sense given above, inasmuch as they are compared to the soul, not as loving and knowing, but as loved and known. His argument holds good in this sense; for if love were in the soul loved as in a subject, it would follow that an accident transcends its subject, since even other things are loved through the soul.

Reply Obj. 6. Although the soul is not composed of matter and form, yet it has an admixture of potentiality, as we have said above,[14] and for this reason it can be the subject of an accident. The statement quoted is verified in God, Who is Pure Act; and it is in treating of this subject that Boethius employs the phrase.

Reply Obj. 7. Rational and sensitive, as differences, are not taken from the powers of sense and reason, but from sensitive and rational soul itself. But because substantial forms, which in themselves are unknown to us, are known by their accidents, nothing prevents us from sometimes substituting accidents for substantial differences.

SECOND ARTICLE
Whether There Are Several Powers of the Soul?

We proceed thus to the Second Article:—

Objection 1. It would seem that there are not several powers of the soul. For the intellectual soul approaches nearest to the likeness of God. But in God there is one simple power. So, too, therefore, in the intellectual soul.

---

[14]Q. 75, a. 5, ad 4.

Obj. 2. Further, the higher a power is, the more unified it is. But the intellectual soul excels all other forms in power. Therefore above all others it has one virtue or power.

Obj. 3. Further, to operate belongs to what is in act. But by the one essence of the soul, man has actual being in the different degrees of perfection, as we have seen above.[15] Therefore by the one power of the soul he performs operations of various degrees.

On the contrary, The Philosopher places several powers in the soul.[16]

I answer that, Of necessity we must place several powers in the soul. To make this evident, we observe that, as the Philosopher says,[17] the lowest order of things cannot acquire perfect goodness, but they acquire a certain imperfect goodness, by few movements. Those which belong to a higher order acquire perfect goodness by many movements. Those yet higher acquire perfect goodness by few movements, and the highest perfection is found in those things which acquire perfect goodness without any movement whatever. Thus he is least of all disposed to health, who can only acquire imperfect health by means of a few remedies. Better disposed is he who can acquire perfect health by means of many remedies, and better still, he who can by few remedies; but best of all is he who has perfect health without any remedies. We conclude, therefore, that things which are below man acquire a certain limited goodness, and so have a few determinate operations and powers. But man can acquire universal and perfect goodness, because he can acquire beatitude. Yet he is in the lowest degree, according to his nature, of those to whom beatitude is possible; and therefore the human soul requires many and various operations and powers. But to angels a smaller variety of powers is sufficient. In God, however, there is not power or action beyond His own Essence.

There is yet another reason why the human soul abounds in a variety of powers:—it is on the confines of spiritual and corporeal creatures, and therefore the powers of both meet together in the soul.

Reply Obj. 1. The intellectual soul approaches to the divine likeness, more than inferior creatures, in being able to acquire perfect goodness, although by many and various means; and in this it falls short of more perfect creatures.

Reply Obj. 2. A unified power is superior if it extends to equal things. But a multiform power is superior to it, if it is over many things.

---

[15]Q. 76, a. 3 and 4.   [16]*De An.*, II, 3 (414 31).   [17]*De Caelo*, II, 12 (292a 22).

Reply Obj. 3. One thing has one substantial being, but may have several operations. So there is one essence in the soul, but several powers.

Whether the Powers Are Distinguished by Their Acts and Objects?

We proceed thus to the Third Article:—

Objection 1. It would seem that the powers of the soul are not distinguished by acts and objects. For nothing is determined to its species by what is subsequent and extrinsic to it. But the act is subsequent to the power, and the object is extrinsic to it. Therefore the soul's powers are not specifically distinct by acts and objects.

Obj. 2. Further, contraries are what differ most from each other. Therefore if the powers are distinguished by their objects, it follows that the same power could not have contrary objects. This is clearly false in almost all the powers, for the power of vision extends to white and black, and the power of taste to sweet and bitter.

Obj. 3. Further, if the cause be removed, the effect is removed. Hence if the difference of powers came from the difference of objects, the same object would not come under different powers. This is clearly false, for the same thing is known by the cognitive power, and desired by the appetitive.

Obj. 4. Further, that which of itself is the cause of anything, is the cause thereof, wherever it is. But various objects which belong to various powers belong also to some one power; as sound and color belong to sight and hearing, which are different powers, yet come under the one power of common sense. Therefore the powers are not distinguished according to the difference of their objects.

On the contrary, Things that are subsequent are distinguished by what precedes. But the Philosopher says that *acts and operations precede the powers according to the reason; and these again are preceded by their opposites,*[18] that is, their objects. Therefore the powers are distinguished according to their acts and objects.

I answer that, A power as such as directed to an act. Therefore we must derive the nature of a power from the act to which it is directed; and consequently the nature of a power is diversified according as the nature of the act is diversified. Now the nature of an act is diversified according to the various natures of the objects. For every act is either of an active power or of a passive power. Now, the object is to the act of a passive power as the principle and moving cause; for color is the principle of vision, inasmuch

---

[18]*De An.*, II, 4 (415a 18).

as it moves the sight. On the order hand, to the act of an active power the object is a term and an end; just as the object of the power of growth is perfect quantity, which is the end of growth. Now, from these two things an act receives its species, namely, from its principle, or from its end or term. For the act of heating differs from the act of cooling in this, that the former proceeds from something hot, which is the active principle, to heat; while the latter proceeds from something cold, which is the active principle, to cold. Therefore the powers are of necessity distinguished by their acts and objects.

Nevertheless, we must observe that things which are accidental do not change the species. For since to be colored is accidental to an animal, its species is not changed by a difference of color, but by a difference in that which belongs to the nature of an animal, that is to say, by a difference in the sensitive soul, which is sometimes found accompanied by reason, and sometimes not. Hence *rational* and *irrational* are differences dividing animal, constituting its various species. In like manner, therefore, not any variety of objects diversifies the powers of the soul, but a difference in that to which the power of its very nature is directed. Thus the senses of their very nature are directed to the passive quality which of itself is divided into color, sound, and the like, and therefore there is one sensitive power with regard to color, namely, sight, and another with regard to sound, namely, hearing. But it is accidental to a passive quality, for instance, to something colored, to be a musician or a grammarian, great or small, a man or a stone. Therefore by reason of such differences the powers of the soul are not distinguished.

Reply Obj. 1. Act, though subsequent in being to power, is, nevertheless, prior to it in intention and logically; as the end is with regard to the agent. And the object, although extrinsic, is, nevertheless, the principle or end of the action; and the conditions which are intrinsic to a thing are proportionate to its principle and end.

Reply Obj. 2. If any power were to have one of two contraries as such for its object, the other contrary would belong to another power. But the power of the soul does not regard the nature of the contrary as such, but rather the common aspect of both contraries; as sight does not regard white as such, but as color. This is because, of two contraries, one, in a manner, includes the nature of the other, since they are to one another as perfect and imperfect.

Reply Obj. 3. Nothing prevents things which coincide in subject from being considered under different aspects; and therefore they can belong to various powers of the soul.

Reply Obj. 4. The higher power of itself regards a more universal formality in its object then the lower power; because the higher a power is, to a greater number of things does it extend. Therefore many things are combined in the one formality of the object, which the higher power considers of itself; while they differ in the formalities regarded by the lower powers of themselves. Thus it is that various objects belong to various lower powers; which objects, however, are subject to one higher power.

FOURTH ARTICLE
Whether Among the Powers of the Soul There Is Order?

We proceed thus to the Fourth Article:—

Objection 1. It would seem that there is no order among the powers of the soul. For in those things which come under one division, there is no before and after, but all are naturally simultaneous. But the powers of the soul are contradistinguished from one another. Therefore there is no order among them.

Obj. 2. Further, the powers of the soul are related to their objects, and to the soul itself. On the part of the soul, there is no order among the powers, because the soul is one. In like manner, there is no order among them in relation to the objects, which are various and dissimilar, as color and sound. Therefore there is no order among the powers of the soul.

Obj. 3. Further, where there is order among powers, we find that the operation of one depends on the operation of another. But the action of one power of the soul does not depend on that of another; for sight can act independently of hearing, and conversely. Therefore there is no order among the powers of the soul.

On the contrary, The Philosopher compares the parts or powers of the soul to figures.[19] But figures have an order among themselves. Therefore the powers of the soul also have order.

I answer that, Since the soul is one, and the powers are many, and since a number of things that proceed from one must proceed in a certain order, there must be some order among the powers of the soul. Accordingly we may observe a triple order among them, two of which correspond to the dependence of one power on another, while the third is taken from the order of the objects. Now the dependence of one power on another can be taken in two ways: according to the order of nature, inasmuch as perfect things are by their nature prior to imperfect things; and according to the order of generation and time, inasmuch as from being imperfect, a thing

---

[19]*Op. cit.*, II, 3 (414b 20).

comes to be perfect. Thus, according to the first kind of order among the powers, the intellectual powers are prior to the sensitive powers; wherefore they direct them and command them. Likewise the sensitive powers are prior according to this order to the powers of the nutritive soul.

In the second kind of order, it is the other way about. For the powers of the nutritive soul are prior in generation to the powers of the sensitive soul; and therefore they prepare the body for the actions of the sensitive powers. The same is to be said of the sensitive powers with regard to the intellectual. But in the third kind of order, certain sensitive powers are ordered among themselves, namely, sight, hearing, and smelling. For the visible comes naturally first, since it is common to higher and lower bodies. On the other hand, sound is audible in the air, which is naturally prior to the mingling of elements, of which odor is the result.

Reply Obj. 1. The species of a given genus are to one another as before and after, like numbers and figures, if considered in their being; although they may be said to be simultaneous, according as they receive the predication of the genus common to them.

Reply Obj. 2. This order among the powers of the soul is both on the part of the soul (which, though it be one according to its essence, is disposed to various acts in a certain order), and on the part of the objects, and furthermore on the part of the acts, as we have said above.

Reply Obj. 3. This argument holds good as regards those powers among which order of the third kind exists. Those powers, however, among which the two other kinds of order exist, are such that the action of one depends on another.

PART ONE
QUESTION 78
The Powers of the Soul in Particular

We next treat of the powers of the soul in particular. The theologian, however, has only to inquire specifically concerning the intellectual and appetitive powers, in which the virtues reside. And since the knowledge of these powers depends to a certain extent on the other powers, our consideration of the powers of the soul in particular will be divided into three parts: first, we shall consider those powers which are a preamble to the intellect; secondly, the intellectual powers[20]; thirdly, the appetitive powers.[21]

FIRST ARTICLE
Whether There Are to Be Distinguished
Five Genera of Powers in the Soul?

We proceed thus to the First Article:—

Objection 1. It would seem that there are not to be distinguished five genera of powers in the soul—namely, vegetative, sensitive, appetitive, locomotive, and intellectual. For the powers of the soul are called its parts. But only three parts of the soul are commonly assigned—namely, the vegetative soul, the sensitive soul, and the rational soul. Therefore there are only three genera of powers in the soul, and not five.

Obj. 2. Further, the powers of the soul are the principles of its vital operations. Now, in four ways is a thing said to live. For the Philosopher says: *In several ways a thing is said to live, and even if only one of these is present, the thing is said to live; as intellect and sense, local movement and rest, and lastly, movement of decrease and increase due to nourishment.*[22] Therefore there are only four genera of powers of the soul, as the appetitive is excluded.

Obj. 3. Further, a special kind of soul ought not to be assigned as regards what is common to all the powers. Now desire is common to each power of the soul. For sight desires its appropriate visible object; whence we read (*Ecclus.* xl. 22): *The eye desireth favor and beauty, but more than*

---

[20]Q. 79.   [21]Q. 80.   [22]*De An.*, II, 2 (413a 22).

these green sown fields. In the same way, every other power desires its appropriate object. Therefore the appetitive power should not be made a special genus of the powers of the soul.

Obj. 4. Further, the moving principle in animals is sense, or intellect, or appetite, as the Philosopher says.[23] Therefore the motive power should not be added to the above as a special genus of soul.

On the contrary, The Philosopher says: *The powers are the vegetative, the sensitive, the appetitive, the locomotive, and the intellectual.*[24]

I answer that, There are five genera among the powers of the soul, as above numbered. Of these, three are called souls, and four are called modes of living. The reason of this diversity is that the various souls are distinguished according as the operation of the soul transcends the operation of the corporeal nature in various ways; for the whole corporeal nature is subject to the soul, and is related to it as its matter and instrument. There exists, therefore, an operation of the soul which so far exceeds the corporeal nature that it is not even performed by any corporeal organ; and such is the operation of the *rational soul.* Below this, there is another operation of the soul, which is indeed performed through a corporeal organ, but not through a corporeal quality, and this is the operation of the *sensitive soul.* For though hot and cold, wet and dry, and other such corporeal qualities are required for the work of the senses, yet they are not required in such a way that the operation of the senses takes place by the power of such qualities; but only for the proper disposition of the organ. The lowest of the operations of the soul is that which is performed by a corporeal organ and by the power of a corporeal quality. Yet this transcends the operation of the corporeal nature; because the movements of bodies are caused by an extrinsic principle, while these operations are from an intrinsic principle. For this is common to all the operations of the soul, since every animate thing, in some way, moves itself. Such is the operation of the *vegetative soul;* for digestion, and what follows, is caused instrumentally by the action of heat, as the Philosopher says.[25]

Now the powers of the soul are distinguished generically by their objects. For the higher a power is, the more universal is the object to which it extends, as we have said above.[26] But the object of the soul's operation may be considered in a triple order. For in the soul there is a power whose object is only the body that is united to that soul; and the powers of this genus are called *vegetative,* for the vegetative power acts

---

[23]*Op. cit.*, III, 10 (433a 9).   [24]*Op. cit.*, II, 3 (414A 31).   [25]Aristotle, *Op. cit.*, II, 4 (416b 25).   [26]Q. 77, a. 3, ad 4.

only on the body to which the soul is united. There is another genus in the powers of the soul which regards a more universal object—namely, every sensible body, and not only the body to which the soul is united. And there is yet another genus in the powers of the soul which regards a still more universal object—namely, not only the sensible body, but universally all being. Therefore it is evident that the latter two genera of the soul's powers have an operation in regard not merely to that which is united to them, but also to something extrinsic. Now, since whatever operates must in some way be united to the object in relation to which it operates, it follows of necessity that this something extrinsic, which is the object of the soul's operation, must be related to the soul in a twofold manner. First, inasmuch as this something extrinsic has a natural aptitude to be united to the soul, and to be by its likeness in the soul. In this way there are two kinds of powers—namely, the *sensitive*, in regard to the less common object, the sensible body; and the *intellectual*, in regard to the most common object, universal being. Secondly, inasmuch as the soul itself has an inclination and tendency to the external thing. And in this way there are again two kinds of powers in the soul: one—the *appetitive*—according to which the soul is referred to something extrinsic as to an end, which is first in the intention; the other—the *locomotive* power—according to which the soul is referred to something extrinsic as to the term of its operation and movement; for every animal is moved for the purpose of realizing its desires and intentions.

The modes of living, on the other hand, are distinguished according to the degrees of living things. There are some living things in which there exists only vegetative power, as plants. There are others in which along with the vegetative there exists also the sensitive, but not the locomotive, power; and such are immovable animals, as shellfish. There are others which, besides this, have locomotive powers, as do the perfect animals, which require many things for their life, and consequently need movement to seek necessaries of life from a distance. And there are some living things which along with these have intellectual power—namely, men. But the appetitive power does not constitute a degree of living things; because *wherever there is sense there is also appetite.*[27]

Thus the first two objections are hereby solved.

Reply Obj. 3. *Natural appetite* is that inclination which each thing has, of its own nature, for something; wherefore by its natural appetite each power desires what is suitable to itself. But *animal appetite* follows from

---

[27] Aristotle, *De An.*, II, 3 (414b 1.)

the apprehended form. This sort of appetite requires a special power in the soul—apprehension alone does not suffice. For a thing is desired according as it exists in its own nature, whereas in the apprehensive power it exists, not according to its own nature, but according to its likeness. Whence it is clear that sight desires naturally a visible object for the purpose of its act only—namely, for the purpose of seeing; but the animal by its appetitive power desires the thing seen, not merely for the purpose of seeing it, but also for other purposes. But if the soul did not require the things perceived by the senses, except for the sake of the actions of the senses (that is, for the purpose of sensing them), there would be no need for a special genus of appetitive power, since the natural appetite of the power would suffice.

Reply Obj. 4. Although sense and appetite are principles of movement in perfect animals, yet sense and appetite, as such, are not sufficient to cause movement, unless another power be added to them; for immovable animals have sense and appetite, and yet they have not the power of motion. Now this motive power is not only in the appetite and sense as commanding the movement, but also in the parts of the body, to make them obey the appetite of the soul which moves them. Of this we have a sign in the fact that when the members are deprived of their natural disposition, they do not move in obedience to the appetite.

SECOND ARTICLE
Whether the Parts of the Vegetative Soul Are Fittingly Enumerated as the Nutritive, Augmentative, and Generative?

We proceed thus to the Second Article:—

Objection 1. It would seem that the parts of the vegetative soul are not fittingly enumerated as the nutritive, augmentative, and generative. For these are called *natural* powers. But the powers of the soul are above the natural powers. Therefore we should not class the above powers as powers of the soul.

Obj. 2. Further, we should not assign a particular power of the soul to that which is common to living and non-living things. But generation is common to all things that can be generated and corrupted, whether living or not living. Therefore the generative power should not be classed as a power of the soul.

Obj. 3. Further, the soul is more powerful than the body. But the body by the same active power gives species and due quantity; much more, therefore, does the soul. Therefore the augmentative power of the soul is not distinct from the generative power.

Obj. 4. Further, everything is preserved in being by that whereby it has being. But the generative power is that whereby a living thing acquires being. Therefore by the same power the living thing is preserved. Now the nutritive power is directed to the preservation of the living thing, being *a power which is capable of preserving whatever receives it.*[28] Therefore we should not distinguish the nutritive power form the generative.

On the contrary, The Philosopher says that the operations of this soul are *generation, the use of food, and growth.*[29]

I answer that, The vegetative part has three powers. For the vegetative part, as we have said, has for its object the body itself, living by the soul; and for this body a triple operation of the soul is required. One is whereby it acquires being, and to this is directed the *generative* power. Another is whereby the living body acquires its due quantity, and to this is directed the *augmentative* power. Another is whereby the body of a living thing is preserved in its being and in its due quantity, and to this is directed the *nutritive* power. We must, however, observe a difference among these powers. The nutritive and the augmentative have their effect where they exist, since the body itself united to the soul grows and is preserved by the augmentative and nutritive powers which exist in one and the same soul. But the generative power has its effect, not in one and the same body, but in another; for a thing cannot generate itself. Therefore the generative power in a way approaches to the dignity of the sensitive soul, which has an operation extending to extrinsic things, although in a more excellent and more universal manner; for that which is highest in an inferior nature approaches to that which is lowest in the higher nature, as is made clear by Dionysius.[30] Therefore, of these three powers, the generative has the greater finality, nobility and perfection, as the Philosopher says, for it belongs to a thing which is already perfect *to produce another like unto itself.*[31] Furthermore, the generative power is served by the augmentative and nutritive powers; and the augmentative power by the nutritive.

Reply Obj. 1. Such powers are called natural, both because they produce an effect like that of nature, which also gives being, quantity and preservation (although the above powers accomplish these things in a more perfect way); and because these powers perform their actions instrumentally, through the active and passive qualities, which are the principles of natural actions.

---

[28] Aristotle, *op. cit.,* II, 4 (416b 14).   [29] *Ibid.* (415a 25; b 23).   [30] *De Div. Nom.,* VII, 3 (PG 3, 872).   [31] Aristotle, *De An.,* II, 4 (416b 24).

Reply Obj. 2. Generation in inanimate things is entirely from an extrinsic source; whereas the generation of living things is in a higher way, through something in the living thing itself, which is the semen containing the formative principle of the body. Therefore, there must be in the living thing a power that prepares this semen; and this is the generative power.

Reply Obj. 3. Since the generation of living things is from a semen, it is necessary that in the beginning an animal of small size be generated. For this reason it must have a power in the soul, whereby it is brought to its appropriate size. But the inanimate body is generated from determinate matter by an extrinsic agent; and therefore it receives at once its nature and its quantity, according to the condition of the matter.

Reply Obj. 4. As we have said above, the operation of the vegetative principle is performed by means of heat, the property of which is to consume humidity. Therefore, in order to restore the humidity thus lost, the nutritive power is required, whereby the food is changed into the substance of the body. This is also necessary for the action of the augmentative and generative powers.

Third Article
Whether the Five Exterior Senses Are Properly Distinguished?

We proceed thus to the Third Article:—

Objection 1. It would seem inaccurate to distinguish five exterior senses. For sense can know accidents. But there are many kinds of accidents. Therefore, since powers are distinguished by their objects, it seems that the senses are multiplied according to the number of the kinds of accidents.

Obj. 2. Further, magnitude and shape, and other so-called *common sensibles*, are *not sensibles by accident*, but are contradistinguished from them by the Philosopher.[32] Now the diversity of the proper objects diversifies the powers. Since, therefore, magnitude and shape are further from color than sound is, it seems that there is much more need for another sensitive power that can grasp magnitude or shape than for that which grasps color or sound.

Obj. 3. Further, once sense regards one contrariety; as sight regards white and black. But the sense of touch grasps several contrarieties, such as hot or cold, moist or dry, and the like. Therefore, it is not a single sense but several. Therefore there are more than five senses.

---

[32]Aristotle, *op. cit.*, II, 6 (418a 8).

Obj. 4. Further, a species is not divided against its genus. But taste is a kind of touch. Therefore it should not be classed as a distinct sense from touch.

On the contrary, The Philosopher says: *There is none other besides the five senses.*[33]

I answer that, The reason of the distinction and number of the senses has been assigned by some on the basis of the organs, in which one or other of the elements preponderates, as water, air, or the like.[34] By others it has been assigned to the medium, which is either in conjunction or extrinsic, and is either water or air, or the like. Others[35] have ascribed it to the diverse natures of the sensible qualities, according as such quality belongs to a simple body or results from complexity.

But none of these explanations is apt. For the powers are not for the organs, but the organs for the powers, and therefore there are not various powers for the reason that there are various organs, but, on the contrary, for this has nature provided a variety of organs, that they might be suitable to the diversity of powers. In the same way, nature provided various mediums for the various senses, according to what suited the acts of the powers. Now to be cognizant of the natures of sensible qualities does not pertain to the senses, but to the intellect. The reason of the number and distinction of the exterior senses must therefore be ascribed to that which belongs to the senses properly and *per se*. Sense is a passive power, and is naturally immuted by the exterior sensible. Hence, the exterior cause of such immutation is what is *per se* perceived by the sense, and according to the diversity of that exterior cause are the sensitive powers diversified.

Now, immutation is of two kinds, one natural, the other spiritual. Natural immutation takes place when the form of that which causes the immutation is received, according to its natural being, into the thing immuted, as heat is received into the thing heated. But spiritual immutation takes place when the form of what causes the immutation is received, according to a spiritual mode of being, into the thing immuted, as the form of color is received into the pupil which does not thereby become colored. Now, for the operation of the senses, a spiritual immutation is required, whereby an intention of the sensible form is effected in the sensile organ. Otherwise, if a natural immutation alone sufficed for the sense's action, all natural bodies would have sensation when they undergo alteration.

---

[33]*Op. cit.*, III, 1 (424b 22). [34]Cf. St. Albert, *Summa de Creatur.*, II, q. 34, a. 4 (XXXV, 304); Alex. of Hales, *Summa Theol.*, II, I, no. 356 (II, 432). [35]Cf. St. Bonaventure, *Itin. Mentis in Deum*, II (V, 300).

But in some senses we find spiritual immutation only, as in *sight*, while in others we find not only a spiritual but also a natural immutation, and this either on the part of the object only, or likewise on the part of the organ. On the part of the object, we find local natural immutation in sound, which is the object of *hearing*; for sound is caused by percussion and commotion of the air. We find natural immutation by alteration in order, which is the object of *smelling*; for in order to give off an odor, a body must be in a measure affected by heat. On the part of the organ, natural immutation takes place in *touch* and *taste*; for the hand that touches something hot becomes hot, while the tongue is moistened by the humidity of flavors. But the organs of smelling and hearing are not affected in their respective operations by any natural immutation, except accidentally.

Now, the sight, which is without natural immutation either in its organ or in its object, is the most spiritual, the most perfect, and the most universal of all the senses. After this comes the hearing and then the smell, which require a natural immutation on the part of the object; while local motion is more perfect than, and naturally prior to, the motion of alteration, as the Philosopher proves.[36] Touch and taste are the most material of all (of their distinction we shall speak later on). Hence it is that the three other senses are not exercised through a medium united to them, to obviate any natural immutation in their organ; as happens as regards these two senses.

Reply Obj. 1. Not every accident has in itself a power of immutation, but only qualities of the third species, according to which there can be alteration. Therefore only such qualities are the objects of the senses, because *the senses are affected by the same things whereby inanimate bodies are affected*, as is stated in Physics vii.[37]

Reply Obj. 2. Size, shape, and the like, which are called *common senibles*, are midway between *accidental sensibles* and *proper sensibles*, where are the objects of the senses. For the proper sensibles first, and of their very nature, affect the senses, since they are qualities that cause alteration. But the common sensibles are all reducible to quantity. As to size and number, it is clear that they are species of quantity. Shape is a quality about quantity, since the nature of shape consists in fixing the bounds of magnitude. Movement and rest are sensed according as the subject is affected in one or more ways in the magnitude of the subject or of its local distance, as in the movement of growth or of locomotion, or again, according as it is affected in some sensible qualities, as in the movement of alteration; and

---

[36]Aristotle, *Phys.*, VIII, 7 (260a 28).   [37]*Op. cit.*, VII, 2 (244b 12).

thus to sense movement and rest is, in a way, to sense one thing and many. Now quantity is the proximate subject of the qualities that cause alteration, as surface is of color. Therefore the common sensibles do not move the senses first and of their own nature, but by reason of sensible quality; as the surface by reason of color. Yet they are not accidental sensibles, for they product a certain diversity in the immutation of the senses. For sense is immuted differently by a large and by a small surface; since whiteness itself is said to be great or small, and therefore is divided according to its proper subject.

Reply Obj. 3. As the Philosopher seems to say, the sense of touch is generically one, but is divided into several specific senses, and for this reason it extends to various contrarieties.[38] These senses, however, are not separate from one another in their organ, but are spread together throughout the whole body, so that their distinction is not evident. But taste, which perceives the sweet and the bitter, accompanies touch in the tongue, but not in the whole body; so it is easily distinguished from touch. We might also say that all those contrarieties agree, each in some proximate genus, and all in a common genus, which is the common and formal object of touch. Such a common genus is, however, unnamed, just as the proximate genus of hot and cold is unnamed.

Reply Obj. 4. These sense of taste, according to a saying of the Philosopher, is a kind of touch existing only in the tongue.[39] It is not distinct from touch in general, but only from the species of touch distributed in the body. But if touch is only one sense, because of the common formality of its object, we must say that taste is distinguished from touch by reason of a different kind of immutation. For touch involves a natural, and not only a spiritual, immutation in its organ, by reason of the quality which is its proper object. But the organ of taste is not necessarily immuted by a natural immutation according to the quality which is its proper object, so that the tongue itself becomes sweet or bitter, but according to the quality which is a preamble to, and on which is based, the flavor; which quality is moisture, the object of touch.

FOURTH ARTICLE
Whether the Interior Senses Are Suitably Distinguished?

We proceed thus to the Fourth Article:—

Objection 1. It would seem that the interior senses are not suitably distinguished. For the common is not divided against the proper. Therefore

---

[38]*De An.*, II, 11 (422b 17).   [39]*Op. cit.*, II, 9 (421a 18); 11 (423a 17).

the common sense should not be numbered among the interior sensitive powers, in addition to the proper exterior senses.

Obj. 2. Further, there is no need to assign an interior power of apprehension when the proper and exterior sense suffices. But the proper and exterior senses suffice for us to judge of sensible things; for each sense judges of its proper object. In like manner, they seem to suffice for the perception of their own actions; for since the action of the sense is, in a way, between the power and its object, it seems that sight must be much more able to perceive its own vision, as being nearer to it, than the color; and in like manner with the other senses. Therefore for this purpose there is no need to assign an interior power, called the common sense.

Obj. 3. Further, according to the Philosopher, the imagination and the memory are passions of the *first sensitive*.[40] But passion is not divided against its subject. Therefore memory and imagination should not be assigned as powers distinct from sense.

Obj. 4. Further, the intellect depends on the senses less than any power of the sensitive part. But the intellect knows nothing but what it receives from the senses; whence we read that *those who lack one sense lack one kind of knowledge*.[41] Therefore much less should we assign to the sensitive part a power, which they call the *estimative* power, for the perception of representations which the sense does not perceive.

Obj. 5. Further, the action of the *cogitative* power, which consists in comparing, uniting and dividing, and the action of the *reminiscence*, which consists in the use of a kind of syllogism for the sake of inquiry, are not less distant from the actions of the *estimative* and *memorative* powers, than the action of the estimative is from the action of the imagination. Therefore either we must add the cogitative and reminiscitive power to the estimative and memorative powers, or the estimative and memorative powers should not be made distinct from the imagination.

Obj. 6. Further, Augustine describes three kinds of vision, namely, corporeal, which is an action of the sense; spiritual, which is an action of the imagination or phantasy; and intellectual, which is an action of the intellect.[42] Therefore there is no interior power between the sense and the intellect, besides the imagination.

On the contrary, Avicenna assigns five interior sensitive powers, namely, *common sense, phantasy, imagination, the estimative and the memorative.*[43]

---

[40]*De Mem. et Rem.*, I (450a 10).   [41]Aristotle, *Post. Anal.*, I, 18 (81a 38).
[42]*De Genesi ad Litt.*, XII, 6; 7; 24 (PL 34, 458; 459; 474).   [43]*De An.*, I, 5 (5rb);
IV, 1 (17va).

I answer that, As nature does not fail in necessary things, there must needs be as many actions of the sensitive soul as may suffice for the life of a perfect animal. If any of these actions cannot be reduced to one and the same principle, they must be assigned to diverse powers; since a power of the soul is nothing else than the proximate principle of the soul's operation.

Now we must observe that for the life of a perfect animal, the animal should apprehend a thing not only at the actual time of sensation, but also when it is absent. Otherwise, since animal motion and action follow apprehension, an animal would not be moved to seek something absent; the contrary of which we may observe especially in perfect animals, which are moved by progression, for they are moved towards something apprehended and absent. Therefore, through the sensitive soul an animal must not only receive the species of sensible things, when it is actually affected by them, but it must also retain and preserve them. Now to receive and retain are, in corporeal things, reduced to diverse principles; for moist things are apt to receive, but retain with difficulty, while it is the reverse with dry things. Therefore, since the sensitive power is the act of a corporeal organ, it follows that the power which receives the species of sensible things must be distinct from the power which preserves them.

Again, we must observe that if an animal were moved by pleasing and disagreeable things only as affecting the sense, there would be no need to suppose that an animal has a power besides the apprehension of those forms which the senses perceive, and in which the animal takes pleasure, or from which is shrinks with horror. But the animal needs to seek or to avoid certain things, not only because they are pleasing or otherwise to the senses, but also because of other advantages and uses, or disadvantages; just as the sheep runs away when it sees a wolf, not because of its color or shape, but as a natural enemy. So, too, a bird gathers together straws, not because they are pleasant to the sense, but because they are useful for building its nest. Animals, therefore, need to perceive such intentions, which the exterior sense does not perceive. Now some distinct principle is necessary for this, since the perception of sensible forms comes by an immutation caused by the sensible, which is not the case with the perception of the above intentions.

Thus, therefore, for the reception of sensible forms, the *proper sense* and the *common sense* are appointed. Of their distinction we shall speak later. But for the retention and preservation of these forms, the *phantasy* or *imagination* is appointed, being as it were a storehouse of forms received through the senses. Furthermore, for the apprehension of intentions which are not received through the senses, the *estimative* power is appointed: and for their preservation, the *memorative* power, which is a storehouse of such intentions. A sign of which we have in the fact that the principle of memory in animals is found in some such intention, for instance, that something is harmful or otherwise. And the very character of something as past, which memory observes, is to be reckoned among these intentions.

Now, we must observe that as to sensible forms there is no difference between man and other animals; for they are similarly immuted by external sensibles. But there is a difference as to the above intentions: for other animals perceive these intentions only by some sort of natural instinct, while man perceives them also by means of a certain comparison. Therefore the power which in other animals is called the *natural estimative* in man is called the *cogitative*, which by some sort of comparison discovers these intentions.[44] Therefore it is also called the *particular reason*, to which medical men assign a particular organ, namely, the middle part of the head;[45] for it compares individual intentions, just as the intellectual reason compares universal intentions. As to the memorative power, man has not only memory, as other animals have, in the sudden recollection of the past, but also *reminiscence*, by seeking syllogistically, as it were, for a recollection of the past by the application of individual intentions. Avicenna,[46] however, assigns between the estimative and the imaginative a fifth power, which combines and divides imaginary forms; as when from the imaginary form of gold, and the imaginary form of a mountain, we compose the one form of a golden mountain, which we have never seen. But this operation is not to be found in animals other than man, in whom the imaginative power suffices for this purpose. Averroes also attributes this action to the imagination, in his book *De sensu et sensibilibus*.[47] So there is no need to assign more than four interior powers of the sensitive part;—namely, the common sense, the imagination, and the estimative and memorative powers.

Reply Obj. 1. The interior sense is called *common* not by predication, as if it were a genus, but as the common root and principle of the exterior senses.

Reply Obj. 2. The proper sense judges of the proper sensible by discerning it from other things which come under the same sense; for instance, by discerning white from black or green. But neither sight nor

---

[44]Cf. Alex. of Hales, *Summa Theol.*, II, I, no. 357 (II, 434).—Cf. also Averroes, *Colliget*, II, 20 (X, 17va).   [45]Avicenna, *De An.*, I, 5 (5rb); Averroes, *Colliget*, II, 20 (X, 17va).   [46]*De An.*, IV, 1 (17va).   [47]*De Sensu et Sensibili* (VI, 193v).

taste can discern white from sweet, because what discerns between two things must know both. Hence, the discerning judgment must be assigned to the common sense. To it, as to a common term, all apprehensions of the senses must be referred, and by it, again, all the intentions of the senses are perceived; as when someone sees that he sees. For this cannot be done by the proper sense, which knows only the form of the sensible by which it is immuted. In this immutation the action of sight is completed, and from it follows another immutation in the common sense which perceives the act of seeing.

Reply Obj. 3. Just as one power arises from the soul by means of another, as we have seen above,[48] so likewise the soul is the subject of one power through another. In this way the imagination and the memory are called passions of the *first sensitive.*

Reply Obj. 4. Although the operation of the intellect has its origin in the senses, yet, in the thing apprehended through the senses, the intellect knows many things which the senses cannot perceive. In like manner does the estimative power, though in a less perfect way.

Reply Obj. 5. The cogitative and memorative powers in man owe their excellence not to that which is proper to the sensitive part, but to a certain affinity and proximity to the universal reason, which, so to speak, over-flows into them. Therefore they are not distinct powers, but the same, yet more perfect than in other animals.

Reply Obj. 6. Augustine calls that vision spiritual which is effected by the images of bodies in the absence of bodies. Whence it is clear that it is common to all interior apprehensions.

---

[48]Q. 77, a. 7.

6

THE INTELLECT: ITS KNOWLEDGE OF MATERIAL THINGS, SELF-KNOWLEDGE, AND KNOWLEDGE OF GOD

Summa Theologica

PART ONE

QUESTION 79

The Intellectual Powers

FIRST ARTICLE
Whether the Intellect Is a Power of the Soul?

We proceed thus to the First Article:—

Objection 1. It would seem that the intellect is not a power of the soul, but the essence of the soul. For the intellect seems to be the same as the mind. Now the mind is not a power of the soul, but the essence; for Augustine says: *Mind and spirit are not names of relations, but denominate the essence.*[1] Therefore the intellect is the essence of the soul.

Obj. 2. Further, different genera of the soul's powers are not united in some one power, but only in the essence of the soul. Now the appetitive and the intellectual are different genera of the soul's powers, as the Philosopher says[2]; but they are united in the mind, for Augustine places the intelligence and will in the mind.[3] Therefore the mind and intellect of man is the very essence of the soul, and not a power.

Obj. 3. Further, according to Gregory, in a homily for the Ascension, *man understands with the angels.*[4] But angels are called *minds* and *intellects.* Therefore the mind and intellect of man is not a power of the soul, but the soul itself.

Obj. 4. Further, a substance is intellectual by the fact that it is immaterial. But the soul is immaterial through its essence. Therefore it seems that the soul must be intellectual through its essence.

---

[1]*De Trin.*, IX, 2 (PL 42, 962).   [2]Aristotle, *De An.*, II, 3 (414a 31).   [3]*De Trin.*, X, 11 (PL 42, 983).   [4]*In Evang.*, II, hom. 29 (PL 76, 1214).

On the contrary, The Philosopher assigns the intellect as a power of the soul.[5]

I answer that, In accordance with what has been already shown, it is necessary to say that the intellect is a power of the soul, and not the very essence of the soul.[6] For the essence of that which operates is then alone the immediate principle of operation, when operation itself is its being; for as power is related to operation as to its act, so is essence related to being. But in God alone is His act of understanding the same as His very Being. Hence, in God alone is His intellect His essence; while in other intellectual creatures, the intellect is a power.

Reply Obj. 1. Sense is sometimes taken for the power, and sometimes for the sensitive soul; for the sensitive soul takes its name from its chief power, which is sense. And in like manner the intellectual soul is sometimes called intellect, as from its chief power; and thus we read that the *intellect is a substance.*[7] And in this sense also Augustine says that the mind is spirit or essence.[8]

Reply Obj. 2. The appetitive and intellectual powers are different genera of powers in the soul, by reason of the different natures of their objects. But the appetitive power agrees partly with the intellectual power, and partly with the sensitive, in its mode of operation either through a corporeal organ or without it; for appetite follows apprehension. It is in this way that Augustine puts the will in the mind; and the Philosopher, in the reason.[9]

Reply Obj. 3. In the angels there is no other power besides the intellect and the will, which follows the intellect. This is the reason why an angel is called a *mind* or an *intellect,* because his whole power consists in this. But the soul has many other powers, such as the sensitive and nutritive powers, and therefore the comparison fails.

Reply Obj. 4. The immateriality of a created intelligent substance is not its intellect; but rather through its immateriality it has the power of understanding. Therefore it follows, not that the intellect is the substance of the soul, but that it is its virtue and power.

SECOND ARTICLE
Whether the Intellect Is a Passive Power?

We proceed thus to the Second Article:—

---

[5]*De An.,* II, 3 (414a 32).   [6]Q. 54, a. 3; q. 77, a. 1.   [7]Aristotle, *De An.,* I, 4 (408b 18).   [8]*De Trin.,* IX, 2; XIV, 16 (PL 42, 962; 1053).   [9]*De An.,* III, 9 (432b 5).

Objection 1. It would seem that the intellect is not a passive power. For everything is passive by its matter, and acts by its form. But the intellectual power results from the immateriality of the intelligent substance. Therefore it seems that the intellect is not a passive power.

Obj. 2. Further, the intellectual power is incorruptible, as we have said above.[10] But *if the intellect is passive, it is corruptible.*[11] Therefore the intellectual power is not passive.

Obj. 3. Further, the *agent is nobler than the patient*, as Augustine[12] and Aristotle[13] say. But all the powers of the vegetative part are active, and yet they are the lowest among the powers of the soul. Much more, therefore, are all the intellectual powers, which are the highest, active.

On the contrary, The Philosopher says that *to understand is in a way to be passive.*[14]

I answer that, To be passive may be taken in three ways. Firstly, in its most strict sense, when from a thing is taken something which belongs to it by virtue either of its nature, or of its proper inclination; as when water loses coolness by heating, and as when a man becomes ill or sad. Secondly, less strictly, a thing is said to be passive when something, whether suitable or unsuitable, is taken away from it. And in this way not only he who is ill is said to be passive, but also he who is healed; not only he that is sad, but also he that is joyful; or whatever way he be altered or moved. Thirdly, in a wide sense a thing is said to be passive, from the very fact that what is in potentiality to something receives that to which is was in potentiality, without being deprived of anything. And accordingly, whatever passes from potentiality to act may be said to be passive, even when it is perfected. It is *thus* that to understand is to be passive. This is clear from the following reason. For the intellect, as we have seen above, has an operation extending to universal being.[15] We may therefore see whether an intellect is in act or potentiality by observing first of all the nature of the relation of the intellect to universal being. For we find an intellect whose relation to universal being is that of the act of all being; and such is the divine intellect, which is the essence of God, in which, originally and virtually, all being pre-exists as in its first cause. Therefore the divine intellect is not potentiality, but is pure act. But no created intellect can be an act in relation to the whole universal being; for then it would needs be an infinite being. Therefore no created intellect, by reason of its very

---

[10]Q. 75, a. 6.   [11]Aristotle, *De An.*, III, 5 (430a 24).   [12]*De Genesi ad Litt.*, XII, 16 (PL 34, 467).   [13]*De An.*, III, 5 (430a 18).   [14]*Op. cit.*, III, 4 (429b 24).   [15]Q. 78, a. 1.

being, is the act of all things intelligible; but it is compared to these intelligible things as a potentiality to act.

Now, potentiality has a double relation to act. There is a potentiality which is always perfected by its act. Such is the case with the matter of the heavenly bodies.[16] And there is another potentiality which is not always in act, but proceeds from potentiality to act; as we observe in things that are corrupted and generated. Hence the angelic intellect is always in act as regards those things which it can understand, by reason of its proximity to the first intellect, which is pure act, as we have said above. But the human intellect, which is the lowest in the order of intellects and most remote from the perfection of the divine intellect, is in potentiality with regard to things intelligible, and is at first *like a clean tablet on which nothing is written*, as the Philosopher says.[17] This is made clear from the fact that at first we are only in potentiality towards understanding, and afterwards we are made to understand actually. And so it is evident that with us to understand is *in a way to be passive*, taking passion in the third sense. And consequently the intellect is a passive power.

Reply Obj. 1. This objection is verified of passion in the first and second senses, which belong to primary matter. But in the third sense, passion is in anything which is reduced from potentiality to act.

Reply Obj. 2. *Passive intellect* is the name given by some to the sensitive appetite, in which are the passions of the soul;[18] which appetite is also called *rational by participation*, because it *obeys the reason*.[19] Others give the name of passive intellect to the cogitative power, which is called the *particular reason*.[20] And in each case *passive* may be taken in the two first senses, since this so-called intellect is the act of a corporeal organ. But the intellect which is in potentiality to things intelligible, and which for this reason Aristotle calls the *possible intellect*,[21] is not passive except in the third sense; for it is not an act of a corporeal organ. Hence it is incorruptible.

Reply Obj. 3. The agent is nobler than the patient, if the action and the passion are referred to the same thing; but not always, if they refer to different things. Now the intellect is a passive power in regard to the whole universal being, while the vegetative power is active in regard to some particular thing, namely, the body as united to the soul. Therefore nothing prevents such a passive power being nobler than such an active one.

---

[16]Q. 58, a. 1.   [17]*De An.*, III, 4 (430a 1).   [18]Themistius, *In De An.*, III, 5 (II, 186).—Cf. Averroes, *In De An.*, III, 20 (VI, 170v).   [19]Aristotle, *Eth.*, I, 13 (1102b 25).   [20]Cf. Averroes, *In De An.*, III, 20 (VI, 171r).   [21]*De An.*, III, 4 (429a 22).

THIRD ARTICLE
Whether There Is an Agent Intellect?

We proceed thus to the Third Article:—

Objection 1. It would seem that there is no agent intellect. For as the senses are to things sensible, so is our intellect to things intelligible. But because sense is in potentiality to things sensible, there is not said to be an *agent sense*, but only a passive one. Therefore, since our intellect is in potentiality to things intelligible, it seems that we cannot say that there is an agent intellect, but only a passive one.[22]

Obj. 2. Further, if we say that also in the senses there is something active, such as light, [23] on the contrary, light is required for sight, inasmuch as it makes the medium to be actually luminous; for color of its own nature moves the luminous medium. But in the operation of the intellect there is no appointed medium that has to be brought into act. Therefore there is no necessity for an agent intellect.

Obj. 3. Further, the likeness of the agent is received into the patient according to the nature of the patient. But the possible intellect is an immaterial power. Therefore its immaterial nature suffices for forms to be received into it immaterially. Now a form is intelligible in act from the very fact that it is immaterial. Therefore there is no need for an agent intellect to make the species actually intelligible.[24]

On the contrary, The Philosopher says: *As in every nature, so in the soul, there is something by which it becomes all things, and something by which it makes all things.*[25] Therefore we must admit an agent intellect.

I answer that, According to the opinion of Plato, there is no need for an agent intellect in order to make things actually intelligible, but perhaps in order to provide intellectual light to the intellect, as will be explained farther on.[26] For Plato supposed that the forms of natural things subsisted apart from matter, and consequently that they are intelligible[27]; for a thing is actually intelligible from the very fact that it is immaterial. And he called such forms *species or ideas.* From a participation in these, he said that even corporeal matter was formed, in order that individuals might be naturally established in their proper genera and species, [28] and also that our intellect was formed by such participation in

---

[22]An argument of William of Auvergne, *De An.*, VII, 4 (II, Suppl., 207). [23]Cf. *ibid.* [24]Cf. *op. cit.*, VII, 5 (II, Suppl., 210). [25]*De An.*, III, 5 (430a 10). [26]A. 4; q. 84, a. 6. [27]Cf. Q. 6, a. 4. [28]Cf. Aristotle, *Metaph.*, I, 9 (991b 3); Plato, *Phaedo* (p. 100d).—Cf. Q. 15, a. 3.

order to have knowledge of the genera and species of things.[29] But since Aristotle did not allow that the forms of natural things exist apart from matter, and since forms existing in matter are not actually intelligible,[30] it follows that the natures or forms of the sensible things which we understand are not actually intelligible. Now nothing is reduced from potentiality to act except by something in act; as the senses are made actual by what is actually sensible. We must therefore assign on the part of the intellect some power to make things actually intelligible, by the abstraction of the species from material conditions. And such is the necessity for positing an agent intellect.

Reply Obj. 1. Sensible things are found in act outside the soul; and hence there is no need for an agent sense. Therefore it is clear that, in the nutritive part, all the powers are active, whereas in the sensitive part all are passive; but in the intellectual part, there is something active and something passive.

Replay Obj. 2. There are two opinions as to the effect of light. For some say that light is required for sight, in order to make colors actually visible.[31] And according to this, the agent intellect is required for understanding in like manner and for the same reason as light is required for seeing. But in the opinion of others, light is required for sight, not for the colors to become actually visible, but in order that the medium may become actually luminous, as the Commentator says on *De Anima* ii.[32] And according to this, Aristotle's comparison of the agent intellect to light[33] is verified in this, that as it is required for understanding, so is light required for seeing; but not for the same reason.

Reply Obj. 3. If the agent pre-exist, it may well happen that its likeness is received variously into various things, because of their dispositions. But if the agent does not pre-exist, the disposition of the recipient has nothing to do with the matter. Now the intelligible in act is not something existing in nature, provided, or course, that we are thinking of the nature of sensible things, which do not subsist without matter. And therefore in order to understand them, the immaterial nature of the possible intellect would not suffice but for the presence of the agent intellect, which makes things actually intelligible by way of abstraction.

---

[29]Cf. below, q. 84, a. 1; a. 4. [30]Cf. *Metaph.*, II, 4 (999b 18); VII, 3 (1043b 19). [31]Avempace: cf. Averroes, *In De An.*, II, comm. 67 (VI, 140r). [32]*Ibid.* [33]*De An.*, III, 5 (430a 15).—Cf. Averroes, *In De An.*, comm. 67 (VI, 140r); III, comm. 18 (VI, 169v).

FOURTH ARTICLE
Whether the Agent Intellect Is Something in the Soul?

We proceed thus to the Fourth Article:—

Objection 1. It would seem that the agent intellect is not something in the soul. For the effect of the agent intellect is to give light for the purpose of understanding. But this is done by something higher than the soul, according to *Jo.* i. 9, *He was the true light that enlighteneth every man coming into this world.* Therefore the agent intellect is not something in the soul.[34]

Obj. 2. Further, the Philosopher says of the agent intellect, *that it does not sometimes understand and sometimes not understand.*[35] But out soul does not always understand, but sometimes it understands, and sometimes it does not understand. Therefore the agent intellect is not something in our soul.[36]

Obj. 3. Further, agent and patient suffice for action. If, therefore, the possible intellect, which is a passive power, is something belonging to the soul; and also the agent intellect, which is an active power:—it follows that man would always be able to understand when he wished, which is clearly false. Therefore the agent intellect is not something in our soul.[37]

Obj. 4. Further, the Philosopher says that the agent intellect is *a substance in actual being.*[38] But nothing can be in potentiality and in act with regard to the same thing. If, therefore, the possible intellect, which is in potentiality to all things intelligible, is something in the soul, it seems impossible for the agent intellect to be also something in our soul.

Obj. 5. Further, if the agent intellect is something in the soul, it must be a power. For it is neither a passion nor a habit, since habits and passions do not have the nature of agents in regard to what the soul receives; but passion is rather the very action of the passive power, while habit is something which results from acts. Now every power flows from the essence of the soul. It would therefore follow that the agent intellect flows from the essence of the soul. And thus it would not be in the soul by way of participation from some higher intellect; which is unfitting. Therefore the agent intellect is not something in our soul.

On the contrary, The Philosopher says that *it is necessary for these differences,* namely, the possible and agent intellect, *to be in the soul.*[39]

---

[34]Cf. William of Auvergne, *De An.*, VII, 6 (II, Suppl., 211).   [35]*De An.*, III, 5 (430a 22).   [36]Cf. William of Auvergne, *De An.*, VII, 3 (II, Suppl., 206).   [37]Cf. *op. cit.*, VII, 4 (II, Suppl., 208).   [38]*De An.*, III, 5 (430a 18).   [39]*Op. cit.*, III, 5 (430a 13).

I answer that, The agent intellect, of which the Philosopher speaks, is something in the soul. In order to make this evident, we must observe that above the intellectual soul of man we must needs suppose a superior intellect, from which the soul acquires the power of understanding. For what is such by participation, and what is moveable, and what is imperfect, always requires the pre-existence of something essentially such, immoveable and perfect. Now the human soul is called intellectual by reason of a participation in intellectual power, a sign of which is that it is not wholly intellectual but only in part. Moreover it reaches to the understanding of truth by reasoning, with a certain discursiveness and movement. Even more, it has an imperfect understanding, both because it does not understand everything, and because, in those things which it does understand, it passes from potentiality to act. Therefore there must needs be some higher intellect, by which the soul is helped to understand.

Therefore some held that this intellect, substantially separate, is the agent intellect,[40] which by lighting up the phantasms, as it were, makes them to be actually intelligible. But, even supposing the existence of such a separate agent intellect, it would still be necessary to assign to the human soul some power participating in that superior intellect, by which power the human soul makes things to be actually intelligible. Such is also the case in other perfect natural things, among which, besides the universal active causes, each one is endowed with its proper powers derived from those universal causes: for the sun alone does not generate man, but in man himself there is power of begetting man; and in like manner with other perfect animals. Now among these sublunary things nothing is more perfect than the human soul. Therefore we must say that in the soul is some power derived from a higher intellect, whereby it is able to illumine the phantasms.

And we know this by experience, since we perceive that we abstract universal forms from their particular conditions; which is to make them actually intelligible. Now no action belongs to anything except through some principle formally inherent therein, as we have said above of the possible intellect.[41] Therefore the power which is the principle of this action must be something in the soul. For this reason Aristotle compared the agent intellect to light, which is something received into the air,[42]

---

[40]Alexander of Aphrodisias, *De Intellectu et Intellecto* (p. 76); Averroes, *In De An.*, III, comm. 18 (VI, 169v); comm. 19 (VI, 170r); Avicenna, *De An.*, V, 5 (25rb); *Metaph.*, IX, 3 (104rb).   [41]Q. 76, a. 1.   [42]*De An.*, III, 5 (430a 15).

while Plato compared the separate intellect, whose light touches the soul, to the sun, as Themistius says in his commentary on *De Anima* iii.[43]

But the separate intellect, according to the teaching of our Faith, is God Himself, Who is the soul's Creator, and only beatitude; as will be shown later on.[44] Therefore the human soul derives its intellectual light from Him, according to *Ps.* iv. 7, *The light of Thy countenance, O Lord, is signed upon us.*

Reply Obj. 1. That true light illumines as a universal cause, from which the human soul derives a particular power, as we have explained.

Reply Obj. 2. The Philosopher says those words not of the agent intellect, but of the intellect in act; of which he had already said: *Knowledge in act is the same as the thing.*[45] Or, if we refer those words to the agent intellect, then they are said because it is not owing to the agent intellect that sometimes we do, and sometimes we do not understand, but to the intellect which is in potentiality.

Reply Obj. 3. If the relation of the agent intellect to the possible intellect were that of an active object to a power (as, for instance, of the visible in act to the sight), it would follow that we could understand all things instantly, since the agent intellect is that which makes all things in act. But the agent intellect is not an object, rather is it that whereby the objects are made to be in act; and for this, besides the presence of the agent intellect, we require the presence of phantasms, the good disposition of the sensitive powers, and practice in this sort of operation. For from one thing understood, other things come to be understood, as from terms propositions are made, and from first principles, conclusions. From this point of view, it matters not whether the agent intellect is something belonging to the soul, or something separate from the soul.

Reply Obj. 4. The intellectual soul is indeed actually immaterial, but it is in potentiality to the determinate species of things. On the contrary, phantasms are actual likenesses of certain species, but they are immaterial in potentiality. Therefore nothing prevents one and the same soul, inasmuch as it is actually immaterial, from having a power by which it makes things actually immaterial, by abstraction from the conditions of individual matter (this power is called the *agent intellect*), and another power, receptive of such species, which is called the *possible intellect* by reason of its being in potentiality to such species.

---

[43] *In De An.*, III, 5 (II, 191); cf. Plato, *Republic*, VI (p. 508).   [44] Q. 90, a. 3; I–II, q. 3, a. 7.   [45] *De An.*, III, 5 (430a 19).

Reply Obj. 5. Since the essence of the soul is immaterial, created by the supreme intellect, nothing prevents the power which it derives from the supreme intellect, and whereby it abstracts from matter, from proceeding from the essence of the soul, in the same way as its other powers.

FIFTH ARTICLE
Whether the Agent Intellect Is One in All?

We proceed thus to the Fifth Article:—

Objection 1. It would seem that there is one agent intellect in all. For what is separate from the body is not multiplied according to the number of bodies. But the agent intellect is *separate*, as the Philosopher says.[46] Therefore it is not multiplied in the multitude of human bodies, but is one for all men.

Obj. 2. Further, the agent intellect is the cause of the universal, which is one in many. But that which is the cause of unity is still more itself one. Therefore the intellect is the same in all.

Obj. 3. Further, all men agree in the first intellectual concepts. But to these they assent by the agent intellect. Therefore all are united in one agent intellect.

On the contrary, The Philosopher says that the agent intellect is as a light.[47] But light is not the same in the various illuminated things. Therefore the same agent intellect is not in various men.

I answer that, The truth about this question depends on what we have already said. For if the agent intellect were not something belonging to the soul, but were some separate substance, there would be one agent intellect for all men. And this is what they mean who hold that there is one agent intellect for all. But if the agent intellect is something belonging to the soul, as one of its powers, we are bound to say that there are as many agent intellects as there are souls, which are multiplied according to the number of men, as we have said above.[48] For it is impossible that one and the same power belong to various substances.

Reply Obj. 1. The Philosopher proves that the agent intellect is separate by the fact that the possible intellect is separate; because, as he says, *the agent is more noble than the patient.*[49] Now the possible intellect is said to be separate because it is not the act of any corporeal organ. And in this sense the agent intellect is also called *separate*; but not as a separate substance.

---

[46]*Ibid.* (420a 17).   [47]*Ibid.* (430a 15).   [48]Q. 76, a. 2.   [49]*De An.*, III, 5 (430a 18).

Reply Obj. 2. The agent intellect is the cause of the universal, by abstracting it from matter. But for this purpose it need not be one in all intelligent beings; but it must be one in relation to all those things from which it abstracts the universal, with respect to which things the universal is one. And this befits the agent intellect inasmuch as it is immaterial.

Reply Obj. 3. All things which are of one species enjoy in common the action which accompanies the nature of the species, and consequently the power which is the principle of such action; but not in such a way that the power be identical in all. Now to know the first intelligible principles is an action belonging to the human species. Therefore all men enjoy in common the power which is the principle of this action; and this power is the agent intellect. But there is no need for it to be identical in all; although it must be derived by all from one principle. And thus the possession by all men in common of first principles proves the unity of the separate intellect, which Plato compares to the sun, but not the unity of the agent intellect, which Aristotle compares to light.[50]

SIXTH ARTICLE
Whether Memory Is in the Intellectual Part of the Soul?

We proceed thus to the Sixth Article:—

Objection 1. It would seem that memory is not in the intellectual part of the soul. For Augustine says that to the higher part of the soul belong those things which are not *common to man and beast*.[51] But memory is common to man and beast, for he says that *beasts can sense corporeal things through the senses of the body, and commit them to memory.*[52] Therefore memory does not belong to the intellectual part of the soul.

Obj. 2. Further, memory is of the past. But the past is said of something according to a fixed time. Memory, therefore, knows a thing under the condition of a fixed time; which involves knowledge under the conditions of *here* and *now*. But this is not the province of the intellect, but of the sense. Therefore memory is not in the intellectual part, but only in the sensitive part.

Obj. 3. Further, in the memory are preserved the species of those things of which we are not actually thinking. But this cannot happen in the intellect, because the intellect is reduced to act by the fact that the intelligible species are received into it. Now for the intellect to be in act is for it to be understanding in act, and therefore the intellect actually

---

[50]*Ibid.* (430a 15).   [51]*De Trin.*, XII, 2; 8 (PL 42, 999; 1005).   [52]*Op. cit.*,
XII, 2 (PL 42, 999).

understands all things of which it has the species. Therefore the memory is not in the intellectual part.

On the contrary, Augustine says that *memory, understanding and will are one mind.*[53]

I answer that, Since it is of the nature of the memory to preserve the species of those things which are not apprehended actually, we must first of all consider whether the intelligible species can thus be preserved in the intellect. For Avicenna held that this was impossible.[54] He admitted that this could happen in the sensitive part, as to some powers, inasmuch as they are acts of corporeal organs, in which certain species may be preserved without actual apprehension; but in the intellect, which has no corporeal organ, nothing but what is intelligible exists. Hence, every thing of which the likeness exists in the intellect must be actually understood. Thus, therefore, according to him, as soon as we cease to understand something actually, the species of that thing ceases to be in our intellect, and if we wish to understand that thing anew, we must turn to the agent intellect, which he held to be a separate substance, in order that the intelligible species may thence flow again into our possible intellect. And from the practice and repetition of turning to the agent intellect there is formed, according to him, a certain aptitude in the possible intellect for turning itself to the agent intellect; which aptitude he calls *the habit of science.* According, therefore, to this supposition, nothing is preserved in the intellectual part that is not actually understood; and hence it would not be possible to admit memory in the intellectual part.

But this opinion is clearly opposed to the teaching of Aristotle. For he says that, when the possible intellect *is identified with each thing as knowing it, it is said to be in act,* and that *this happens when it can operate through itself. And, even then, it is in potentiality, but not in the same way as before learning and discovering.*[55] Now, the possible intellect is said to become each thing, inasmuch as it receives the intelligible species of each thing. To the fact, therefore, that it receives the species of intelligible things it owes its being able to operate when it wills, but not so that it be always operating; for even then it is in potentiality in a certain sense, though otherwise than before the act of understanding—namely, in the sense that whoever has habitual knowledge is in potentiality to actual consideration.

The foregoing opinion is also opposed to reason. For what is received into something is received according to the condition of the recipient. But

---

[53]*Op. cit.,* X, 11 (PL 42, 983).   [54]*De An.,* V, 6 (26rb).   [55]*De An.,* III, 4 (429b 5).

the intellect is of a more stable nature, and is more immovable, than corporeal matter If, therefore, corporeal matter holds the forms which it receives, not only while it actually does something through them, but also after ceasing to act through them, much more does the intellect receive the species unchangeably and lastingly, whether it receive them from things sensible, or from some superior intellect.

Thus, therefore, if we take memory only for the power of retaining species, we must say that it is in the intellectual part. But if in the notion of memory we include its object as something past, then the memory is not in the intellectual, but only in the sensitive part, which apprehends individual things. For past, as past, since it signifies being under a condition of fixed time, is something individual.

Reply Obj. 1. Memory, if considered as retentive of species, is not common to us and other animals. For species are not retained in the sensitive part of the soul only, but rather in the body and soul united, since the memorative power is the act of some organ. But the intellect in itself is retentive of species, without the association of any corporeal organ. Therefore the Philosopher says that *the soul is the seat of the species, not the whole soul, but the intellect.*[56]

Reply Obj. 2. The condition of *pastness* may be referred to two things—namely, to the object known, and to the act of knowledge. These two are found together in the sensitive part, which apprehends something from the fact of its being immuted by a present sensible. Therefore, at one and the same time an animal remembers that he sensed before in the past, and that he sensed some past sensible thing. But as concerns the intellectual part, the past is accidental, and is not in itself a part of the object of the intellect, for the intellect understands man as man; and to man, as man, it is accidental that he exist in the present, past, or future. But on the part of the act, the condition of being past, even as such, may be understood to be in the intellect, as well as in the senses. For our soul's act of understanding is an individual act, existing in this or that time, inasmuch as a man is said to understand now, or yesterday, or tomorrow. And this is not incompatible with what is intellectual, for such an act of understanding, though something individual, is yet an immaterial act, as we have said above of the intellect.[57] And therefore, just as the intellect understands itself, though it be itself an individual intellect, so also it understands its act of understanding, which is an individual act, in the past, present, or future. In this way, then, the notion of memory, in as far as it regards past

---

[56] *Ibid.* (429a 27).   [57] Q. 76, a. 1.

events, is preserved in the intellect, according as it understands that it previously understood; but not in the sense that it understands the past as something *here* and *now*.

Reply Obj. 3. The intelligible species is sometimes in the intellect only in potentiality, and then the intellect is said to be in potentiality. Sometimes the intelligible species is in the intellect according to the ultimate completion of the act, and then the intellect understands in act. And sometimes the intelligible species is in a middle state, between potentiality and act; and then we have habitual knowledge. In this last way the intellect retains the species, even when it does not understand in act.

PART ONE

QUESTION 84

How the Soul While United to the Body Understands Corporeal Things Beneath It

We now have to consider the acts of the soul in regard to the intellectual and the appetitive powers, for the other powers of the soul do not come directly under the consideration of the theologian. Now the acts of the appetitive part of the soul come under the consideration of the science of morals, and so we shall treat of them in the second part of this work, to which the consideration of moral matters belongs. But of the acts of the intellectual part we shall treat now. In treating of these acts, we shall proceed in the following order. First, we shall inquire how the soul understands when united to the body; secondly, how it understands when separated from the body.[58]

The former of these inquiries will be threefold: (1) How the soul understands bodies, which are beneath it. (2) How it understands itself and things contained in itself.[59] (3) How it understands immaterial substances, which are above it.[60]

In treating of the knowledge of corporeal things, there are three points to be considered: (1) Through what does the soul know them? (2) How and in what order does it know them?[61] (3) What does it know in them?[62]

FIRST ARTICLE
Whether the Soul Knows Bodies Through the Intellect?

We proceed thus to the First Article:—

Objection 1. It would seem that the soul does not know bodies through the intellect. For Augustine says that *bodies cannot be understood by the intellect: nor indeed anything corporeal unless it can be perceived by the senses.*[63] He says also that intellectual vision is of those things that are in the soul by their essence.[64] But such are not bodies. Therefore the soul cannot know bodies through the intellect.

Obj. 2. Further, as sense is to the intelligible, so is the intellect to the

---

[58]Q. 89.   [59]Q. 87.   [60]Q. 88.   [61]Q. 85.   [62]Q. 86.
[63]*Solil.*, II, 4 (PL 32, 888).   [64]*De Genesi ad Litt.*, XII, 24 (PL 34, 474).

sensible. But the soul can by no means, through the senses, understand spiritual things, which are intelligible. Therefore by no means can it, through the intellect, know bodies, which are sensible.

Obj. 3. Further, the intellect is concerned with things that are necessary and unchangeable. But all bodies are movable and changeable. Therefore the soul cannot know bodies through the intellect.

On the contrary, Science is in the intellect. If, therefore, the intellect does not know bodies, it follows that there is no science of bodies; and thus perishes the science of nature, which treats of movable bodies.

I answer, In order to elucidate this question, that the early philosophers, who inquired into the natures of things, thought there was nothing in the world save bodies.[65] And because they observed that all bodies are subject to motion, and considered them to be ever in a state of flux, they were of the opinion that we can have no certain knowledge of the reality of things. For what is in a continual state of flux cannot be grasped with any degree of certitude, for it passes away before the mind can form a judgment on it. As Heraclitus said, *it is not possible to touch the water in a passing stream twice* (as the Philosopher relates[66]).

After these came Plato, who, wishing to save the certitude of our knowledge of truth through the intellect, maintained that, besides these corporeal things, there is another genus of beings, separate from matter and movement, which he called *species* or *ideas*, by participation in which each one of these singular and sensible things is said to be either a man, or a horse, or the like.[67] And so, he said that sciences and definitions, and whatever pertains to the act of the intellect, is not referred to these sensible bodies, but to those immaterial and separate beings[68]; so that, according to this, the soul does not understand these corporeal things, but their separated species.

Now this is clearly false for two reasons. First, because, since those species are immaterial and immovable, knowledge of movement and matter (which is proper to natural philosophy) would be excluded from among the sciences, and likewise all demonstration through moving and material causes. Secondly, because it seems ridiculous, when we seek for knowledge of things which are to us manifest, to introduce other beings, which cannot be the substances of the things with which we began, since they differ from them in being. Hence, granted that we have a knowledge

---

[65]Cf. q. 44, a. 2.   [66]*Metaph*, III, 5 (1010a 14).   [67]Cf. Aristotle, *op. cit.*, I, 6 (987b 6; b7); I, 9 (992b 7).—Cf. also Plato, *Theaetet.* (p 156a).   [68]Cf. Avicenna, *Metaph.*, VII, 2 (96ra).

of those separate substances, we cannot for that reason claim to form judgments concerning these sensible things.

Now it seems that Plato strayed from the truth because, having observed that all knowledge takes place through some kind of similitude[69], he thought that the form of the thing known must of necessity be in the knower in the same manner as in the thing known itself. But it was his opinion that the form of the thing understood is in the intellect under conditions of universality, immateriality, and immobility; which is apparent from the very operation of the intellect, whose act of understanding is universal, and characterized by a certain necessity; for the mode of action corresponds to the mode of the agent's form. Therefore he concluded that the things which we understand must subsist in themselves under the same conditions of immateriality and immobility.

But there is no necessity for this. For even in sensible things it is to be observed that the form is otherwise in one sensible than in another. For instance, whiteness may be of great intensity in one, and of a less intensity in another; in one we find whiteness with sweetness, in another without sweetness. In the same way, the sensible form is in one way in the thing which is external to the soul, and in another way in the senses, which receive the forms of sensible things without receiving matter, such as the color of gold without receiving gold. So, too, the intellect, according to its own mode, receives under conditions of immateriality and immobility the species of material and movable bodies; for the received is in the receiver according to the mode of the receiver. We must conclude, therefore, that the soul knows bodies through the intellect by a knowledge which is immaterial, universal and necessary.

Reply Obj. 1. These words of Augustine are to be understood as referring to the medium of intellectual knowledge, and not to its object. For the intellect knows bodies by understanding them, not indeed through bodies, nor through material and corporeal likenesses, but through immaterial and intelligible species, which can be in the soul by their own essence.

Reply Obj. 2. As Augustine says, it is not correct to say that as the sense knows only bodies so the intellect knows only spiritual things[70]; for it would follow that God and the angels would not know bodies. The reason for this diversity is that the lower power does not extend to those things

---

[69]Cf. *ibid.* (96rb).—Cf. also, Aristotle, *De An.*, I, 2 (404b 17).   [70]*De Civit. Dei*, XXII, 29 (PL 41, 800)

that belong to the higher power; whereas the higher power accomplishes in a more excellent manner what belongs to the lower power.

Reply Obj. 3. Every movement presupposes something immovable. For when a change of quality occurs, the substance remains unmoved; and when there is a change of substantial form, matter remains unmoved. Moreover, mutable things have immovable dispositions; for instance, though Socrates be not always sitting, yet it is an immovable truth that whenever he does sit he remains in one place. For this reason there is nothing to hinder our having an immovable science of movable things.

SECOND ARTICLE
Whether the Soul Understands Corporeal Things Through Its Essence?

We proceed thus to the Second Article:—

Objection 1. It would seem that the soul understands corporeal things through its essence. For Augustine says that the soul *collects and lays hold of the images of bodies which are formed in the soul and of the soul; for in forming them it gives them something of its own substance.*[71] But the soul understands bodies by the likenesses of bodies. Therefore the soul knows bodies through its essence, which it employs for the formation of such likenesses, and from which it forms them.

Obj. 2. Further, the Philosopher says that *the soul, after a fashion, is everything.*[72] Since, therefore, like is known by like, it seems that the soul knows corporeal things through itself.

Obj. 3. Further, the soul is superior to corporeal creatures. Now lower things are in higher things in a more eminent way than in themselves, as Dionysius says.[73] Therefore all corporeal creatures exist in a more excellent way in the essence of the soul than in themselves. Therefore the soul can know corporeal creatures through its essence.

On the contrary, Augustine says that *the mind gathers the knowledge of corporeal things through the bodily senses.*[74] But the soul itself cannot be known through the bodily senses. Therefore it does not know corporeal things through itself.

I answer that, The ancient philosophers held that the soul knows bodies through its essence. For it was universally admitted that *like is known by like.*[75] But they thought that the form of the thing known is in the

---

[71]*De Trin.* X, 5 (PL 42, 977). [72]*De An.,* III, 8 (431b 21). [73]*De Cael.*
Hier., XII, 2 (PG 3, 293). [74]*De Trin.,* IX, 3 (PL 42, 963). [75]Cf.
Aristotle, *De An.,* I, 5 (409b 24).

knower in the same way as in the thing known. The Platonists however were of a contrary opinion. For Plato, having observed that the intellectual soul has an immaterial nature,[76] and an immaterial mode of knowing,[77] held that the forms of the things known subsist immaterially. But the earlier natural philosophers, observing that the things known are corporeal and material, held that they must exist materially even in the soul that knows them. And therefore, in order to ascribe to the soul a knowledge of all things, they held that it has the same nature in common with all.[78] And because the nature of an effect is determined by its principles, they ascribed to the soul the nature of a principle.[79] Hence it is that those who thought fire to be the principle of all, held that the soul had the nature of fire,[80] and in like manner as to air[81] and water.[82] Lastly, Empedocles, who held the existence of four material elements and two principles of movement,[83] said that the soul was composed of these.[84] Consequently, since they held that things existed in the soul materially, they maintained that all the soul's knowledge is material, thus failing to distinguish intellect from sense.[85]

But this opinion will not hold. First, because in the material principle of which they were speaking, effects do not exist save in potentiality. But a thing is not known according as it is in potentiality, but only according as it is in act, as is shown in *Metaph.* ix.[86]; therefore neither is a power known except through its act. It was therefore insufficient to ascribe to the soul the nature of the principles of things in order to guarantee to the soul a knowledge of all things; it was further necessary to admit in the soul the natures and forms of each individual effect, for instance, of bone, flesh, and the like. Thus does Aristotle argue against Empedocles.[87] Secondly, because if it were necessary for the thing known to exist materially in the knower, there would be no reason why things which have a material existence outside the soul should be devoid of knowledge; why, for instance, if

---

[76]Cf. Nemesius, *De Nat. Hom.*, II (PG 40, 572); St. Augustine, *De Civit. Dei*, VIII, 5 (PL 41, 230). [77]Cf. Aristotle, *Metaph.*, I, 6 (987b 6). [78]Cf. Aristotle, *De An.*, I, 5 (409b 24). [79]Cf. *op. cit.*, I, 2 (404b 110). [80]A theory of Democritus, according to Aristotle, *De An.*, I, 2 (405a 5). [81]A theory of Diogenes, according to Aristotle, *ibid.*, (405a 21); and of Anaximenes, according to Macrobius, *In Somn. Scipion.*, I, 14 (p. 543). [82]A theory of Hippo, according to Aristotle, *De An.*, I, 2 (405b 1). [83]Cf. Aristotle, *De Gener.*, I, 1 (314a 16). [84]Cf. Aristotle, *De An.*, I, 5 (410a 3); I, 4 (408a 19). [85]Cf. *op. cit.*, III, 3 (427a 21). [86]Aristotle, *Metaph.*, VIII, 9 (1051a 29). [87]*De An.*, I, 5 (409b 23).

by fire the soul knows fire, that fire also which is outside the soul should not have knowledge of fire.

We must conclude, therefore, that the material things known must needs exist in the knower, not materially, but rather immaterially. The reason for this is that the act of knowledge extends to things outside the knower; for we know even the things that are outside us. Now by matter the form of a thing is determined to some one thing. Therefore it is clear that knowledge is in inverse ratio to materiality. Consequently, things that are not receptive of forms, save materially, have no power of knowledge whatever—such as plants, as the Philosopher says.[88] But the more immaterially a being receives the form of the thing known, the more perfect is its knowledge. Therefore the intellect, which abstracts the species not only from matter, but also from the individuating conditions of matter, knows more perfectly than the senses, which receive the form of the thing known, without matter indeed, but subject to material conditions. Moreover, among the senses themselves, sight has the most perfect knowledge, because it is the least material, as we have remarked above.[89] So, too, among intellects, the more perfect is the more immaterial.

It is therefore clear from the foregoing, that if there be an intellect which knows all things by its essence, then its essence must needs have all things in itself immaterially; much as the early philosophers held that the essence of the soul must be composed actually of the principles of all material things in order to know all things. Now it is proper to God that His essence comprise all things immaterially, as effects pre-exist virtually in their cause. God alone, therefore, understands all things through His essence; but neither the human soul nor the angels can do so.

Reply Obj. 1. Augustine in that passage is speaking of an imaginary vision, which takes place through the images of bodies. To the formation of such images the soul gives part of its substance, just as a subject is given in order to be informed by some form. In this way the soul makes such images from itself; not that the soul or some part of the soul be turned into this or that image, but just as we say that a body is made into something colored because of its being informed with color. That this is the sense is clear from the sequel. For he says that the soul *keeps something*—namely, not informed with such an image—*which is able freely to judge of the species of these images*, and that this is the *mind* or *intellect*.[90] And he says that the part which is informed with these images—namely, the imagination—is *common to us and beasts*.

---

[88]*Op. cit.*, II, 12 (424a 32).   [89]Q. 78, a. 3.   [90]*De Trin.*, X, 5 (PL 42, 977).

Reply Obj. 2. Aristotle did not hold that the soul was actually composed of all things, as did the earlier naturalists; he said that the soul is all things, *after a fashion*, inasmuch as it is in potentiality to all—through the senses, to all sensible things; through the intellect, to all intelligible things.

Reply Obj. 3. Every creature has a finite and determinate being. Therefore, although the essence of a higher creature has a certain likeness to a lower creature, inasmuch as they share in a common genus, yet it has not a complete likeness thereof, because it is determined to a certain species other than the species of the lower creature. But the divine essence is a perfect likeness of all that may be found to exist in things created, being the universal principle of all.

THIRD ARTICLE
Whether the Soul Understands
All Things Through Innate Species?

We proceed thus to the Third Article:—

Objection 1. It would seem that the soul understands all things through innate species. For Gregory says, in a homily for the Ascension, that *man has understanding in common with the angels.*[91] But angels understand all things through innate species: wherefore in the *Book of Causes* it is said that *every intelligence is full of forms.*[92] Therefore the soul also has innate species of things, by means of which it understands corporeal things.

Obj. 2. Further, the intellectual soul is more excellent than corporeal primary matter. But primary matter was created by God under the forms to which it has potentiality. Therefore much more is the intellectual soul created by God with intelligible species. And so the soul understands corporeal things through innate species.

Obj. 3. Further, no one can answer the truth except concerning what he knows. But even a person untaught, and devoid of acquired knowledge, answers the truth to every question if put to him in orderly fashion, as we find related in the *Meno* of Plato concerning a certain individual.[93] Therefore we have some knowledge of things even before we acquire knowledge; which would not be the case unless we had innate species. Therefore the soul understands corporeal things through innate species.

On the contrary, The Philosopher, speaking of the intellect, says that it is like a *tablet on which nothing is written.*[94]

---

[91]*In Evang.*, II, hom. 29 (PL 76, 1214). [92]*De Causis*, X (p. 170). [93]*Meno* (p. 82b).—Cf. St. Augustine, *De Trin.*, II, 15 (PL 42, 1011). [94]*De An.*, III, 4 (430a 1).

I answer that, Since form is the principle of action, a thing must be related to the form which is the principle of an action in the same way as it is to that action. For instance, if upward motion is from lightness, then that which moves upwards only potentially must needs be only potentially light, but that which actually moves upwards must needs be actually light. Now we observe that man sometimes is only a potential knower, both as to sense and as to intellect. And he is reduced from such potentiality to act:—through the action of sensible objects on his senses, to the act of sensation; by instruction or discovery, to the act of understanding. Therefore we must say that the cognitive soul is in potentiality both to the likenesses which are the principles of sensing, and to the likenesses which are the principles of understanding. For this reason Aristotle held that the intellect by which the soul understands has no innate species, but is at first in potentiality to all such species.[95]

But since that which actually has a form is sometimes unable to act according to that form because of some hindrance (as a light thing may be hindered from moving upwards), for this reason Plato held that man's intellect is naturally filled with all intelligible species, but that, by being united to the body, it is hindered from the realization of its act.[96] But this seems to be unreasonable. First, because, if the soul has a natural knowledge of all things, it seems impossible for the soul so far to forget the existence of such knowledge as not to know itself to be possessed of it. For no man forgets what he knows naturally, *e.g.*, that every whole is larger than its part, and the like. And especially unreasonable does this seem if we suppose that it is natural to the soul to be united to the body, as we have established above;[97] for it is unreasonable that the natural operation of a thing be totally hindered by that which belongs to it naturally. Secondly, the falseness of this opinion is clearly proved from the fact that if a sense be wanting, the knowledge of what is apprehended through that sense is also wanting. For instance, a man who is born blind can have no knowledge of colors. This would not be the case if the soul had innate likenesses of all intelligible things. We must therefore conclude that the soul does not know corporeal things through innate species.

Reply Obj. 1. Man indeed has understanding in common with the angels, but not in the same degree of perfection; just as the lower grades of bodies, which merely exist, according to Gregory, have not the same degree of perfection as the higher bodies. For the matter of the lower bodies is not totally completed by its form, but is in potentiality to forms

---

[95]*Ibid.* (429b 30).   [96]Cf. Aristotle, *Metaph.*, I, 9 (993a 1).   [97]Q. 76, a. 1.

which it has not; whereas the matter of the heavenly bodies is totally completed by its form, so that it is not in potentiality to any other form, as we
have said above.[98] In the same way the angelic intellect is perfected by
intelligible species, in accordance with its nature; whereas the human
intellect is in potentiality to such species.

Reply Obj. 2. Primary matter has substantial being through its form,
and consequently it had need to be created under some form; for otherwise it would not be in act. But when once it exists under one form it is in
potentiality to others. On the other hand, the intellect does not receive
substantial being through the intelligible species; and therefore there is no
comparison.

Reply Obj. 3. If questions be put in an orderly fashion, they proceed
from universal self-evident principles to what is particular. Now by such a
process knowledge is produced in the soul of the learner. Therefore, when
he answers the truth to a subsequent question, this is not because he had
knowledge previously, but because he then acquires such knowledge for
the first time. For it matters not whether the teacher proceed from universal principles to conclusions by questioning or by asserting; for in either
case the intellect of the listener is assured of what follows by that which
preceded.

FOURTH ARTICLE
Whether the Intelligible Species Are Derived by the Soul from Certain Separate Forms?

We proceed thus to the Fourth Article:—

Objection 1. It would seem that the intelligible species are derived by
the soul from some separate forms. For whatever is such by participation
is caused by what is such essentially; for instance, that which is on fire is
reduced to fire as its cause. But the intellectual soul, in so far as it is actually understanding, participates in the intelligibles themselves; for, in a
manner, the intellect in act is the thing understood in act. Therefore that
which in itself and in its essence is understood in act, is the cause that the
intellectual soul actually understands. Now that which in its essence is
actually understood is a form existing without matter. Therefore the intelligible species, by which the soul understands, are caused by some separate forms.

Obj. 2. Further, the intelligible is to the intellect as the sensible is to
the sense. But the sensible species which are in the senses, and by which

---

[98]Q. 66, a. 2.

we sense, are caused by the sensible things which exist actually outside the soul. Therefore the intelligible species, by which our intellect understands, are caused by some things actually intelligible, existing outside the soul. But these can be nothing else than forms separate from matter. Therefore the intelligible forms of our intellect are derived from some separate substances.

Obj. 3. Further, whatever is in potentiality is reduced to act by something actual. If, therefore, our intellect, previously in potentiality, afterwards actually understands, this must needs be caused by some intellect which is always in act. But this is a separate intellect. Therefore the intelligible species, by which we actually understand, are caused by some separate substances.

On the contrary, If this were true, we should not need the senses in order to understand. And this is proved to be false especially from the fact that if a man be wanting in a sense, he cannot have any knowledge of the sensibles corresponding to that sense.

I answer that, Some have held that the intelligible species of our intellect are derived from certain separate Forms or substances. And this in two ways. For Plato, as we have said, held that the forms of sensible things subsist by themselves without matter: *e.g.*, the Form of a man which he called man-in-himself, and the Form or Idea of a horse which he called horse-in-itself, and so forth. He said therefore that these Forms are participated both by our soul and by corporeal matter: by our soul, for knowledge,[99] and by corporeal matter for being[100]; so that, just as corporeal matter, by participating the Idea of a stone, becomes an individual stone, so our intellect, by participating the Idea of a stone, is made to understand a stone. Now the participation of an Idea takes place by some likeness of the Idea in the participator, in the way that a model is participated by a copy.[101] So just as he held that the sensible forms, which are in corporeal matter, are derived from the Ideas as certain likenesses of them, so he held that the intelligible species of our intellect are likenesses of the Ideas, derived therefrom.[102] And for this reason, as we have said above, he referred sciences and definitions to those Ideas.

But since it is contrary to the nature of sensible things that their forms should subsist without matter, as Aristotle proves in many ways,[103] Avi-

---

[99]Cf. St. Augustine, *Lib. 83 Quaest.*, q. 46 (PL 40, 30). [100]Cf. Aristotle, *Metaph.*, I, 9 (991b 3).—Plato, *Phaedo* (p. 100d). [101]Cf. Aristotle, *Metaph.*, I, 9 (991a 21).—Plato, *Timaeus* (pp. 28a, 30c). [102]Cf. Avicenna, *De An.*, V, 5 (25rb); *Metaph.*, IX, 4 (105ra). [103]*Metaph.*, VI, 14 (1039a 24).

cenna, setting this opinion aside, held that the intelligible species of all sensible things, instead of subsisting in themselves without matter, pre-exist immaterially in some separate intellects.[104] From the first of these intellects, said he, such species are derived by a second, and so on to the last separate intellect, which he called the *agent intellect*. From the agent intellect, according to him, intelligible species flow into our souls, and sensible species into corporeal matter.[105] And so Avicenna agrees with Plato in this, that the intelligible species of our intellect are derived from certain separate Forms; but these Plato held to subsist of themselves, while Avicenna placed them in the agent intellect. They differ, too, in this respect, that Avicenna held that the intelligible species do not remain in our intellect after it has ceased actually to understand, and that it needs to turn [to the agent intellect] in order to receive them anew.[106] Conse-quently, he does not hold that the soul has innate knowledge, as Plato, who held that the participations of the Ideas remain immovably in the soul.[107]

But in this opinion no sufficient reason can be assigned for the soul being united to the body. For it cannot be said that the intellectual soul is united to the body for the sake of the body, since neither is form for the sake of matter, nor is the mover for the sake of the thing moved, but rather the reverse. Especially does the body seem necessary to the intellectual soul for the latter's proper operation, which is to understand; since as to its being, the soul does not depend on the body. But if the soul by its very nature had an inborn aptitude for receiving intelligible species only through the influence of certain separate principles, and were not to receive them from the senses, it would not need the body in order to understand. Hence, it would be united to the body to no purpose.

But if it be said that our soul needs the senses in order to understand, in that it is in some way awakened by them to the consideration of those things whose intelligible species it receives from the separate principles,[108] even this seems an insufficient explanation. For this awakening does not seem necessary to the soul, except in as far as it is overcome by sleep, as the Platonists expressed it, and by forgetfulness, through its union with the body[109]; and thus the senses would be of no use to the intellectual soul

---

[104]*De An.*, V, 5 (25rb); *Metaph.*, IX, 4 (105ra).   [105]*De An.*, V, 6 (26rb); *Metaph.*, IX, 5 (105rb).—Cf. q. 65, a. 4.   [106]*De An.*, V, 6 (26rb).—Cf. *C. G.*, II, 74.   [107]Cf. Aristotle, *Metaph.*, I, 7 (988b 3); *Top.*, II, 7 (113a 27). [108]Cf. William of Auvergne, *De Univ.*, IIa IIae, 76 (I, pt. II, 929); IIIa IIae, 3 (I, pt. II, 1018).   [109]Pseudo-Augustine (Alcher of Clairvaux, *De Spir. et An.*, I (PL 40, 781).

except for the purpose of removing the obstacle which the soul encounters through its union with the body.[110] Consequently, the reason for the union of the soul with the body still remains unexplained.

And if it be said, with Avicenna, that the senses are necessary to the soul because by them it is roused to turn to the agent intellect from which it receives the species,[111] neither is this a sufficient explanation. Because if it is natural for the soul to understand through species derived from the agent intellect, it would follow that the soul can turn to the agent intellect from the inclination of its very nature, or through being roused by another sense to turn to the agent intellect, and receive the species of those sensible things for which we are missing a sense. And thus a man born blind could have knowledge of colors; which is clearly untrue. We must therefore conclude that the intelligible species, by which our soul understands, are not derived from separate forms.

Reply Obj. 1. The intelligible species which are participated by our intellect are reduced, as to their first cause, to a first principle which is by its essence intelligible—namely, God. But they proceed from that principle by way of the forms of sensible and material things, from which we gather knowledge, as Dionysius says.[112]

Reply Obj. 2. Material things, as to the being which they have outside the soul, may be actually sensible, but not actually intelligible. Therefore there is no comparison between sense and intellect.

Reply Obj. 3. Our possible intellect is reduced from potentiality to act by some being in act, that is, by the agent intellect, which is a power of the soul, as we have said[113]; and not by any separate intellect, as a proximate cause, although perchance as a remote cause.

FIFTH ARTICLE
Whether the Intellectual Soul Knows Material Things in the Eternal Exemplars?

We proceed thus to the Fifth Article:—

Objection 1. It would seem that the intellectual soul does not know material things in the eternal exemplars. For that in which anything is known must itself be known more and antecedently. But the intellectual soul of man, in the present state of life, does not know the eternal exemplars, for it does not know God in Whom the eternal exemplars exist, but

---

[110]Cf. below, q. 89, a. 1.   [111]*De An.*, V, 5 (25rb).   [112]*De Div. Nom.*, VII, 2 (PG 3, 886).   [113]Q. 79, a. 4.

is *united to God as to the unknown*, as Dionysius says.[114] Therefore the soul does not know all in the eternal exemplars.

Obj. 2. Further, it is written (*Rom.* i. 20) that *the invisible things of God are clearly seen . . . by the things that are made*. But among the invisible things of God are the eternal exemplars. Therefore the eternal exemplars are known through creatures, and not the converse.

Obj. 3. Further, the eternal exemplars are nothing else but ideas, for Augustine says that *ideas are permanent exemplars existing in the divine mind*.[115] If therefore we say that the intellectual soul knows all things in the eternal exemplars, we come back to the opinion of Plato who said that all knowledge is derived from them.

On the contrary, Augustine says: *If we both see that what you say is true, and if we both see that what I say is true, where do we see this, I pray? Neither do I see it in you, nor do you see it in me; but we both see it in the unchangeable truth which is above our minds*.[116] Now the unchangeable truth is contained in the eternal exemplars. Therefore the intellectual soul knows all truths in the eternal exemplars.

I answer that, As Augustine says: *If those who are called philosophers said by chance anything that was true and consistent with our faith, we must claim it from them as from unjust possessors. For some of the doctrines of the pagans are spurious imitations or superstitious inventions, which we must be careful to avoid when we renounce the society of the pagans*.[117] Consequently whenever Augustine, who was imbued with the doctrines of the Platonists, found in their teaching anything consistent with faith, he adopted it; and those things which he found contrary to faith he amended. Now Plato held, as we have said above, that the forms of things subsist of themselves apart from matter. These he called Ideas, and he said that our intellect knows all things by participation in them; so that just as corporeal matter, by participating in the Idea of a stone, becomes a stone, so our intellect, by participating in the same Idea, has knowledge of a stone. But it seems contrary to faith that the forms of things should subsist of themselves without matter outside the things themselves, as the Platonists held, asserting that *life-in-itself* and *wisdom-in-itself* are certain creative substances, as Dionysius relates.[118] Therefore, in the place of the Ideas defended by Plato, Augustine said that the exemplars of all creatures existed in the divine

---

[114]*De Myst. Theol.*, I, 3 (PG 3, 1001); cf. *De Div. Nom.*, I, 1 (PG 3, 585).
[115]*Lib. 83 Quaest.*, q. 46 (PL 40, 30).   [116]*Confess.*, XII, 25 (PL 32, 840).
[117]*De Doc. Christ.*, II, 40 (PL 34, 63).   [118]*De Div. Nom.*, XI, 6 (PG 3, 956).

mind. It is according to these that all things are formed, as well as that the human soul knows all things.[119]

When, therefore, the question is asked: Does the human soul know all things in the eternal exemplars? we must reply that one thing is said to be known in another in two ways. First, as in an object itself known; as one may see in a mirror the images of the things reflected therein. In this way the soul, in the present state of life, cannot see all things in the eternal exemplars; but thus the blessed, who see God and all things in Him, know all things in the eternal exemplars. Secondly, one thing is said to be known in another as in a principle of knowledge; and thus we might say that we see in the sun what we see by the sun. And thus we must needs say that the human soul knows all things in the eternal exemplars, since by participation in these exemplars we know all things. For the intellectual light itself, which is in us, is nothing else than a participated likeness of the uncreated light, in which are contained the eternal exemplars. Whence it is written (*Ps.* iv. 6, 7), *Many say: who showeth us good things?* which question the Psalmist answers, *The light of Thy countenance, O Lord, is signed upon us*; as though to say: By the seal of the divine light in us, all things are made known to us.

But since besides the intellectual light which is in us, intelligible species, which are derived from things, are required in order that we may have knowledge of material things, therefore this knowledge is not due merely to a participation of the eternal exemplars, as the Platonists held, maintaining that the mere participation in the Ideas sufficed for knowledge.[120] Therefore Augustine says: *Although the philosophers prove by convincing arguments that all things occur in time according to the eternal exemplars, were they able to see in the eternal exemplars, or to find out from them, how many kinds of animals there are and the origin of each? Did they not seek for this information from the story of times and places?*[121]

Now that Augustine did not understand all things to be known in their *eternal exemplars* or in *the unchangeable truth*, as though the eternal exemplars themselves were seen, is clear from what he says, viz., that *not each and every rational soul can be said to be worthy of that vision*, namely, of the eternal exemplars, *but only those that are holy and pure*,[122] such as the souls of the blessed.

From what has been said the objections are easily solved.

---

[119] *Lib. 83 Quaest.*, q. 46 (PL 40,30)   [120] Cf. below, q. 87, a. 1.—Cf. also St. Bonaventure, *Quaest. Disp. de Scientia Dei*, q. 4 (V, 17).   [121] *De Trin.*, IV, 16 (PL 42, 902).   [122] *Lib. 83 Quaest.*, q. 46 (PL 40, 30).

SIXTH ARTICLE
Whether Intellectual Knowledge Is
Derived from Sensible Things?

We proceed thus to the Sixth Article:—

Objection 1. It would seem that intellectual knowledge is not derived from sensible things. For Augustine says that *we cannot expect to acquire the pure truth from the senses of the body.*[123] This he proves in two ways. First, because, *whatever the bodily senses reach is continually being changed; and what is never the same cannot be perceived.* Secondly, because, *whatever we perceive by the body, even when not present to the senses, may be present in their images, is when we are asleep or angry; yet we cannot discern by the senses whether what we perceive be the sensible things themselves, or their deceptive images. Now nothing can be perceived which cannot be distinguished from its counterfeit.* And so he concludes that we cannot expect to learn the truth from the senses. But intellectual knowledge apprehends the truth. Therefore intellectual knowledge cannot be conveyed by the senses.

Obj. 2. Further, Augustine says: *We must not think that the body can make any impression on the spirit, as though the spirit were to subject itself like matter to the body's action; for that which acts is in every way more excellent than that which it acts on.*[124] Whence he concludes that *the body does not cause its image in the spirit, but the spirit itself causes it in itself.* Therefore intellectual knowledge is not derived from sensible things.

Obj. 3. Further, an effect does not surpass the power of its cause. But intellectual knowledge extends beyond sensible things, for we understand some things which cannot be perceived by the senses. Therefore intellectual knowledge is not derived from sensible things.

On the contrary, The Philosopher proves that the origin of knowledge is from the senses.[125]

I answer that, On this point the philosophers held three opinions. For Democritus held that *all knowledge is caused by images issuing from the bodies we think of and entering into our souls,* as Augustine says in his letter to Dioscorus.[126] And Aristotle says that Democritus held that knowledge is caused by a *discharge of images.*[127] And the reason for this opinion was that both Democritus and the other early philosophers did not distinguish between intellect and sense, as Aristotle relates.[128] Consequently, since the sense is immuted by the sensible, they thought that all our knowledge is

---

[123]*Op. cit.*, q. 9 (PL 40, 13).   [124]*De Genesi ad Litt.*, XII, 16 (PL 34, 467).
[125]*Metaph.*, I, 1 (981a 2); *Post. Anal.*, II, 15 (100a 3).   [126]*Epist.* CXVIII, 4 (PL 33, 446).   [127]*De Divinat.*, II (464a 5).   [128]*De An.*, III, 3 (427a 17).

caused merely by an immutation from sensible things. This immutation Democritus held to be caused by a discharge of images.

Plato, on the other hand, held that the intellect differs from sense, and that it is an immaterial power not making use of a corporeal organ for its action.[129] And since the incorporeal cannot be affected by the corporeal, he held that intellectual knowledge is not brought about by sensible things immuting the intellect, but by the participation in separate intelligible forms by the intellect, as we have said above. Moreover he held that sense is a power operating through itself. Consequently not even the sense itself, since it is a spiritual power, is affected by sensible things; but the sensible organs are affected by the sensible, with the result that the soul is in a way roused to form within itself the species of the sensible. Augustine seems to touch on this opinion where he says that the *body feels not, but the soul through the body, which it makes use of as a kind of messenger, for reproducing within itself what is announced from without.*[130] Thus according to Plato, neither does intellectual knowledge proceed from sensible knowledge, nor does sensible knowledge itself come entirely from sensible things; but these rouse the sensible soul to sensation, and the senses likewise rouse the intellect to the act of understanding.

Aristotle chose a middle course. For with Plato he agreed that intellect and sense are different.[131] But he held that the sense has not its proper operation without the cooperation of the body; so that *to sense is not an act of the soul alone*, but of the *composite*.[132] And he held the same in regard to all the operations of the sensitive part. Since, therefore, it is not incongruous that the sensible things which are outside the soul should produce some effect in the *composite*, Aristotle agreed with Democritus in this, that the operations of the sensitive part are caused by the impression of the sensible on the sense; not indeed by a discharge, as Democritus said, but by some kind of operation. Democritus, it must be remembered, maintained that every action is by way of a discharge of atoms, as we gather from *De Gener.* i.[133] But Aristotle held that the intellect has an operation in which the body does not share.[134] Now nothing corporeal can make an impression on the incorporeal. And therefore, in order to cause the intellectual operation, according to Aristotle, the impression caused by sensible bodies does not suffice, but something more noble is required, *for the*

---

[129]Cf. above, q. 75, a. 3.   [130]*De Genesi ad Litt.*, XII, 24 (PL 34, 475).
[131]*De An.*, III, 3 (427b 6).   [132]*De Somno*, I (454a 7).   [133]Aristotle, *De Gener.*, I, 8 (324b 25).   [134]*De An.*, III, 4 (429a 24).

agent is more noble than the patient, as he says.[135] Not, be it observed, in the sense that the intellectual operation is effected in us by the mere impression of some superior beings, as Plato held; but that the higher and more noble agent which he calls the agent intellect, of which we have spoken above,[136] causes the phantasms received from the senses to be actually intelligible, by a process of abstraction.

According to this opinion, then, on the part of the phantasms, intellectual knowledge is caused by the senses. But since the phantasms cannot of themselves immute the possible intellect, but require to be made actually intelligible by the agent intellect, it cannot be said that sensible knowledge is the total and perfect cause of intellectual knowledge, but rather is in a way the matter of the cause.

Reply Obj. 1. These words of Augustine mean that truth is not entirely from the senses For the light of the agent intellect is needed, through which we know the truth of changeable things unchangeably, and discern things themselves from their likenesses.

Reply Obj. 2. In this passage Augustine speaks not of intellectual but of imaginary knowledge. And since, according to the opinion of Plato, the imagination has an operation which belongs to the soul only, Augustine, in order to show that corporeal images are impressed on the imagination, not by bodies but by the soul, uses the same argument as Aristotle does in proving that the agent intellect must be separate, namely, because *the agent is more noble than the patient*.[137] And without doubt, according to the above opinion, in the imagination there must needs be not only a passive but also an active power. But if we hold, according to the opinion of Aristotle,[138] that the action of the imaginative power is an action of the *composite*, there is no difficulty; because the sensible body is more noble than the organ of the animal, in so far as it is compared to it as a being in act to a being in potentiality; even as the object actually colored is compared to the pupil which is potentially colored. Now, although the first immutation of the imagination is through the agency of the sensible, since *the phantasm is a movement produced in accordance with sensation*,[139] nevertheless, it may be said that there is in man an operation which by division and composition forms images of various things, even of things not perceived by the senses. And Augustine's words may be taken in this sense.

---

[135]*Op. cit.*, III, 5 (430a 18).   [136]Q. 79, a. 3 and 4.   [137]*De An.*, III, 5 (430a 18).   [138]*Op. cit.*, I, 1 (403a 5).   [139]*Op. cit.*, III, 3 (429a 1).

Reply Obj. 3. Sensitive knowledge is not the entire cause of intellectual knowledge. And therefore it is not strange that intellectual knowledge should extend beyond sensitive knowledge.

SEVENTH ARTICLE

**Whether the Intellect Can Understand Actually
Through the Intelligible Species of Which It Is Possessed,
Without Turning to the Phantasms?**

We proceed thus to the Seventh Article:—

Objection 1. It would seem that the intellect can understand actually through the intelligible species of which it is possessed, without turning to the phantasms. For the intellect is made actual by the intelligible species by which it is informed. But if the intellect is in act, it understands. Therefore the intelligible species suffices for the intellect to understand actually without turning to the phantasms.

Obj. 2. Further, the imagination is more dependent on the senses than the intellect on the imagination. But the imagination can actually imagine in the absence of the sensible. Therefore much more can the intellect understand without turning to the phantasms.

Obj. 3. There are no phantasms of incorporeal things, for the imagination does not transcend time and space. If, therefore, our intellect cannot understand anything actually without turning to the phantasms, it follows that it cannot understand anything incorporeal. Which is clearly false, for we understand truth, and God, and the angels.

On the contrary, The Philosopher says that *the soul understands nothing without a phantasm.*[140]

I answer that, In the state of the present life, in which the soul is united to a corruptible body, it is impossible for our intellect to understand anything actually, except by turning to phantasms. And of this there are two indications. First of all because the intellect, being a power that does not make use of a corporeal organ, would in no way be hindered in its act through the lesion of a corporeal organ, if there were not required for its act the act of some power that does make use of a corporeal organ. Now sense, imagination and the other powers belonging to the sensitive part make use of a corporeal organ. Therefore it is clear that for the intellect to understand actually, not only when it acquires new knowledge, but also when it uses knowledge already acquired, there is need for the act of the imagination and of the other powers. For when the act of the imagination is

---

[140]*Op. cit.,* III, 7 (431a 16).

hindered by a lesion of the corporeal organ, for instance, in a case of frenzy, or when the act of the memory is hindered, as in the case of lethargy, we see that a man is hindered from understanding actually even those things of which he had a previous knowledge. Secondly, anyone can experience this of himself, that when he tries to understand something, he forms certain phantasms to serve him by way of examples, in which as it were he examines what he is desirous of understanding. For this reason it is that when we wish to help someone to understand something, we lay examples before him, from which he can form phantasms for the purpose of understanding.

Now the reason for this is that the power of knowledge is proportioned to the thing known. Therefore the proper object of the angelic intellect, which is entirely separate from a body, is an intelligible substance separate from a body. Whereas the proper object of the human intellect, which is united to a body, is the quiddity or nature existing in corporeal matter; and it is through these natures of visible things that it rises to a certain knowledge of things invisible. Now it belongs to such a nature to exist in some individual, and this cannot be apart from corporeal matter; for instance, it belongs to the nature of a stone to be in an individual stone, and to the nature of a horse to be in an individual horse, and so forth. Therefore the nature of a stone or any material thing cannot be known completely and truly, except in as much as it is known as existing in the individual. Now we apprehend the individual through the sense and the imagination. And, therefore, for the intellect to understand actually its proper object, it must of necessity turn to the phantasms in order to perceive the universal nature existing in the individual. But if the proper object of our intellect were a separate form, or if, as the Platonists say, the natures of sensible things subsisted apart from the individual, there would be no need for the intellect to turn to the phantasms whenever it understands.

Reply Obj. 1. The species preserved in the possible intellect exist there habitually when it does not understand them actually, as we have said above.[141] Therefore for us to understand actually, the fact that the species are preserved does not suffice; we need further to make use of them in a manner befitting the things of which they are the species, which things are natures existing in individuals.

Reply Obj. 2. Even the phantasm is the likeness of an individual thing; and so the imagination does not need any further likeness of the individual, whereas the intellect does.

---

[141]Q. 79, a. 6.

Reply Obj. 3. Incorporeal beings, of which there are no phantasms, are known to us by comparison with sensible bodies of which there are phantasms. Thus we understand truth by considering a thing in which we see the truth; and God, as Dionysius says,[142] we know as cause, by way of excess and by way of remotion. Other incorporeal substances we know, in the state of the present life, only by way of remotion or by some comparison to corporeal things. Hence, when we understand something about these beings, we need to turn to the phantasms of bodies, although there are no phantasms of these beings themselves.

EIGHTH ARTICLE
Whether the Judgment of the Intellect is Hindered Through Suspension of the Sensitive Powers?

We proceed thus to the Eighth Article:—

Objection 1. It would seem that the judgment of the intellect is not hindered by suspension of the sensitive powers. For the superior does not depend on the inferior. But the judgment of the intellect is higher than the senses. Therefore the judgment of the intellect is not hindered through suspension of the senses.

Obj. 2. Further, to syllogize is an act of the intellect. But during sleep the senses are suspended, as is said in *De Somno et Vigilia*,[143] and yet it sometimes happens to us to syllogize while asleep. Therefore the judgment of the intellect is not hindered through suspension of the senses.

On the contrary, What a man does while asleep, against the moral law, is not imputed to him as a sin, as Augustine says.[144] But this would not be the case if man, while asleep, had free use of his reason and intellect. Therefore the judgment of the intellect is hindered by suspension of the senses.

I answer that, As we have said above, our intellect's proper and proportionate object is the nature of a sensible thing. Now a perfect judgment concerning anything cannot be formed, unless all that pertains to that thing be known; especially if that be ignored which is the term and end of judgment. For the Philosopher says that *as the end of practical science is a work, so the end of the science of nature is that which is perceived principally through the senses.*[145] For the smith does not seek the knowledge of a knife except for the purpose of producing this individual knife; and in like manner the natural philosopher does not seek to know the nature of a

---

[142]*De Div. Nom.*, I, 5 (PG 3, 593). [143]Aristotle, *De Somno*, I (454b 13).
[144]*De Genesi ad Litt.*, XII, 15 (PL 34, 466). [145]*De Caelo*, III, 7 (306a 16).

stone and of a horse, save for the purpose of knowing the essential properties of those things which he perceives with his senses. Now it is clear that a smith cannot judge perfectly of a knife unless he knows what making this particular knife means; and in like manner the natural philosopher cannot judge perfectly of natural things, unless he knows sensible things. But in the present state of life, whatever we understand we know by comparison with natural sensible things. Consequently it is not possible for our intellect to form a perfect judgment while the senses are suspended, through which sensible things are known to us.

Reply Obj. 1. Although the intellect is superior to the senses, nevertheless in a manner it receives from the senses, and its first and principal objects are founded in sensible things. Hence, suspension of the senses necessarily involves a hindrance to the judgment of the intellect.

Reply Obj. 2. The senses are suspended in the sleeper through certain evaporations and the escape of certain exhalations, as we read in *De Somno et Vigilia*.[146] And, therefore, according to the disposition of such evaporation, the senses are more or less suspended. For when the movement of the vapors is very agitated, not only are the senses suspended, but also the imagination, so that there are no phantasms; as happens especially when a man falls asleep after much eating and drinking. If, however, the movement of the vapors be somewhat less violent, phantasms appear, but distorted and without sequence; as happens in a case of fever. And if the movement be still more attenuated, the phantasms will have a certain sequence; as happens especially towards the end of sleep, and in sober men and those who are gifted with a strong imagination. If the movement be very slight, not only does the imagination retain its freedom, but even the common sense is partly freed; so that sometimes while asleep a man may judge that what he sees is a dream, discerning, as it were, between things and their images. Nevertheless, the common sense remains partly suspended, and therefore, although it discriminates some images from reality, yet it is always deceived in some particular. Therefore, while a man is asleep, according as sense and imagination are free, so is the judgment of his intellect unfettered, though not entirely. Consequently, if a man syllogizes while asleep, when he wakes up he invariably recognizes a flaw in some respect.

---

[146] Aristotle, *De Somno*, III (456b 17).

Summa Theologica

PART ONE

QUESTION 85

The Mode and Order of Understanding

FIRST ARTICLE
Whether Our Intellect Understands Corporeal and Material Things by Abstraction from Phantasms?

We proceed thus to the First Article:—

Objection 1. It would seem that our Intellect does not understand corporeal and material things by abstraction from the phantasms. For the intellect is false if it understands a thing otherwise than as it is. Now the forms of material things do not exist in abstraction from the particular things represented by the phantasms. Therefore, if we understand material things by the abstraction of species from phantasms, there will be error in the intellect.

Obj. 2. Further, material things are those natural things which include matter in their definition. But nothing can be understood apart from that which enters into its definition. Therefore material things cannot be understood apart from matter. Now matter is the principle of individuation. Therefore material things cannot be understood by the abstraction of the universal from the particular; and this is to abstract intelligible species from the phantasm.

Obj. 3. Further, the Philosopher says that the phantasm is to the intellectual soul what color is to the sight.[147] But seeing is not caused by abstraction of species from color, but by color impressing itself on the sight. Therefore neither does the act of understanding take place by the abstraction of something from the phantasms, but by the phantasms impressing themselves on the intellect.

Obj. 4. Further, the Philosopher says that there are two things in the intellectual soul— the possible intellect and the agent intellect.[148] But it does not belong to the possible intellect to abstract the intelligible species from the phantasm, but to receive them already abstracted. Neither does it seem to be the function of the agent intellect, which is related to phan-

---

[147]Aristotle, *De An.*, III, 7 (431a 14).   [148]*Op. cit.*, III, 5 (430a 14).

tasms as light is to colors; since light does not abstract anything from colors, but rather acts on them. Therefore in no way do we understand by abstraction from phantasms.

Obj. 5. Further, the Philosopher says that *the intellect understands the species in the phantasms*[149]; and not, therefore, by abstraction.

On the contrary, The Philosopher says that *things are intelligible in proportion as they are separable from matter.*[150] Therefore material things must needs be understood according as they are abstracted from matter and from material images, namely, phantasms.

I answer that, As stated above, the object of knowledge is proportionate to the power of knowledge.[151] Now there are three grades of the cognitive powers. For one cognitive power, namely, the sense, is the act of a corporeal organ. And therefore the object of every sensitive power is a form as existing in corporeal matter; and since such matter is the principle of individuation, therefore every power of the sensitive part can have knowledge only of particulars. There is another grade of cognitive power which is neither the act of a corporeal organ, nor in any way connected with corporeal matter. Such is the angelic intellect, the object of whose cognitive power is therefore a form existing apart from matter; for though angels know material things, yet they do not know them save in something immaterial, namely, either in themselves or in God. But the human intellect holds a middle place; for it is not the act of an organ, and yet it is a power of the soul, which is the form of the body, as is clear from what we have said above.[152] And therefore it is proper to it to know a form existing individually in corporeal matter, but not as existing in this individual matter. But to know what is in individual matter, yet not as existing in such matter, is to abstract the form from individual matter which is represented by the phantasms. Therefore we must needs say that our intellect understands material things by abstracting from phantasms; and that through material things thus considered we acquire some knowledge of immaterial things, just as, on the contrary, angels know material things through the immaterial.

But Plato, considering only the immateriality of the human intellect, and not that it is somehow united to the body, held that the objects of the intellect are separate Ideas, and that we understand, not by abstraction, but rather by participating in abstractions, as was stated above.[153]

---

[149]*Op. cit.*, III, 7 (431b 2). [150]*Op. cit.*, III, 4 (429b 21). [151]Q. 84, a. 7.
[152]Q. 76, a. 1. [153]Q. 84, a. 1.

Reply Obj. 1. Abstraction may occur in two ways. First, by way of composition and division, and thus we may understand that one thing does not exist in some other, or that it is separate from it. Secondly, by way of a simple and absolute consideration; and thus we understand one thing without considering another. Thus, for the intellect to abstract one from another things which are not really abstract from one another, does, in the first mode of abstraction, imply falsehood. But, in the second mode of abstraction, for the intellect to abstract things which are not really abstract from one another, does not involve falsehood, as clearly appears in the case of the senses. For if we said that color is not in a colored body, or that it is separate from it, there would be error in what we thought or said. But if we consider color and its properties, without reference to the apple which is colored, or if we express in word what we thus understand, there is no error in such an opinion or assertion; for an apple is not essential to color, and therefore color can be understood independently of the apple. In the same way, the things which belong to the species of a material thing, such as a stone, or a man, or a horse, can be thought without the individual principles which do not belong to the notion of the species. This is what we mean by abstracting the universal from the particular, or the intelligible species from the phantasm; in other words, this is to consider the nature of the species apart from its individual principles represented by the phantasms. If, therefore, the intellect is said to be false when it understands a thing otherwise than as it is, that is so, if the word *otherwise* refers to the thing understood; for the intellect is false when it understands a thing to be otherwise than as it is. Hence, the intellect would be false if it abstracted the species of a stone from its matter in such a way as to think that the species did not exist in matter, as Plato held.[154] But it is not so, if the word *otherwise* be taken as referring to the one who understands. For it is quite true that the mode of understanding, in one who understands, is not the same as the mode of a thing in being; since the thing understood is immaterially in the one who understands, according to the mode of the intellect, and not materially, according to the mode of a material thing.

Reply Obj. 2. Some have thought that the species of a natural thing is a form only, and that matter is not part of the species.[155] If that were so, matter would not enter into the definition of natural things. Therefore we must disagree and say that matter is twofold, common and *signate*, or indi-

---

[154]Cf. above, q. 84, a. 4.   [155]Averroes, *In Metaph.*, VII, comm. 21 (VIII, 80v; 81r); comm. 34 (VIII, 87r).—Cf. St. Thomas, *In Metaph.*, VII, lect. 9.

vidual: common, such as flesh and bone; individual, such as this flesh and these bones. The intellect therefore abstracts the species of a natural thing from the individual sensible matter, but not from the common sensible matter. For example, it abstracts the species of *man* from *this flesh and these bones*, which do not belong to the species as such, but to the individual,[156] and need not be considered in the species. But the species of man cannot be abstracted by the intellect from *flesh and bones*.

Mathematical species, however, can be abstracted by the intellect not only from individual sensible matter, but also from common sensible matter. But they cannot be abstracted from common intelligible matter, but only from individual intelligible matter. For sensible matter is corporeal matter as subject to sensible qualities, such as being cold or hot, hard or soft, and the like; while intelligible matter is substance as subject to quantity. Now it is manifest that quantity is in substance before sensible qualities are. Hence quantities, such as number, dimension, and figures, which are the terminations of quantity, can be considered apart from sensible qualities, and this is to abstract them from sensible matter. But they cannot be considered without understanding the substance which is subject to the quantity, for that would be to abstract them from common intelligible matter. Yet they can be considered apart from this or that substance, and this is to abstract them from individual intelligible matter.

But some things can be abstracted even from common intelligible matter, such as *being, unity, potency, act*, and the like, all of which can exist without matter, as can be verified in the case of immaterial substances. And because Plato failed to consider the twofold kind of abstraction, as above explained, he held that all those things which we have stated to be abstracted by the intellect, are abstract in reality.[157]

Reply Obj. 3. Colors, as being in individual corporeal matter, have the same mode of being as the power of sight; and therefore they can impress their own image on the eye. But phantasms, since they are images of individuals, and exist in corporeal organs, have not the same mode of being as the human intellect, as is clear from what we have said, and therefore they have not the power of themselves to make an impression on the possible intellect. But through the power of the agent intellect, there results in the possible intellect a certain likeness produced by the turning of the agent intellect toward the phantasms. This likeness represents what is in the phantasms, but includes only the nature of the species. It is thus that the

---

[156]Aristotle, *Metaph.*, VI, 10 (1035b 28).   [157]Cf. above, q. 84, a. 1; cf. also q. 50, a. 2.

intelligible species is said to be abstracted from the phantasm; not that the identical form which previously was in the phantasm is subsequently in the possible intellect, as a body transferred from one place to another.

Reply Obj. 4. Not only does the agent intellect illumine phantasms, it does more; by its power intelligible species are abstracted from phantasms. It illumines phantasms because, just as the sensitive part acquires a greater power by its conjunction with the intellectual part, so through the power of the agent intellect phantasms are made more fit for the abstraction of intelligible intentions from them. Now the agent intellect abstracts intelligible species from phantasms inasmuch as by its power we are able to take into our consideration the natures of species without individual conditions. It is in accord with their likenesses that the possible intellect is informed.

Reply Obj. 5. Our intellect both abstracts the intelligible species *from* phantasms, inasmuch as it considers the natures of things universally, and yet understands these natures *in* the phantasms, since it cannot understand the things, of which it abstracts the species, without turning to phantasms, as we have said above.[158]

SECOND ARTICLE
Whether the Intelligible Species Abstracted from Phantasms Are Related to Our Intellect as That Which Is Understood?

We proceed thus to the Second Article:—

Objection 1. It would seem that the intelligible species abstracted from phantasms are related to our intellect as that which is understood. For the understood in act is in the one who understands: since the understood in act is the intellect itself in act. But nothing of what is understood is in the actually understanding intellect save the abstracted intelligible species. Therefore this species is what is actually understood.

Obj. 2. Further, what is actually understood must be in something; or else it would be nothing. But it is not in something outside the soul; for, since what is outside the soul is material, nothing therein can be actually understood. Therefore what is actually understood is in the intellect. Consequently it can be nothing else than the aforesaid intelligible species.

Obj. 3. Further, the Philosopher says that *words are signs of the passions in the soul*.[159] But words signify the things understood, for we express by word what we understand. Therefore these passions of the soul, viz., the intelligible species, are what is actually understood.

---

[158]Q. 84, a. 7.   [159]*Perih.*, I, 1 (16a 3).

On the contrary, The intelligible species is to the intellect what the sensible species is to the sense. But the sensible species is not *what* is perceived, but rather that *by which* the sense perceives. Therefore the intelligible species is not what is actually understood, but that by which the intellect understands.

I answer that, Some[160] have asserted that our intellectual powers know only the impressions made on them; as, for example, that sense is cognizant only of the impression made on its own organ. According to this theory, the intellect understands only its own impressions, namely, the intelligible species which it has received.

This is, however, manifestly false for two reasons. First, because the things we understand are also the objects of science. Therefore, if what we understand is merely the intelligible species in the soul, it would follow that every science would be concerned, not with things outside the soul, but only with the intelligible species within the soul; just as, according to the teaching of the Platonists, all the sciences are about Ideas, which they held to be that which is actually understood.[161] Secondly, it is untrue, because it would lead to the opinion of the ancients who maintained that *whatever seems, is true*,[162] and that consequently contradictories are true simultaneously. For if a power knows only its own impressions, it can judge only of them. Now a thing *seems* according to the impression made on the cognitive power. Consequently the cognitive power will always judge of its own impression as such; and so every judgment will be true. For instance, if taste perceived only its own impression, when anyone with a healthy taste perceives that honey is sweet, he would judge truly, and if anyone with a corrupt taste perceives that honey is bitter, this would be equally true; for each would judge according to the impression on his taste. Thus every opinion, in fact, every sort of apprehension, would be equally true.

Therefore it must be said that the intelligible species is related to the intellect as that by which it understands. Which is proved thus. Now action is twofold, as it is said in *Metaph.* ix[163]: one which remains in the agent (for instance, to see and to understand), and another which passes into an external object (for instance, to heat and to cut). Each of these actions proceeds in virtue of some form. And just as the form from which proceeds an act tending to something external is the likeness of the object

[160]The reference seems to be to Protagoras and to Heraclitus: cf. Aristotle, *Metaph.*, VIII, 3 (1047a 6); III, 3 (1005b 25).   [161]Q. 84, a. 1 and 4.
[162]Cf. Aristotle, *Metaph.*, III, 5 (1009a 8).   [163]*Op. cit.*, VIII, 8 (1050a 23).

of the action, as heat in the heater is a likeness of the thing heated, so the form from which proceeds an action remaining in the agent is a likeness of the object. Hence that by which the sight sees is the likeness of the visible thing; and the likeness of the thing understood, that is, the intelligible species, is the form by which the intellect understands. But since the intellect reflects upon itself, by such reflection it understands both its own act of understanding, and the species by which it understands. Thus the intelligible species is secondarily that which is understood; but that which is primarily understood is the thing, of which the species is the likeness.

This also appears from the opinion of the ancient philosophers, who said that *like is known by like.*[164] For they said that the soul knows the earth outside itself by the earth within itself; and so of the rest. If, therefore, we take the species of the earth instead of the earth, in accord with Aristotle who says *that a stone is not in the soul, but only the likeness of the stone,*[165] it follows that by means of its intelligible species the soul knows the things which are outside it.

Reply Obj. 1. The thing understood is in the knower by its own likeness. It is in this sense that we say that the thing actually understood is the intellect in act, because the likeness of the thing understood is the form of the intellect, just as the likeness of a sensible thing is the form of the sense in act. Hence it does not follow that the abstracted intelligible species is what is actually understood; but rather that it is the likeness thereof.

Reply Obj. 2. In these words *the thing actually understood* there is a double meaning—the thing which is understood, and the fact that it is understood. In like manner, the words *abstract universal* mean two things, the nature of a thing and its abstraction or universality. Therefore the nature itself which suffers the act of being understood, or the act of being abstracted, or the intention of universality, exists only in individuals; but that it is understood, abstracted or considered as universal is in the intellect. We see something similar to this in the senses. For the sight sees the color of the apple apart from its smell. If therefore it be asked where is the color which is seen apart from the smell, it is quite clear that the color which is seen is only in the apple; but that it be perceived apart from the smell, this is owing to the sight, inasmuch as sight receives the likeness of color and not of smell. In like manner, the humanity which is understood exists only in this or that man; but that humanity be apprehended without the conditions of individuality, that is, that it be abstracted and conse-

---

[164]The opinion of Empedocles, according to Aristotle, *De An.*, I, 5 (409b 26); and of Plato: cf. *op. cit.*, I, 2 (404b 17).   [165]*Op. cit.*, III, 8 (431b 29).

quently considered as universal, befalls humanity inasmuch as it is per-ceived by the intellect, in which there is a likeness of the specific nature, but not of the individual principles.

Reply Obj. 3. There are two operations in the sensitive part. One is limited to immutation, and thus the operation of the senses takes place when the senses are impressed by the sensible. The other is formation, inasmuch as the imagination forms for itself an image of an absent thing, or even of something never seen. Both of these operations are found in the intellect. For in the first place there is the passion of the possible intellect as informed by the intelligible species; and then the possible intellect, as thus informed, then forms a definition, or a division, or a composition, which is expressed by language. And so, the notion signified by a *term* is a definition; and a *proposition* signifies the intellect's division or composi-tion. Words do not therefore signify the intelligible species themselves; but that which the intellect forms for itself for the purpose of judging of external things.

THIRD ARTICLE
Whether the More Universal Is First in Our Intellectual Cognition?

We proceed thus to the Third Article:—

Objection 1. It would seem that the more universal is not first in our intellectual cognition. For what is first and more known in its own nature is secondarily and less known in relation to ourselves. But universals come first as regards their nature, because *that is first which does not involve the existence of its correlative.* Therefore universals are secondarily known by our intellect.

Obj. 2. Further, the composite precedes the simple in relation to us. But universals are the more simple. Therefore they are known secondarily by us.

Obj. 3. Further, the Philosopher says that the object defined comes in our knowledge before the parts of its definition.[166] But the more universal is part of the definition of the less universal, as *animal* is part of the defini-tion of *man*. Therefore universals are secondarily known by us.

Obj. 4. Further, we know causes and principles by their effects. But universals are principles. Therefore universals are secondarily known by us.

On the contrary, We must proceed from the universal to the singular.[167]

---

[166]*Phys.*, I, 1 (184b 11).   [167]*Ibid.* (184a 23).

I answer that, In our knowledge there are two things to be considered. First, that intellectual knowledge in some degree arises from sensible knowledge. Now because sense has singular and individual things for its object, and intellect has the universal for its object, it follows that our knowledge of the former comes before our knowledge of the latter. Secondly, we must consider that our intellect proceeds from a state of potentiality to a state of actuality; and that every power thus proceeding from potentiality to actuality comes first to an incomplete act, which is intermediate between potentiality and actuality, before accomplishing the perfect act. The perfect act of the intellect is complete knowledge, when the object is distinctly and determinately known; whereas the incomplete act is imperfect knowledge, when the object is known indistinctly, and as it were confusedly. A thing thus imperfectly known is known partly in act and partly in potentiality. Hence the Philosopher says that *what is manifest and certain is known to us at first confusedly; afterwards we know it by distinguishing its principles and elements.*[168] Now it is evident that to know something that comprises many things, without a proper knowledge of each thing contained in it, is to know that thing confusedly. In this way we can have knowledge not only of the universal whole, which contains parts potentially, but also of the integral whole; for each whole can be known confusedly, without its parts being known distinctly. But to know distinctly what is contained in the universal whole is to know the less common; and thus to know *animal* indistinctly is to know it as *animal*, whereas to know *animal* distinctly is to know it as *rational* or *irrational animal*, that is, to know a man or a lion. And so our intellect knows *animal* before it knows man; and the same reason holds in comparing any more universal concept with the less universal.

Moreover, as sense, like the intellect, proceeds from potentiality to act, the same order of knowledge appears in the senses. For by sense we judge of the more common before the less common, in reference both to place and time. In reference to place, when a thing is seen afar off it is seen to be a body before it is seen to be an animal, and to be an animal before it is seen to be a man, and to be a man before it is seen to be Socrates or Plato. The same is true as regards time, for a child can distinguish man from not-man before he distinguishes this man from that, and therefore *children at first call all men fathers, and later on distinguish each one from the others.*[169] The reason of this is clear: he who knows a thing indistinctly is in a state of potentiality as regards its principle of distinction; just as he who

---

[168] *Ibid.* (184a 21).   [169] *Ibid.* (184b 12).

knows *genus* is in a state of potentiality as regards *difference*. Thus it is evident that indistinct knowledge is midway between potentiality and act.

We must therefore conclude that knowledge of the singular and individual is prior, as regards us, to the knowledge of the universal, just as sensible knowledge is prior to intellectual knowledge. But in both sense and intellect the knowledge of the more common precedes the knowledge of the less common.

Reply Obj. 1. The universal can be considered in two ways. First, the universal nature may be considered together with the intention of universality. And since the intention of universality—viz., the relation of one and the same to many—is due to intellectual abstraction, the universal thus considered is subsequent in our knowledge. Hence it is said that the *universal animal is either nothing or something subsequent.*[170] But according to Plato, who held that universals are subsistent, the universal considered thus would be prior to the particular, for the latter, according to him, are mere participations in the subsistent universals which he called Ideas.[171]

Secondly, the universal can be considered according to the nature itself (for instance, *animality* or *humanity*) as existing in the individual. And thus we must distinguish two orders of nature: one, by way of generation and time; and thus the imperfect and the potential come first. In this way the more common comes first in the order of nature. This appears clearly in the generation of man and animal; for *the animal is generated before man*, as the Philosopher says.[172] The other order is the order of perfection or of the intention of nature. For instance, act considered absolutely is naturally prior to potentiality, and the perfect to the imperfect; and thus the less common comes naturally before the more common, as man comes before animal. For the intention of nature does not stop at the generation of animal, but aims at the generation of man.

Reply Obj. 2. The more common universal may be compared to the less common as a whole, and as a part. As a whole, inasmuch as in the more universal there is potentially contained not only the less universal, but also other things; as in *animal* is contained not only *man* but also *horse*. As a part, inasmuch as the less common universal contains in its notion not only the more common, but also more; as *man* contains not only *animal* but also *rational*. Therefore *animal* considered in itself is in our knowledge before *man*; but *man* comes before *animal* considered as a part of the notion of man.

---

[170]Aristotle, *De An.*, I, 1 (402b 7).   [171]Cf. above, q. 84, a. 1.   [172]Aristotle, *De Gener. Anim.*, II, 3 (736b 2).

Reply Obj. 3. A part can be known in two ways. First, absolutely considered in itself; and thus nothing prevents the parts from being known before the whole, as stones are known before a house is known. Secondly, as belonging to a certain whole; and thus we must needs know the whole before its parts. For we know a house confusedly before we know its different parts. So, likewise, that which defines is known before the thing defined is known; otherwise the thing defined would not be made known by the definition. But as parts of the definition they are known after. For we know man confusedly as man before we know how to distinguish all that belongs to human nature.

Reply Obj. 4. The universal, as understood with the intention of universality, is, in a certain manner, a principle of knowledge, in so far as the intention of universality results from the mode of understanding, which is by way of abstraction. But that which is a principle of knowledge is not of necessity a principle of being, as Plato thought, since at times we know a cause through its effect, and substance through accidents. Therefore the universal thus considered, according to the opinion of Aristotle, is neither a principle of being, nor a substance, as he makes clear.[173] But if we consider the generic or specific nature itself as existing in the singular, thus in a way it has the character of a formal principle in regard to singulars; for the singular is the result of matter, while the nature of the species is from the form. But the generic nature is compared to the specific nature rather after the fashion of a material principle, because the generic nature is taken from that which is material in a thing, while the nature of the species is taken from that which is formal. Thus the notion of animal is taken from the sensitive part, whereas the notion of man is taken from the intellectual part. Thus it is that the ultimate intention of nature is towards the species and not the individual, or the genus; because the form is the end of generation, while matter is for the sake of the form. Neither is it necessary that the knowledge of any cause or principle should be subsequent in relation to us, since through sensible causes we sometimes become acquainted with unknown effects, and sometimes conversely.

FOURTH ARTICLE
Whether We Can Understand Many Things at the Same Time?

We proceed thus to the Fourth Article:—

Objection 1. It would seem that we can understand many things at the same time. For intellect is above time, whereas the succession of before

---

[173]Aristotle, *Metaph.*, VI, 13 (1038b 8).

and after belongs to time. Therefore the intellect does not understand different things in succession, but at the same time.

Obj. 2. Further, there is nothing to prevent different forms not opposed to each other from actually being in the same subject, as, for instance, color and smell are in the apple. But intelligible species are not opposed to each other. Therefore there is nothing to prevent the same intellect from being in act as regards different intelligible species. Thus it can understand many things at the same time.

Obj. 3. Further, the intellect understands a whole at the same time, such as a man or a house. But a whole contains many parts. Therefore the intellect understands many things at the same time.

Obj. 4. Further, we cannot know the difference between two things unless we know both at the same time[174]; and the same is to be said of any other comparison. But our intellect knows the difference between one thing and another. Therefore it knows many things at the same time.

On the contrary, It is said that *understanding is of one thing only, science is of many.*[175]

I answer that, The intellect can, indeed, understand many things as one, but not as many, that is to say, by *one* but not by *many* intelligible species. For the mode of every action follows the form which is the principle of that action. Therefore whatever things the intellect can understand under one species, it can understand together. Hence it is that God sees all things at the same time, because He sees all in one, that is, in His essence. But whatever things the intellect understands under different species, it does not understand at the same time. The reason for this is that it is impossible for one and the same subject to be perfected at the same time by many forms of one genus and diverse species, just as it is impossible for one and the same body at the same time to have different colors or different shapes. Now all intelligible species belong to one genus, because they are the perfections of one intellectual power even though the things which the species represent belong to different genera. Therefore it is impossible for one and the same intellect to be perfected at the same time by different intelligible species so as actually to understand different things.

Reply Obj. 1. The intellect is above that time which is the measure of the movement of corporeal things. But the multitude itself of intelligible species causes a certain succession of intelligible operations, according as

---

[174]Aristotle, *De An.*, III, 2 (426b 22).   [175]Aristotle, *Top.*, II, 10 (114b 34).

one operation is prior to another. And this succession is called time by Augustine, who says that *God moves the spiritual creature through time.*[176]

Reply Obj. 2. Not only is it impossible for opposite forms to exist at the same time in the same subject, but neither can any forms belonging to the same genus, although they be not opposed to one another, as is clear from the examples of colors and shapes.

Reply Obj. 3. Parts can be understood in two ways. First, in a confused way, as existing in the whole; and thus they are known through the one form of the whole, and so are known together. In another way, they are known distinctly; and thus each is known by its species, and hence they are not understood at the same time.

Reply Obj. 4. If the intellect sees the difference or comparison between one thing and another, it knows both in relation to their difference or comparison; just as it knows the parts in the whole, as we said above.

FIFTH ARTICLE
Whether Our Intellect Understands by Composition and Division?

We proceed thus to the Fifth Article:—

Objection 1. It would seem that our intellect does not understand by composition and division. For composition and division are only of many, whereas the intellect cannot understand many things at the same time. Therefore it cannot understand by composition and division.

Obj. 2. Further, every composition and division implies past, present, or future time. But the intellect abstracts from time, as also from other particular conditions. Therefore the intellect does not understand by composition and division.

Obj. 3. Further, the intellect understands things by an assimilation to them. But composition and division are not in things; for nothing is in things but the thing which is signified by the predicate and the subject, and which is one and the same thing, provided that the composition be true; for *man* is truly what *animal* is. Therefore the intellect does not act by composition and division.

On the contrary, Words signify the conceptions of the intellect, as the Philosopher says.[177] But in words we find composition and division, as appears in affirmative and negative propositions. Therefore the intellect acts by composition and division.

---

[176]*De Genesi ad Litt.,* VIII, 20; 22 (PL 34, 388; 389).   [177]*Perih.,* I, 1 (16a 3).

I answer that, The human intellect must of necessity understand by composition and division. For since the intellect passes from potentiality to act, it has a likeness to generable things, which do not attain to perfection all at once but acquire it by degrees. In the same way, the human intellect does not acquire perfect knowledge of a thing by the first apprehension; but it first apprehends something of the thing, such as its quiddity, which is the first and proper object of the intellect; and then it understands the properties, accidents, and various dispositions affecting the essence. Thus it necessarily relates one thing with another by composition or division; and from one composition and division it necessarily proceeds to another, and this is *reasoning.*

But the angelic and the divine intellects, like all incorruptible beings, have their perfection at once from the beginning. Hence the angelic and the divine intellect have the entire knowledge of a thing at once and perfectly; and hence, in knowing the quiddity of a thing, they know at once whatever we can know by composition, division and reasoning. Therefore the human intellect knows by composition, division and reasoning. But the divine and the angelic intellects have a knowledge of composition, division, and reasoning, not by the process itself, but by understanding the simple essence.

Reply Obj. 1. Composition and division of the intellect are made by differentiating and comparing. Hence the intellect knows many things by composition and division, by knowing the difference and comparison of things.

Reply Obj. 2. Although the intellect abstracts from phantasms, it does not understand actually without turning to the phantasms, as we have said.[178] And in so far as the intellect turns to phantasms, composition and division involve time.

Reply Obj. 3. The likeness of a thing is received into the intellect according to the mode of the intellect, not according to the mode of the thing. Hence, although something on the part of the thing corresponds to the composition and division of the intellect, still, it does not exist in the same way in the intellect and in the thing. For the proper object of the human intellect is the quiddity of a material thing, which is apprehended by the senses and the imagination. Now in a material thing there is a twofold composition. First, there is the composition of form with matter. To this corresponds that composition of the intellect whereby the universal whole is predicated of its part: for the genus is derived from common matter, while the difference that completes the species is derived from the

---

[178]A. 1; q. 84, a. 7.

form, and the particular from individual matter. The second composition is of accident with subject; and to this composition corresponds that composition of the intellect whereby accident is predicated of subject, as when we say the *man is white*. Nevertheless, the composition of the intellect differs from the composition of things; for the components in the thing are diverse, whereas the composition of the intellect is a sign of the identity of the components. For the above composition of the intellect was not such as to assert that *man is whiteness*; but the assertion, *the man is white*, means that *the man is something having whiteness*. In other words, *man* is identical in subject with the *being having whiteness*. It is the same with the composition of form and matter. For *animal* signifies that which has a sensitive nature; *rational*, that which has an intellectual nature; *man*, that which has both; and *Socrates*, that which has all these things together with individual matter. And so, according to this kind of identity our intellect composes one thing with another by means of predication.

SIXTH ARTICLE
Whether the Intellect Can Be False?

We proceed thus to the Sixth Article:—

Objection 1. It would seem that the intellect can be false, for the Philosopher says that *truth and falsehood are in the mind.*[179] But the *mind* and *intellect* are the same, as is shown above.[180] Therefore falsehood may be in the intellect.

Obj. 2. Further, opinion and reasoning belong to the intellect. But falsehood exists in both. Therefore falsehood can be in the intellect.

Obj. 3. Further, sin is in the intellectual part. But sin involves falsehood, for *those err that work evil* (*Prov.* xiv. 22). Therefore falsehood can be in the intellect.

On the contrary, Augustine says that *everyone who is deceived, does not rightly understand that wherein he is deceived.*[181] And the Philosopher says that *the intellect is always true.*[182]

I answer that, The Philosopher compares the intellect with the sense on this point.[183] For the sense is not deceived in its proper object (as sight in regard to color), save accidentally, through some hindrance to the sensible organ. For example, the taste of a fever-stricken person judges a sweet thing to be bitter, because his tongue is vitiated by ill humors. The sense, however, may be deceived as regards common sensible objects, as

---

[179]*Metaph.*, V, 4 (1027b 27).   [180]Q. 72.   [181]*Lib. 83 Quaest.*, q. 32 (PL 40, 22).   [182]*De An.*, III, 10 (433a 26).   [183]*Op. cit.*, III, 6 (430b 29).

size or figure; as when, for example, it judges the sun to be only a foot in diameter, whereas in reality it exceeds the earth in size. Much more is the sense deceived concerning accidental sensible objects; as when it judges that vinegar is honey because the color is similar. The reason of this is evident. Every power, as such, is essentially directed to its proper object; and things of this kind are always uniform. Hence, so long as the power exists, its judgment concerning its own proper object does not fail. Now the proper object of the intellect is the *quiddity* in a thing. Hence, properly speaking, the intellect is not in error concerning this quiddity; whereas it may go astray as regards the accompaniments of the essence or quiddity in the thing, either in referring one thing to another, in what concerns composition or division, or also in the process of reasoning. That is why it is also true that the intellect cannot err in regard to those propositions which are understood as soon as their terms are understood. Such is the case with first principles, from which there also arises infallible truth in the certitude of science with respect to its conclusions.

The intellect, however, may be accidentally deceived in the quiddity of composite things, not by the defect of its organ, for the intellect is a power that is independent of an organ, but on the part of the composition affecting the definition. This may happen, for instance, when the definition of a thing is false in relation to something else, as the definition of a circle predicated of a triangle; or when a definition is false in itself as involving the composition of things incompatible, as, for instance, to describe anything as *a rational winged animal*. Hence as regards simple things, in whose definitions there is no composition, we cannot be deceived; but if we fail, we fail completely in understanding them, as is said in *Metaph.* ix.[184]

Reply Obj. 1. The Philosopher says that falsehood is in the intellect in regard to composition and division. The same answer applies to the *second objection* concerning opinion and reasoning; as well as to the *third objection*, concerning the error of the sinner, who errs in the practical judgment of the appetible object. But in the absolute consideration of the quiddity of a thing, and of those things which are known thereby, the intellect is never deceived. In this sense are to be understood the authorities quoted in proof of the opposite conclusion.

---

[184]Aristotle, *Metaph.*, VIII, 10 (1052a 1).

PART ONE

QUESTION 87

How the Intellectual Soul Knows Itself and All That Is Within Itself

FIRST ARTICLE
Whether the Intellectual Soul Knows Itself by Its Essence?

We proceed thus to the First Article:—

Objection 1. It would seem that the intellectual soul knows itself by its own essence. For Augustine says that *the mind knows itself by itself, because it is incorporeal.*[185]

Obj. 2. Further, both angels and human souls belong to the genus of intellectual substance. But an angel understands himself by his own essence. Therefore so does the human soul.

Obj. 3. Further, *in things without matter, the intellect and that which is understood are the same.*[186] But the human mind is without matter, not being the act of a body, as was stated above.[187] Therefore the intellect and its object are the same in the human mind; and therefore the human mind understands itself by its own essence.

On the contrary, It is said that the *intellect understands itself in the same way as it understands other things.*[188] But it understands other things, not by their essence, but by their likenesses. Therefore it does not understand itself by its own essence.

I answer that, Everything is knowable so far as it is in act, and not so far as it is in potentiality[189]; for a thing is a being, and is true, and therefore knowable, according as it is actual. This is quite clear as regards sensible things, for the eye does not see what is potentially, but what is actually, colored. In like manner, it is clear that the intellect, so far as it knows material things, does not know save what is in act; and hence it does not know primary matter except as proportionate to form, as is stated *Physics* i.[190] Consequently immaterial substances are intelligible by their own essence,

---

[185]*De Trin.*, IX, 3 (PL 42, 963).   [186]Aristotle, *De An.*, III, 4 (430a 3).
[187]Q. 76, a.1.   [188]Aristotle, *De An.*, III, 4 (430a 2).   [189]Aristotle,
Metaph., VIII, 9 (1051a 29).   [190]Aristotle, *Phys.*, I, 7 (191a 8).

according as each one is actual by its own essence.

Therefore it is that the essence of God, the pure and perfect act, is absolutely and perfectly in itself intelligible; and hence God by His own essence knows Himself, and all other things also. The angelic essence belongs, indeed, to the genus of intelligible things as *act*, but not as a *pure act*, nor as a *complete act*; and hence the angel's act of intelligence is not completed by his essence. For, although an angel understands himself by his own essence, still he cannot understand all other things by his own essence; he rather knows things other than himself by their likenesses. Now the human intellect is only potential in the genus of intelligible beings, just as primary matter is potential in the genus of sensible beings; and hence it is called *possible*.[191] Therefore in its essence the human intellect is potentially understanding. Hence it has in itself the power to understand, but not to be understood, except as it is made actual. For even the Platonists asserted that an order of intelligible beings existed above the order of intellects, since the intellect understands only by participation in the intelligible;[192] for that which participates is below what it participates.

If, therefore, the human intellect, as the Platonists held, became actual by participating in separate intelligible Forms, it would understand itself by such a participation in incorporeal beings. But as in this life our intellect has material and sensible things for its proper object, as was stated above,[193] it understands itself according as it is made actual by the species abstracted from sensible things, through the light of the agent intellect, which not only actualizes the intelligibles themselves, but also, by their instrumentality, actualizes the possible intellect. Therefore the intellect knows itself, not by its essence, but by its act. This happens in two ways: In the first place, singularly, as when Socrates or Plato perceives that he has an intellectual soul because he perceives that he understands. In the second place, universally, as when we consider the nature of the human mind from a knowledge of the intellectual act. It is true, however, that the judgment and power of this knowledge, by which we know the nature of the soul, comes to us according to the derivation of our intellectual light from the divine truth which contains the exemplars of all things, as was stated above.[194] Hence Augustine says: *We gaze on the inviolable truth whence we can as perfectly as possible define, not what each man's mind is, but*

---

[191] Aristotle, *De An.*, III, 4 (428a 22).   [192] Cf. Dionysius, *De Div. Nom.*, IV, 1 (PG 3, 693); *De Causis*, IX (p. 169). Cf. Also Proclus, *Elem. of Theol.*, prop. 163 and 163 (p. 142).   [193] Q. 84, a. 7.   [194] Q. 84, a. 5.

what it ought to be in the light of the eternal exemplars.[195] There is, however, a difference between these two kinds of knowledge, and it consists in this that the mere presence of the mind suffices for the first; since the mind itself is the principle of action whereby it perceives itself, and hence it is said to know itself by its own presence. But as regards the second kind of knowledge, the mere presence of the mind does not suffice, but there is further required a careful and subtle inquiry. Hence many are ignorant of the soul's nature, and many have erred about it. So Augustine says concerning such mental inquiry: *Let the mind strive not to see itself as if it were absent, but to discern itself as present*[196]—*i.e.*, to know how it differs from other things; which is to know its essence and nature.

Reply Obj. 1. The mind knows itself by means of itself, because at length it arrives at a knowledge of itself, though led thereto by its own act:—because it is itself that it knows, since it loves itself, as Augustine says in the same passage. Now a thing can be called self-evident in two ways, either because we can know it by nothing else except itself, as first principles are called self-evident; or because it is not accidentally knowable, as color is visible of itself, whereas substance is visible accidentally.

Reply Obj. 2. The essence of an angel is as an act in the genus of intelligible beings, and therefore it is both intellect and the thing understood. Hence an angel apprehends his own essence through himself; not so the human intellect, which is either altogether in potentiality to intelligible things,—as is the possible intellect,—or is the act of the intelligible abstracted from the phantasms,—as is the agent intellect.

Reply Obj. 3. This saying of the Philosopher is universally true in every kind of intellect. For as the sense in act is the sensible in act, by reason of the sensible likeness which is the form of sense in act, so likewise the intellect in act is the object understood in act, by reason of the likeness of the thing understood, which is the form of the intellect in act. So the human intellect, which becomes actual by the species of the thing understood, is itself understood by the same species as by its own form. Now to say that in *things without matter the intellect and what is understood are the same,* is equal to saying that *as regards things actually understood the intellect and what is understood are the same.* For a thing is actually understood in that it is immaterial. But a distinction must be drawn, since the essences of some things are immaterial, as the separate substances called angels, each of which is understood and understands; whereas there are other things whose essences are not without matter but only their abstract like-

---

[195]*De Trin.*, IX, 6 (PL 42, 966).   [196]*Op. cit.*, X, 9 (PL 42, 980).

nesses. Hence the Commentator says that the proposition quoted is true only of separate substances[197]; because in a sense it is verified in their regard, and not in regard to other substances, as was already stated.

SECOND ARTICLE

**Whether Our Intellect Knows the
Habits of the Soul by Their Essence?**

We proceed thus to the Second Article:—

Objection 1. It would seem that our intellect knows the habits of the soul by their essence. For Augustine says: *Faith is not seen in the heart wherein it abides in the same way as the soul of a man may be seen by another from the movement of the body; but we know most certainly that it is there, and conscience proclaims its existence.*[198] The same applies to the other habits of the soul. Therefore the habits of the soul are not known by their acts, but by themselves.

Obj. 2, Further, material things outside the soul are known because their likenesses are present in the soul, and are said therefore to be known by their likenesses. But the soul's habits are present by their essence in the soul. Therefore the habits of the soul are known by their essence.

Obj. 3. Further, *whatever is the cause that a thing is such, is still more so.* But habits and intelligible species cause things to be known by the soul. Therefore they are still more known by the soul in themselves.

On the contrary, Habits, like powers, are the principles of acts. But, as it is said, *acts and operations are logically prior to powers.*[199] Therefore in the same way they are prior to habits; and thus habits, like the powers, are known by their acts.

I answer that, A habit is intermediate between mere power and mere act. Now, it has been said that nothing is known but as it is actual; and therefore so far as a habit fails in being a perfect act, it falls short in being of itself knowable, and can be known only by its act. Thus, for example, anyone knows he has a habit from the fact that he can produce the act proper to that habit; or he may inquire into the nature and character of the habit by considering the act. The first kind of knowledge of the habit arises from its being present, for the very fact of its presence causes the act whereby it is known. The second kind of knowledge of the habit arises from a careful inquiry, as was explained above concerning the mind.

---

[197]*In De An.*, III, comm. 15 (VI 169r).   [198]*De Trin.*, XIII, 1 (PL 42, 1014).
[199]Aristotle, *De An.*, II, 4 (415a 18).

Reply Obj. 1. Although faith is not known by external movements of the body, it is perceived by the subject wherein it resides by the interior act of the heart. For no one knows that he has faith except because he knows that he believes.

Reply Obj. 2. Habits are present in our intellect, not as its object,— since, in the present state of life, our intellect's object is the nature of a material thing, as was stated above[200]—but as that by which it understands.

Reply Obj. 3. The axiom, *whatever is the cause that a thing is such, is still more so*, is true of things that are of the same order, for instance, of the same kind of cause. For example, we may say that health is desirable because of life, and therefore that life is more desirable still. But if we take things of different orders, the axiom is not true; for we may say that health is caused by medicine, but it does not follow that medicine is more desirable than health, for health belongs to the order of final causes, whereas medicine belongs to the order of efficient causes. So of two things belonging essentially to the order of the objects of knowledge, the one which causes the other to be known will be the more known, as principles are more known than conclusions. But a habit as such does not belong to the order of objects of knowledge; nor are things known because of the habit as because of an object known, but rather as because of a disposition or form whereby the subject knows. Therefore the argument does not hold.

THIRD ARTICLE
Whether Our Intellect Knows Its Own Act?

We proceed thus to the Third Article:—

Objection 1. It would seem that our intellect does not know its own act. For what is known is the object of the knowing power. But the act differs from the object. Therefore the intellect does not know its own act.

Obj. 2. Further, whatever is known is known by some act. If, then, the intellect knows its own act, it knows it by some act, and again it knows that act by some other act. This is to proceed indefinitely, which seems impossible.

Obj. 3. Further, the intellect has the same relation to its act as sense has to its act. But the proper sense does not perceive its own act, for this belongs to the common sense, as is stated in *De Anima* iii.[201] Therefore neither does the intellect understand its own act.

On the contrary, Augustine says: *I understand that I understand.*[202]

---

[200]Q. 84, a. 7; q. 85, a. 8; q. 86, a. 2.   [201]Aristotle, *De An.*, III, 2 (425b 12).
[202]*De Trin.*, X, 11 (PL 42, 983).

I answer that, As was stated above, a thing is known according as it is in act. Now the ultimate perfection of the intellect consists in its own operation. For this is not an act tending to something else in which lies the perfection of the work accomplished, as building is the perfection of the thing built; but it remains in the agent as its perfection and act, as is said in *Metaph.* ix.[203] Therefore the first thing of the intellect that is understood is its own act of understanding. This occurs in different ways with different intellects. For there is an intellect, namely, the divine, which is its own act of understanding, so that in God the understanding of His understanding and the understanding of His essence are one and the same act, because His essence is His act of understanding. But there is another intellect, the angelic, which is not its own act of understanding, as we have said above[204]; and yet the first object of that act is the angelic essence. Therefore, although there is a logical distinction between the act whereby he understands that he understands, and that whereby he understands his essence, yet he understands both by one and the same act, because to understand his own essence is the proper perfection of his essence, and by one and the same act is a thing, together with its perfection, understood. And there is yet another, namely, the human intellect, which is not its own act of understanding, nor is its own essence the first object of its act of understanding, for this object is the nature of a material thing. And therefore that which is first known by the human intellect is an object of this kind, and that which is known secondarily is the act by which that object is known; and through the act the intellect itself is known, whose perfection is the act itself of understanding. For this reason did the Philosopher assert that objects are known before acts, and acts before powers.[205]

Reply Obj. 1. The object of the intellect is something universal, namely, *being* and *the true*, in which the act of understanding is itself comprised. Therefore the intellect can understand its own act; but not primarily, since the first object of our intellect, in this state of life, is not every being and everything true, but *being* and *true* as found in material things, as we have said above,[206] from which it acquires knowledge of all other things.

Reply Obj. 2. The act of the human intellect is not the act and perfection of the nature understood, as if the nature of the material thing and the act of the intellect could be understood by one act; just as a thing and its perfection are understood by one act. Hence the act whereby the intel-

---

[203] Aristotle, *Metaph.*, VIII, 8 (1050a 36).   [204] Q. 79, a. I.   [205] *De An.*, II, 4 (415a 16).   [206] Q. 84, a. 7.

lect understands a stone is distinct from the act whereby it understands that it understands a stone; and so on. Nor is it incongruous for the intellect to be infinite potentially, as was explained above.[207]

Reply Obj. 3. The proper sense perceives by reason of the immutation in the material organ caused by the external sensible. A material thing, however, cannot immute itself, but one is immuted by another; and therefore the act of the proper sense is perceived by the common sense. The intellect, on the contrary, does not have understanding by the material immutation of an organ; and so there is no comparison.

FOURTH ARTICLE
Whether the Intellect Understands the Act of the Will?

We proceed thus to the Fourth Article:—

Objection 1. It would seem that the intellect does not understand the act of the will. For nothing is known by the intellect, unless it be in some way present in the intellect. But the act of the will is not in the intellect, since the will and the intellect are distinct powers. Therefore the act of the will is not known by the intellect.

Obj. 2. Further, the act is specified by the object. But the object of the will is not the same as the object of the intellect. Therefore the act of the will also is specifically distinct from the object of the intellect. Therefore the act of the will is not known by the intellect.

Obj. 3. Augustine says of the soul's affections that *they are known neither by images, as bodies are known; nor by their presence, like the arts; but by certain notions.*[208] Now it does not seem that there can be in the soul any other notions of things except either the essences of the things known or their likenesses. Therefore it seems impossible for the intellect to know the affections of the soul, which are the acts of the will.

On the contrary, Augustine says: *I understand that I will.*[209]

I answer that, As was stated above, the act of the will is nothing but an inclination consequent on the form understood; just as natural appetite is an inclination consequent on the natural form.[210] Now the inclination of a thing resides in it according to its mode of being; and hence natural inclination resides in a natural thing naturally and the inclination called the sensible appetite is in the sensible thing sensibly; and likewise the intelligible inclination, which is the act of the will, is in the intelligent being intelligibly, as in its principle and proper subject. Hence the Philosopher

---

[207]Q. 86, a. 2.   [208]*Confess.*, X, 17 (PL 32, 790).   [209]*De Trin.*, X, 11 (PL 42, 983).   [210]Q. 59, a. 1.

expresses himself thus, that *the will is in the reason.*[211] Now whatever is intelligibly in an intelligent subject is understood by that subject. Therefore the act of the will is understood by the intellect, both inasmuch as one perceives that one wills, and inasmuch as one knows the nature of this act, and consequently, the nature of the principle which is the habit or power.

Reply Obj. 1. This argument would hold good if the will and the intellect were in different subjects, in addition to being distinct powers; for then whatever was in the will would not be in the intellect. But as both are rooted in the same substance of the soul, and since one is in a way the principle of other, consequently what is in the will is, in a way, also in the intellect.

Reply Obj. 2. The *good* and the *true*, which are the objects of the will and of the intellect, differ logically, but one is contained in the other, as we have said above;[212] for the true is a particular good, and the good is a particular true. Therefore the objects of the will fall under the intellect, and those of the intellect can fall under the will.

Reply Obj. 3. The affections of the soul are in the intellect, not by likeness only, as are bodies, nor as being present in their subject, as are the arts; but as the thing caused is in its principle, which contains some notion of the thing caused. And so Augustine says that the soul's affections are in the memory by certain notions.

---

[211]*De An.*, III, 9 (432b 5).   [212]Q. 16, a. 4, ad 1; q. 82, a. 4, ad 1.

PART ONE
QUESTION 88
How the Human Soul Knows What Is Above Itself

FIRST ARTICLE
Whether the Human Soul in the Present State of Life Can Understand Immaterial Substances in Themselves?

We proceed thus to the First Article:—

Objection 1. It would seem that the human soul in the present state of life can understand immaterial substances in themselves. For Augustine says: *As the mind itself acquires the knowledge of corporeal things by means of the corporeal senses, so it gains through itself the knowledge of incorporeal things.*[213] But these are the immaterial substances. Therefore the human mind understands immaterial substances.

Obj. 2. Further, like is known by like. But the human mind is more akin to immaterial than to material things; since its own nature is immaterial, as is clear from what we have said above.[214] Since then our mind understands material things, much more is it able to understand immaterial things.

Obj. 3. Further, the fact that objects which are in themselves most eminently sensible are not most perceived by us, comes from the fact that sense is corrupted by their very excellence. But the intellect is not subject to such a corrupting influence from the excellence of its object, as is stated in *De Anima* iii.[215] Therefore things which are in themselves in the highest degree of intelligibility are likewise to us most intelligible. Since material things, however, are intelligible only so far as we make them actually so, by abstracting them from material conditions, it is clear that those substances are more intelligible in themselves whose nature is immaterial. Therefore they are much more known to us than are material things.

Obj. 4. Further, the Commentator says that, *nature would be frustrated in its end* were we unable to understand abstract substances, *because it would have made what in itself is naturally intelligible not to be understood at*

---

[213]*De Trin.*, IX, 3 (PL 42, 963).   [214]Q. 76, a. 1.   [215]Aristotle, *De An.*, III, 4 (429b 2).

all.[216] But in nature nothing is idle or purposeless. Therefore immaterial substances can be understood by us.

Obj. 5. Further, as the sense is to the sensible, so is the intellect to the intelligible. But our sight can see all things corporeal, whether superior and incorruptible, or sublunary and corruptible. Therefore our intellect can understand all intelligible substances, including the superior and immaterial.

On the contrary, It is written (*Wis.* ix. 16): *The things that are in heaven who shall search out?* But these substances are said to be in heaven, according to *Matthew* xviii. 10, *Their angels in heaven*, etc. Therefore immaterial substances cannot be known by human investigation.

I answer that, In the opinion of Plato, immaterial substances are not only understood by us, but are also the objects we understand first of all. For Plato taught that immaterial subsisting Forms, which he called *Ideas*, are the proper objects of our intellect, and are thus first and essentially understood by us.[217] Furthermore, material things are known by the soul inasmuch as imagination and sense are joined to the intellect.[218] Hence the purer the intellect is, so much the more clearly does it perceive the intelligible reality of immaterial things.[219]

But in Aristotle's opinion, which experience corroborates, our intellect in its present state of life has a natural relation to the natures of material things[220]; and therefore it can understand only by turning to the phantasms, as we have said above.[221] Thus it clearly appears that immaterial substances, which do not fall under sense and imagination, cannot be known by us first and essentially, according to the mode of knowledge of which we have experience.

Nevertheless Averroes teaches that in this present life man can in the end arrive at the knowledge of separate substances by being joined or united to some separate substance, which he calls the *agent intellect*, and which, being a separate substance itself, can naturally understand separate substances.[222] Hence, when it is perfectly united to us, so that through it we are able to understand perfectly, we too shall be able to understand separate substances; just as in the present life, through the possible intellect united to us, we can understand material things.

---

[216]*In Metaph.*, II, comm. 1 (VIII, 14v).   [217]Cf. q. 84, a. 4.   [218]Cf. Macrobius, *In Somn. Scipion.*, I, 12 (pp. 531–532).   [219]Cf. Cicero, *Tusc. Disp.*, I, 30 (p. 254).—Cf. also Plato, *Phaedo* (p. 80).   [220]*De An.*, III, 7 (431a 16).   [221]Q. 84, a. 7.   [222]*In De An.*, III, comm. 36, pt. 5 (VI, 178v).

Now he said that the agent intellect is united to us as follows.[223] For since we understand by means of both the agent intellect and intelligible objects (as, for instance, we understand conclusions by principles understood), the agent intellect must be compared to the objects understood, either as the principle agent is to the instrument, or as form to matter: For an action is ascribed to two principles in one of these two ways: to a principal agent and to an instrument, as cutting to the workman and the saw; to a form and its subject, as heating to heat and fire. In both these ways the agent intellect can be compared to the intelligible object as perfection is to the perfectible, and as act is to potentiality. Now a subject is made perfect and receives its perfection at one and the same time, as the reception of what is actually visible synchronizes with the reception of light in the eye. Therefore the possible intellect receives the intelligible object and the agent intellect together. And the more numerous the intelligible objects received, so much the nearer do we come to the point of perfect union between ourselves and the agent intellect; so much so, that when we shall have understood all the intelligible objects, the agent intellect will become perfectly united to us, and through it we shall understand all things material and immaterial. In this he makes the ultimate happiness of man to consist.[224] Nor, as regards the present inquiry, does it matter whether the possible intellect in that state of happiness understands separate substances through the agent intellect, as he himself maintains, or whether (as he imputes to Alexander) the possible intellect can never understand separate substances (because according to him it is corruptible), but man understands separate substances through the agent intellect.[225]

All this, however, is untrue. First, because, supposing the agent intellect to be a separate substance, we could not formally understand through it; for the formal medium of an agent's action is its form and act, since every agent acts according to its actuality, as was said of the possible intellect.[226] Secondly, this opinion is untrue because the agent intellect, supposing it to be a separate substance, would not be joined to us in its substance, but only in its light, as participated in what we understood. But this would not extend to the other acts of the agent intellect so as to enable us to understand immaterial substances; just as when we see colors set off by the sun, we are not united to the substance of the sun so as to act like the sun, but only its light is united to us, that we may see the colors.

---

[223] *Ibid.* (VI, 179rv). [224] *De An. Beatitud.*, I (IX, 64ra).—Cf. Avicenna, *De An.*, V, 6 (26va). [225] Averroes, *In De An.*, III, comm. 36, pt. 2 (VI, 176r). [226] Q. 76, a. 1.

Thirdly, this opinion is untrue because, granted that, as was above explained, the agent intellect were united to us in substance, still it is not said that it is wholly united to us on the basis of one intelligible object, or two; but rather on the basis of all intelligible objects. But all such objects together do not equal the power of the agent intellect, as it is a much greater thing to understand separate substances than to understand all material things. Hence it clearly follows that the knowledge of all material things would not make the agent intellect to be so united to us as to enable us to understand separate substances through it.

Fourthly, this opinion is untrue because it is hardly possible for anyone in this world to understand all material things, and thus no one, or very few, would reach perfect felicity. This is against what the Philosopher says, that happiness is a *kind of common good, communicable to all capable of virtue.*[227] Further, it is against reason that only the few of any species attain to the end of the species.

Fifthly, the Philosopher expressly says that happiness is *an operation according to perfect virtue*[228]; and after enumerating many virtues in the tenth book of the *Ethics,* he concludes that ultimate happiness, consisting in the knowledge of the highest things intelligible, is attained through the virtue of *wisdom,*[229] which in the sixth book he had named as *the chief of the speculative sciences.*[230] Hence Aristotle clearly placed the ultimate felicity of man in that knowledge of separate substances which is obtainable by speculative science; and not in any union with the agent intellect, as some have imagined.

Sixthly, as was shown above,[231] the agent intellect is not a separate substance, but a power of the soul, extending itself actively to the same objects to which the possible intellect extends receptively; because, as Aristotle states, the possible intellect is *all things potentially,* and the agent intellect is *all things in act.*[232] Therefore both intellects, according to the present state of life, extend only to material things, which are made actually intelligible by the agent intellect, and are received in the possible intellect. Hence, in the present state of life, we cannot understand separate immaterial substances in themselves, either by the possible or by the agent intellect.

Reply Obj. 1. Augustine may be taken to mean that the knowledge of

---

[227]*Eth.*, I, 9 (1099b 18). (1177a 21); 8 (1179a 30). [228]*Op. cit.*, I, 10 (1101a 14). [230]*Op. cit.*, VI, 7 (1141a 20). [229]*Op. cit.*, X, 7 [231]Q. 79, a. 4. [232]Aristotle, *De An.*, III, 5 (430a 14).

incorporeal things in the mind can be gained through the mind itself. This is so true that philosophers also say that the knowledge concerning the soul is a principle for the knowledge of separate substances.[233] For by knowing itself, the soul attains to some knowledge of incorporeal substances, such as is within its compass; not that the knowledge of itself gives it a perfect and absolute knowledge of them.

Reply Obj 2. The likeness of nature is not a sufficient principle of knowledge. Otherwise what Empedocles said would be true—that the soul needs to have the nature of all in order to know all.[234] But knowledge requires that the likeness of the thing known be in the knower, as a kind of form in the knower. Now our possible intellect, in the present state of life, is such that it can be informed with the likenesses abstracted from phantasms: and therefore it knows material things rather than immaterial substances.

Reply Obj. 3. There must needs be some proportion between the object and the power of knowledge; such as of the active to the passive, and of perfection to the perfectible. Hence that sensible objects of great excellence are not grasped by the senses is due not merely to the fact that they corrupt the organ, but also to their not being proportionate to the sensitive powers. And it is thus that immaterial substances are not proportionate to our intellect, in our present state of life, so that it cannot understand them.

Reply Obj. 4. This argument of the Commentator fails in several ways. First, because if separate substances are not understood by us, it does not follow that they are not understood by any intellect; for they are understood by themselves, and by one another.

Secondly, to be understood by us is not the end of separate substances and only that is vain and purposeless which fails to attain its end. It does not follow, therefore, that immaterial substances are purposeless, even if they are not at all understood by us.

Reply Obj. 5. Sense knows bodies, whether superior or inferior, in the same way, that is, by the sensible thing acting on the organ. But we do not understand material and immaterial substances in the same way. The former we understand by abstraction, which is impossible in the case of the latter, for there are no phantasms of what is immaterial.

---

[233] Averroes, *In De An.*, I, comm. 2 (VI 108v); III, comm. 5 (VI, 166r).   [234] Cf. Aristotle, *De An.*, I, 2 (404b 11).

SECOND ARTICLE
Whether Our Intellect Can Come to Understand Immaterial Substances Through Its Knowledge of Material Things?

We proceed thus to the Second Article:—

Objection 1. It would seem that our intellect can come to know immaterial substances through the knowledge of material things. For Dionysius says that *the human mind cannot be raised up to immaterial contemplation of the heavenly hierarchies, unless it uses thereto material guidance according to its own nature.*[235] Therefore we can be led by material things to know immaterial substances.

Obj. 2. Further, science resides in the intellect. But there are sciences and definitions of immaterial substances; for Damascene defines an angel,[236] and we find angels discussed both in theology and in philosophy. Therefore immaterial substances can be understood by us.

Obj. 3. Further, the human soul belongs to the genus of immaterial substances. But it can be understood by us through its act, by which it understands material things. Therefore other immaterial substances also can be understood by us, through their effects in material things.

Obj. 4. Further, the only cause which cannot be comprehended through its effects is that which infinitely transcends them, and this belongs to God alone. Therefore other created immaterial substances can be understood by us through material things.

On the contrary, Dionysius says that *intelligible things cannot be understood through sensible things, nor composite things through simple, nor incorporeal things through corporeal.*[237]

I answer that, Averroes says that a philosopher named Avempace taught that by the understanding of material substances we can be led, according to true philosophical principles, to the knowledge of immaterial substances.[238] For since the nature of our intellect is to abstract the quiddity of material things from matter, anything material residing in that abstracted quiddity can again be made subject to abstraction; and as the process of abstraction cannot go on forever, it must arrive at length at the understanding of a quiddity that is absolutely without matter; and this would be the understanding of immaterial substance.

---

[235]*De Cael. Hier.*, I, 3 (PG 3, 124).   [236]*De Fide Orth.*, II, 3 (PG 94, 865).
[237]*De Div. Nom.*, I, 1 (PG 3, 588).   [238]*In De An.*, III, comm., 36, pt. 3 (VI,
177v–178v).

Now this opinion would be true, were immaterial substances the forms and species of these material things, as the Platonists supposed.[239] But supposing, on the contrary, that immaterial substances differ altogether from the quiddity of material things, it follows that, however much our intellect may abstract the quiddity of a material thing from matter, it could never arrive at anything like an immaterial substance. Therefore we are not able to understand immaterial substances perfectly through material substances.

Reply Obj. 1. From material things we can rise to some sort of knowledge of immaterial things, but not to a perfect knowledge; for there is no proper and adequate proportion between material and immaterial things, and the likenesses drawn from material things for the understanding of immaterial things are very unlike them, as Dionysius says.[240]

Reply Obj. 2. Science treats of higher things principally by way of remotion. Thus Aristotle explains the heavenly bodies by denying to them the properties of sublunary bodies.[241] Hence it follows that much less can immaterial substances be known by us in such a way as to make us know their quiddity; but we may have a knowledge of them from the sciences by way of negation and by their relation to material things.

Reply Obj. 3. The human soul understands itself through its own act of understanding, which is proper to it, showing perfectly its power and nature. But the power and nature of immaterial substances cannot be perfectly known through such an act, nor through any other and material thing, because there is no proportion between the latter and the power of the former.

Reply Obj. 4. Created immaterial substances are not in the same natural genus as material substances, for they do not agree in power or in matter; but they belong to the same logical genus, because even immaterial substances are in the predicament of substance, since their essence is distinct from their being. But God has no community with material things either in a natural genus or in a logical genus; because God is not in a genus at all, as was stated above.[242] Hence through the likenesses derived from material things we can know something positive concerning the angels, according to some common notion, though not according to their specific nature; whereas we cannot acquire any such knowledge at all about God.

---

[239]Cf. above, q. 84, a. 1. [240]*De Cael. Hier.*, II, 2 (PG 3, 137). [241]*De Caelo*, I, 3 (269b 18). [242]Q. 3, a. 5.

THIRD ARTICLE
Whether God Is the First Object Known by the Human Mind?

We proceed thus to the Third Article:—

Objection 1. It would seem that God is the first object known by the human mind. For that object in which all others are known, and by which we judge others, is the first thing known to us; as light is to the eye, and first principles to the intellect. But we know all things in the light of the first truth, and thereby judge of all things, as Augustine says.[243] Therefore God is the first object known to us.

Obj. 2. Further, whatever causes a thing to be such is more so. But God is the cause of all our knowledge; for He is *the true light which enlighteneth every man that cometh into this world (Jo.* i. 9). Therefore God is our first and most known object.

Obj. 3. Further, what is first known in an image is the exemplar to which the image is formed. But in our mind is *the image of God,* as Augustine says.[244] Therefore God is the first object known to our mind.

On the contrary, No man hath seen God at any time (Jo. i. 18).

I answer that, Since the human intellect in the present state of life cannot understand immaterial created substances, much less can it understand the essence of the uncreated substance. Hence it must be said absolutely that God is not the first object of our knowledge. Rather do we know God through creatures, according to the Apostle (*Rom.* i. 20): *the invisible things of God are clearly seen, being understood by the things that are made.* Now the first object of our knowledge in this life is the *quiddity of a material thing,* which is the proper object of our intellect, as appears above in many passages.[245]

Reply Obj. 1. We see and judge of all things in the light of the first truth, insofar as the light itself of our intellect, whether natural or gratuitous, is nothing else than an impression of the first truth upon it, as was stated above.[246] Hence, since the light itself of our intellect is not that which the intellect understands, but the medium whereby it understands, much less can it be said that God is the first thing known by our intellect.

Reply Obj. 2. The axiom, *Whatever causes a thing to be such is more so,* must be understood of things belonging to one and the same order, as was explained above.[247] Other things than God are known because of God, not

---

[243]*De Trin.,* XII, 2 (PL 42, 999); *De Vera Relig.,* XXXI (PL 34, 147); *Confess.,* XII, 25 (PL 32, 840).   [244]*De Trin.,* XII, 4 (PL 42, 1000).   [245]Q. 84, a. 7; q. 85, a. 8; q. 87, a. 2, ad 2.   [246]Q. 12, a. 11, ad 3; q. 84, a. 5.   [247]Q. 87, a. 2, ad 3.

as if He were the first known object, but because He is the first cause of our power of knowledge.

Reply Obj. 3. If there existed in our souls a perfect image of God, as the Son is the perfect image of the Father, our mind would know God at once. But the image in our mind is imperfect; and hence the argument does not hold.

PART ONE

QUESTION 89

The Knowledge of the Separated Soul

FIRST ARTICLE
Whether the Separated Soul Can Understand Anything?

We proceed thus to the First Article:—

Objection 1. It would seem that the soul separated from the body can understand nothing at all. For the Philosopher says that *the understanding is corrupted together with its interior principle.*[248] But by death all human interior principles are corrupted. Therefore understanding itself is corrupted.

Obj. 2. Further, the human soul is hindered from understanding when the senses are impeded, and by a distracted imagination, as was explained above.[249] But death destroys the senses and imagination, as we have shown above.[250] Therefore after death the soul understands nothing.

Obj. 3. Further, if the separated soul understands, this must be by means of some species. But it does not understand by means of innate species, because it has none such, being at first *like a tablet on which nothing is written.* Nor does it understand by species abstracted from things, for it does not then possess the organs of sense and imagination which are necessary for the abstraction of species; nor yet does it understand by means of species formerly abstracted and retained in the soul, for if that were so, a child's soul would have no means of understanding at all; nor finally does it understand by means of intelligible species divinely infused, for such knowledge would not be natural, such as we treat of now, but the effect of grace. Therefore the soul apart from the body understands nothing.

On the contrary, The Philosopher says: *If the soul had no proper operation, it could not be separated from the body.*[251] But the soul is separated from the body, and therefore it has a proper operation, and especially that which consists in understanding. Therefore the soul can understand when it is apart from the body.

---

[248]*De An.*, I, 4 (408b 24).   [249]Q. 84, a. 7 and 8.   [250]Q. 77, a. 8.
[251]*De An.*, I, 1 (403a 11).

I answer that, The difficulty in solving this question arises from the fact that the soul united to the body can understand only by turning to the phantasms, as experience shows. Did this not proceed from the soul's very nature, but accidentally, through its being bound up with the body, as the Platonists said,[252] the difficulty would vanish; for in that case, when the burden of the body was once removed,[253] the soul would at once return to its own nature, and would understand intelligible things simply, without turning to phantasms, as is exemplified in the case of other separate substances. In that case, however, the union of soul and body would not be for the soul's good, for evidently it would understand worse in the body than out of it; but the union would be for the good of the body, which would be absurd, since matter exists for the sake of the form, and not the form for the sake of the matter. But if we hold that the nature of the soul requires it to understand by turning to the phantasms, it will seem, since death does not change its nature, that it can then naturally understand nothing, since the phantasms are wanting to which it may turn.

To solve this difficulty, we must consider that nothing acts except so far as it is actual, and therefore the mode of action in every agent follows from the mode of its being. Now the soul has one mode of being when in the body, and another when apart from it, though its nature remains the same. But this does not mean that its union with the body is accidental, for, on the contrary, such a union belongs to it according to the very character of its nature, just as the nature of a light body is not changed when it is in its proper place, which is natural to it, and outside its proper place, which is beside its nature. The soul, therefore, when united to the body, consistently with that mode of being, has a mode of understanding by turning to corporeal phantasms, which are in corporeal organs; but when it is separated from the body, it has a mode of understanding by turning to pure intelligibles, as is proper to other separate substances. Hence it is as natural for the soul to understand by turning to the phantasms, as it is for it to be joined to the body. But to be separated from the body is not in accordance with its nature, and likewise to understand without turning to the phantasms is not natural to it. That is why it is united to the body in order that it may have a mode of being and operation suitable to its nature. But here again a difficulty arises. For since a being is always ordered to what is best and since it is better to understand by turning to pure intelligibles than by turning to the phantasms, God should have established the soul's

---

[252]Cf. Cicero, *Tusc. Disp.*, I, 31 (pp. 255–256).—Cf. also Plato, *Phaedo* (p. 67d).
[253]Cf. Avicenna, *De An.*, V, 5 (25va).

nature in such a way that the nobler way of understanding would have been natural to it, and it would not have needed the body for that purpose.

In order to resolve this difficulty, we must consider that while it is true that in itself it is nobler to understand by turning to something higher than to understand by turning to phantasms, nevertheless such a mode of understanding was less perfect if we consider to what extent it lay within the power of the soul. This will appear if we consider that every intellectual substance possesses intellective power by the influence of the divine light. This light is one and simple in its first principle, and the farther off intellectual creatures are from the first principle so much the more is the light divided and diversified, as is the case with lines radiating from the center of a circle. Hence it is that God by His essence understands all things, while the superior intellectual substances understand by means of a number of species, which nevertheless are fewer and more universal and bestow a deeper comprehension of things, because of the efficaciousness of the intellectual power of such natures; but inferior intellectual natures possess a greater number of species, which are also less universal, and bestow a lower degree of comprehension, in proportion as they recede from the intellectual power of the higher intellectual substances. If, therefore, inferior substances received species in the same degree of universality as the superior substances, since they are not so strong in understanding, the knowledge which they would derive through these species would be imperfect, and of a general and confused nature. We can see this to a certain extent in men, for those who are of weaker intellect fail to acquire perfect knowledge through the universal conceptions of those who have a better understanding, unless things are explained to them singly and in detail. Now it is clear that in the order of nature human souls hold the lowest place among intellectual substances; for the perfection of the universe required various grades of being. If, therefore, God had willed human souls to understand in the same way as separate substances, it would follow that human knowledge, so far from being perfect, would be confused and general. Therefore, to make it possible for human souls to possess a perfect and proper knowledge of things, they were so made that their nature required them to be joined to bodies, and thus to receive a proper knowledge of sensible things from the sensible things themselves. So, too, we see in the case of uneducated men that they have to be taught by sensible examples.

It is clear then that it was for the soul's good that it was united to a body, and that it understands by turning to the phantasms. Nevertheless it is possible for it to exist apart from the body, and also to understand in another way.

Reply Obj. 1. The Philosopher's words, if carefully examined, will show that he said this on the basis of a previous supposition, namely, that understanding is a movement of body and soul as united, just as is sensation, for he had not as yet explained the difference between intellect and sense.[254] We may also say that he is referring to the way of understanding by turning to phantasms.

This is also the meaning of the second objection.

Reply Obj. 3. The separated soul does not understand by innate species, nor by species then abstracted, nor only by retained species, as the objection proves: but the soul in that state understands by means of participated species resulting from the influence of the divine light, shared by the soul as by other separate substances, though in a lesser degree. Hence, as soon as it ceases to act by turning to the body, the soul turns at once to what is above it; nor is this way of knowledge unnatural, for God is the author of the influx both of the light of grace and of the light of nature.

---

[254]*De An.*, I, 4 (408b 6).

7

HUMAN AGENCY:
THE WILL AND FREE CHOICE

Summa Theologica

PART ONE
QUESTION 82
The Will

FIRST ARTICLE
Whether the Will Desires Something of Necessity?

We proceed thus to the First Article:—

Objection 1. It would seem that the will desires nothing of necessity. For Augustine says that if anything is necessary, it is not voluntary.[1] But whatever the will desires is voluntary. Therefore nothing that the will desires is desired of necessity.

Obj. 2. Further, *the rational powers*, according to the Philosopher, *extend to opposite things.*[2] But the will is a rational power, because, as he says, *the will is in the reason.*[3] Therefore the will extends to opposite things, and hence is determined to nothing of necessity.

Obj. 3. Further, by the will we are masters of our own actions. But we are not masters of that which is of necessity. Therefore the act of the will cannot be necessitated.

On the contrary, Augustine says that *all desire happiness with one will.*[4] Now if this were not necessary, but contingent, there would at least be a few exceptions. Therefore the will desires something of necessity.

I answer that, The word *necessity* is employed in many ways. For that which must be is necessary. Now that a thing must be may belong to it by an intrinsic principle:—either material, as when we say that everything composed of contraries is of necessity corruptible;—or formal, as when

---

[1]*De Civit. Dei*, V, 10 (PL 41, 152).   [2]*Metaph.*, VIII, 2 (1046b 5).
[3]Aristotle, *De An.*, III, 9 (432b 5).   [4]*De Trin.*, XIII, 4 (PL 42, 1018).

we say that it is necessary for the three angles of a triangle to be equal to two right angles. And this is *natural* and *absolute necessity.* In another way, that a thing must be belongs to it by reason of something extrinsic, which is either the end or the agent. The necessity is imposed on something by the end when without it the end is not to be attained or so well attained: for instance, food is said to be necessary for life, and a horse is necessary for a journey. This is called the *necessity of the end*, and sometimes also *utility.* The necessity is imposed by the agent when someone is forced by some agent, so that he is not able to do the contrary. This is called the *necessity of coercion.*

Now this necessity of coercion is altogether repugnant to the will. For we call *violent* that which is against the inclination of a thing. But the very movement of the will is an inclination to something. Therefore, just as a thing is called *natural* because it is according to the inclination of nature, so a thing is called *voluntary* because it is according to the inclination of the will. Therefore, just as it is impossible for a thing to be at the same time violent and natural, so it is impossible for a thing to be absolutely coerced, or violent, and voluntary.

But the necessity of the end is not repugnant to the will, when the end cannot be attained except in one way; and thus from the will to cross the sea arises in the will the necessity to desire a ship.

In like manner, neither is natural necessity repugnant to the will. Indeed, just as the intellect of necessity adheres to first principles, so the will must of necessity adhere to the last end, which is happiness; for the end is in practical matters what the principle is in speculative matters, as is said in *Physics* ii.[5] For what befits a thing naturally and immovably must be the root and principle of all else pertaining thereto, since the nature of a thing is the first in everything, and every movement arises from something immovable.

Reply Obj. 1. The words of Augustine are to be understood of the necessity of coercion. But natural necessity *does not take away the liberty of the will*, as he himself says in the same work.[6]

Reply Obj. 2. The will, so far as it desires a thing naturally, corresponds rather to the intellect of natural principles than to the reason, which extends to contraries. Hence, in this respect, it is rather an intellectual than a rational power.

Reply Obj. 3. We are masters of our own actions by reason of our being able to choose this or that. But choice regards, not the end, but *the means*

---

[5]Aristotle, *Phys.*, II, 9 (200a 21).   [6]*De Civit. Dei*, V, 10 (PL 41, 152).

to the end, as the Philosopher says.[7] Consequently, the desire of the ultimate end is not among those actions of which we are masters.

SECOND ARTICLE
Whether the Will Desires of Necessity Whatever It Desires?

We proceed thus to the Second Article:—

Objection 1. It would seem that the will desires of necessity all that it desires. For Dionysius says that *evil is outside the scope of the will.*[8] Therefore the will tends of necessity to the good which is proposed to it.

Obj. 2. Further, the object of the will is compared to the will as the mover to the movable thing. But the movement of the movable necessarily follows the mover. Therefore it seems that the will's object moves it of necessity.

Obj. 3. Further, just as the thing apprehended by sense is the object of the sensitive appetite, so the thing apprehended by the intellect is the object of the intellectual appetite, which is called the will. But what is apprehended by the sense moves the sensitive appetite of necessity, for Augustine says that *animals are moved by things seen.*[9] Therefore it seems that whatever is apprehended by the intellect moves the will of necessity.

On the contrary, Augustine says that *it is the will by which we sin and live well.*[10] Thus, the will extends to opposites. Therefore it does not desire of necessity all things whatsoever it desires.

I answer that, The will does not desire of necessity whatsoever it desires. In order to make this evident we must observe that, just as the intellect naturally and of necessity adheres to first principles, so the will adheres to the last end, as we have said already. Now there are some intelligible things which have no necessary connection with first principles: *e.g.,* contingent propositions, the denial of which does not involve a denial of first principles. And to such the intellect does not assent of necessity. But there are some propositions which have a necessary connection with first principles, namely, demonstrable conclusions, a denial of which involves a denial of first principles. And to these the intellect assents of necessity, when once it is aware (by demonstration) of the necessary connection of these conclusions with the principles; but it does not assent of necessity until through the demonstration it recognizes the necessity of such a connection.

---

[7]Aristotle, *Eth.*, III, 2 (111b 27).   [8]*De Div. Nom.*, IV, 32 (PG 3, 732).
[9]*De Genesi ad Litt.*, IX, 14 (PL 34, 402).   [10]*Retract.*, I, 9 (PL 32, 596); *De Civit. Dei*, V, 10 (PL 41, 152).

It is the same with the will. For there are certain particular goods which have not a necessary connection with happiness, because without them a man can be happy; and to such the will does not adhere of necessity. But there are some things which have a necessary connection with happiness, namely, those by means of which man adheres to God, in Whom alone true happiness consists. Nevertheless, until through the certitude produced by seeing God the necessity of such a connection be shown, the will does not adhere to God of necessity, nor to those things which are of God. But the will of the man who sees God in His essence of necessity adheres to God, just as now we desire of necessity to be happy. It is therefore clear that the will does not desire of necessity whatever it desires.

Reply Obj. 1. The will can tend to nothing except under the aspect of good. But because good is of many kinds, for this reason the will is not of necessity determined to one.

Reply Obj 2. The mover of necessity causes movement in the movable thing only when the power of the mover exceeds the movable thing in such a way that its entire capacity is subject to the mover. But as the capacity of the will is for the universal and perfect good, it is not subjected to any particular good. And therefore it is not of necessity moved by it.

Reply Obj. 3. The sensitive power does not compare different things with each other, as reason does; but it apprehends simply some one thing. Therefore, according to that one thing, it moves the sensitive appetite in a determinate way. But the reason is a power that compares several things together. Therefore the intellectual appetite—that is, the will—may be moved by several things, but not of necessity by one thing.

THIRD ARTICLE
Whether the Will Is a Higher Power Than the Intellect?

We proceed thus to the Third Article:—

Objection 1. It would seem that the will is a higher power than the intellect. For the object of the will is the good and the end. But the end is the first and highest cause. Therefore the will is the first and highest power.

Obj. 2. Further, in the order of natural things we observe a progress from imperfect things to perfect. And this also appears in the powers of the soul, for sense precedes the intellect, which is more noble. Now the act of the will, according to a natural order, follows the act of the intellect. Therefore the will is a more noble and perfect power than the intellect.

Obj. 3. Further, habits are proportioned to their powers, as perfections to what they make perfect. But the habit which perfects the will—namely, charity—is more noble than the habits which perfect the intellect; for it is written (*I Cor.* xiii. 2): *If I should know all mysteries, and if I should have all faith, and have not charity, I am nothing.* Therefore the will is a higher power than the intellect.

On the contrary, The Philosopher holds the intellect to be the highest power of the soul.[11]

I answer that, The superiority of one thing over another can be considered in two ways: *absolutely* and *relatively.* Now a thing is considered to be such absolutely when it is considered such in itself; but relatively, when it is such in relation to something else. If therefore the intellect and will be considered with regard to themselves, then the intellect is the higher power. And this is clear if we compare their respective objects to one another. For the object of the intellect is more simple and more absolute than the object of the will. For the object of the intellect is the very notion of the appetible good; and the appetible good, the notion of which is in the intellect, is the object of the will. Now the more simple and the more abstract a thing is, the nobler and higher it is in itself; and therefore the object of the intellect is higher than the object of the will. Therefore, since the proper nature of a power is according to its order to its object, it follows that the intellect, in itself and absolutely, is higher and nobler than the will.

But relatively, and by comparison with something else, we find that the will is sometimes higher than the intellect; and this happens when the object of the will occurs in something higher than that in which occurs the object of the intellect. Thus, for instance, I might say that hearing is relatively nobler than sight, inasmuch as something in which there is sound is nobler than something in which there is color, though color is nobler and simpler than sound. For, as we have said above, the act of the intellect consists in this—that the likeness of the thing understood is in the one who understands[12]; while the act of the will consists in this—that the will is inclined to the thing itself as existing in itself. And therefore the Philosopher says in *Metaph.* vi. that *good and evil,* which are objects of the will, *are in things,* but *truth and error,* which are objects of the intellect, *are in the mind.*[13] When, therefore, the thing in which there is good is nobler than the soul itself, in which is the understood likeness, then, by comparison with such a thing, the will is higher than the intellect. But when the

---

[11]*Eth.,* X, 7 (1177a 20).   [12]Q. 16, a. 1; q. 27, a. 4.   [13]*Metaph.,* V, 4 (1027b 25).

thing which is good is less noble than the soul, then, even in comparison with that thing, the intellect is higher than the will. Hence, the love of God is better than the knowledge of God; but, on the contrary, the knowledge of corporeal things is better than the love of them. Absolutely, however, the intellect is nobler than the will.

Reply Obj. 1. The notion of cause is perceived by comparing one thing to another, and in such a comparison the notion of good is found to be nobler; but truth signifies something more absolutely, and extends to the notion of good itself. Thus, the good is something true. But, again, the true is something good. For the intellect is a given reality, and truth is its end. And among other ends this is the most excellent: just as is the intellect among the other powers.

Reply Obj. 2. What precedes in the order of generation and time is less perfect, for in one and the same thing potentiality precedes act, and imperfection precedes perfection. But what precedes absolutely and in the order of nature is more perfect; for thus act precedes potentiality. And in this way the intellect precedes the will, as the motive power precedes the movable thing, and as the active precedes the passive; for it is the *apprehended* good that moves the will.

Reply Obj. 3. This argument is verified of the will as compared with what is above the soul. For charity is the virtue by which we love God.

FOURTH ARTICLE
Whether the Will Moves the Intellect?

We proceed thus to the Fourth Article:—

Objection 1. It would seem that the will does not move the intellect. For what moves excels and precedes what is moved, because what moves is an agent, and *the agent is nobler than the patient*, as Augustine says,[14] and the Philosopher.[15] But the intellect excels and precedes the will, as we have said above. Therefore the will does not move the intellect.

Obj. 2. Further, what moves is not moved by what is moved, except perhaps accidentally. But the intellect moves the will, because the good apprehended by the intellect moves without being moved; whereas the appetite is a moved mover. Therefore the intellect is not moved by the will.

Obj. 3. Further, we can will nothing but what we understand. If, therefore, in order to understand, the will moves by willing to understand, that act of the will must be preceded by another act of the intellect, and this

---

[14]*De Genesi ad Litt.*, XII, 16 (PL 34, 467).   [15]*De An.*, III, 5 (430a 18).

act of the intellect by another act of the will, and so on indefinitely, which is impossible. Therefore the will does not move the intellect.

On the contrary, Damascene says: *It is in our power to learn an art or not, as we will.*[16] But a thing is in our power by the will, and we learn an art by the intellect. Therefore the will moves the intellect.

I answer that, A thing is said to move in two ways: First, as an end, as when we say that the end moves the agent. In this way the intellect moves the will, because the understood good is the object of the will, and moves it as an end. Secondly, a thing is said to move as an agent, as what alters moves what is altered, and what impels moves what is impelled. In this way the will moves the intellect, and all the powers of the soul, as Anselm says.[17] The reason is, because wherever we have order among a number of active powers, that power which is related to the universal end moves the powers which refer to particular ends. And we may observe this both in nature and in political things. For the heavens, which aims at the universal preservation of things subject to generation and corruption, moves all inferior bodies, each of which aims at the preservation of its own species or of the individual. So, too, a king, who aims at the common good of the whole kingdom, by his rule moves all the governors of cities, each of whom rules over his own particular city. Now the object of the will is the good and the end in general, whereas each power is directed to some suitable good proper to it, as sight is directed to the perception of color, and the intellect to the knowledge of truth. Therefore the will as an agent moves all the powers of the soul to their respective acts, except the natural powers of the vegetative part, which are not subject to our choice.

Reply Obj. 1. The intellect may be considered in two ways: as apprehensive of universal being and truth, and as a reality and a particular power having a determinate act. In like manner also the will may be considered in two ways: according to the common nature of its object—that is to say, as appetitive of universal good—and as a determinate power of the soul having a determinate act. If, therefore, the intellect and will be compared with one another according to the universality of their respective objects, then, as we have said above, the intellect is absolutely higher and nobler than the will. If, however, we take the intellect in relation to the common nature of its object and the will as a determinate power, then again the intellect is higher and nobler than the will, because under the notion of being and truth is contained both the will itself, its act, and its object. Therefore the intellect understands the will, its act, and its object,

---

[16]*De Fide Orth.*, II, 26 (PG 94, 960).   [17]Eadmer, *De Similit.*, II (PL 159, 605).

just as it understands other species of things, as stone or wood, which are contained in the common notion of being and truth. But if we consider the will in relation to the common nature of its object, which is good, and the intellect as a reality and a special power, then the intellect itself, its act, and its object, which is the true, each of which is some species of good, are contained under the common notion of good. And in this way the will is higher than the intellect, and can move it. From this we can easily understand why these powers include one another in their acts, because the intellect understands that the will wills, and the will wills the intellect to understand. In the same way, the good is contained under the true, inasmuch as it is an understood truth, and the true under the good, inasmuch as it is a desired good.

Reply Obj. 2. The intellect moves the will in one sense, and the will moves the intellect in another, as we have said above.

Reply Obj. 3. There is no need to go on indefinitely, but we must stop at the intellect as preceding all the rest. For every movement of the will must be preceded by apprehension, whereas every apprehension is not preceded by an act of the will; but the principle of counselling and understanding is an intellectual principle higher than our intellect—namely, God; as Aristotle also says, explaining in this way that there is no need to proceed indefinitely.[18]

FIFTH ARTICLE
Whether We Should Distinguish Irascible and Concupiscible Parts in the Superior Appetite?

We proceed thus to the Fifth Article:—

Objection 1. It would seem that we ought to distinguish irascible and concupiscible parts in the superior appetite, which is the will. For the concupiscible power is so called from *concupiscere* [*to desire*], and the irascible part from *irasci* [*to be angry*]. But there is a concupiscence which cannot belong to the sensitive appetite, but only to the intellectual, which is the will: *e.g.*, the concupiscence of wisdom, of which it is said (*Wis.* vi. 21): *The concupiscence of wisdom bringeth to the eternal kingdom.* There is also a certain anger which cannot belong to the sensitive appetite, but only to the intellectual; as when our anger is directed against vice. And so, Jerome commenting on *Matt.* xiii. 33, warns us *to have the hatred of vice in the irascible part.*[19] Therefore we should distinguish irascible and concupiscible parts in the intellectual soul as well as in the sensitive.

---

[18]*Eth. Eudem.*, VII, 14 (1248a 26).   [19]*In Matt.*, I, super XIII, 33 (PL 26, 94).

Obj. 2. Further, as is commonly said, charity is in the concupiscible, and hope in the irascible part. But they cannot be in the sensitive appetite, because their objects are not sensible, but intellectual. Therefore we must assign an irascible and a concupiscible power to the intellectual part.

Obj. 3. Further, it is said that *the soul has these powers*—namely, the irascible, concupiscible and rational—*before it is united to the body.*[20] But no power of the sensitive part belongs to the soul alone, but to the soul and body united, as we have said above.[21] Therefore the irascible and concupiscible powers are in the will, which is the intellectual appetite.

On the contrary, Gregory of Nyssa says that the irrational part of the soul is divided into the desiderative and irascible,[22] and Damascene says the same.[23] And the Philosopher says *that the will is in the reason, while in the irrational part of the soul are concupiscence and anger, or desire and spirit.*[24]

I answer that, The irascible and concupiscible are not parts of the intellectual appetite, which is called the will. For, as was said above, a power which is directed to an object according to some common notion is not differentiated by special differences which are contained under that common notion.[25] For instance, because sight is related to what is visible under the common notion of something colored, the visual power is not multiplied according to the different kinds of color; but if there were a power concerned with white as white, and not as something colored, it would be distinct from a power concerned with black as black.

Now the sensitive appetite is not related to the common notion of good, because neither do the senses apprehend the universal. Therefore the parts of the sensitive appetite are differentiated by the different notions of particular good; for the concupiscible is related to its proper sort of good, which is something pleasant to the senses and suitable to nature; whereas the irascible is related to that sort of good which is something that wards off and repels what is hurtful. But the will is related to the good according to the common notion of good, and therefore in the will, which is the intellectual appetite, there is no differentiation of appetitive powers, so that there be in the intellectual appetite an irascible power distinct from a concupiscible power; just as neither on the part of the

---

[20]Pseudo-Augustine (Alcher of Clairvaux), *De Spir. et An.*, XVI (PL 40, 791). [21]Q. 77, a. 5 and 8.   [22]Cf. Nemesius, *De Nat. Hom.*, XVI; XVII (PG 40, 672; 676).   [23]*De Fide Orth.*, XII (PG 94, 928).   [24]*De An.*, III, 11 (432b 5). [25]Q. 59, a. 4; q. 79, a. 7.

intellect are the apprehensive powers multiplied, although they are on the part of the senses.

Reply Obj. 1. Love, concupiscence and the like can be understood in two ways. Sometimes they are taken as passions—arising, that is, with a certain commotion of spirit. And thus they are commonly understood, and in this sense they are only in the sensitive appetite. They may, however, be taken in another way, in so far as they are simple affections without passion or commotion of spirit, and thus they are acts of the will. And in this sense, too, they are attributed to the angels and to God. But if taken in this sense, they do not belong to different powers, but only to one power, which is called the will.

Reply Obj. 2. The will itself may be said to be irascible, insofar as it wills to repel evil, not from any sudden movement of passion, but from a judgment of the reason. And in the same way the will may be said to be concupiscible because of its desire for good. And thus in the irascible and concupiscible are charity and hope—that is, in the will as ordered to such acts.

And in this way, too, we may understand the words quoted from the *De Spiritu et Anima*, namely, that the irascible and concupiscible powers are in the soul before it is united to the body (as long as we understand priority of nature, and not of time); although there is no need to have faith in what that book says.

Whence the answer to the third objection is clear.

Summa Theologica

PART ONE
QUESTION 83
Free Choice

FIRST ARTICLE
Whether Man Has Free Choice?

We proceed thus to the First Article: —

Objection 1. It would seem that man has not free choice. For whoever has free choice does what he wills. But man does not what he wills, for it is written (*Rom.* vii. 19): *For the good which I will I do not, but the evil which I will not, that I do.* Therefore man has not free choice.

Obj. 2. Further, whoever has free choice has in his power to will or not to will, to do or not to do. But this is not in man's power, for it is written (*Rom.* ix. 16): *It is not of him that willeth*—namely, to will—*nor of him that runneth*—namely, to run. Therefore man has not free choice.

Obj. 3. Further, he is free who is his own master, as the Philosopher says.[26] Therefore what is moved by another is not free. But God moves the will, for it is written (*Prov.* xxi. 1): *The heart of the king is in the hand of the Lord; whithersoever He will He shall turn it*; and (*Phil.* ii. 13): *It is God Who worketh in you both to will and to accomplish.* Therefore man has not free choice.

Obj. 4. Further, whoever has free choice is master of his own actions. But man is not master of his own actions, for it is written (*Jer.* x. 23): *The way of a man is not his, neither is it in a man to walk.* Therefore man has not free choice.

Obj. 5. Further, the Philosopher says: *According as each one is, such does the end seem to him.*[27] But it is not in our power to be such as we are, for this comes to us from nature. Therefore it is natural to us to follow some particular end, and therefore we are not free in so doing.

On the contrary, It is written (*Ecclus.* xv. 14): *God made man from the beginning, and left him in the hand of his own counsel*; and the *Gloss* adds: *That is, in the liberty of choice.*[28]

---

[26]Aristotle, *Metaph.*, I, 2 (982b 26).   [27]*Eth.*, 111, 5 (III4a 32).   [28]*Glossa interl.*, (III, 401V); cf. *Glossa ordin.* (III, 401E).

I answer that, Man has free choice, or otherwise counsels, exhortations, commands, prohibitions, rewards and punishments would be in vain. In order to make this evident, we must observe that some things act without judgment, as a stone moves downwards; and in like manner all things which lack knowledge. And some act from judgment, but not a free judgment; as brute animals. For the sheep, seeing the wolf, judges it a thing to be shunned, from a natural and not a free judgment; because it judges, not from deliberation, but from natural instinct. And the same thing is to be said of any judgment in brute animals. But man acts from judgment, because by his apprehensive power he judges that something should be avoided or sought. But because this judgment, in the case of some particular act, is not from a natural instinct, but from some act of comparison in the reason, therefore he acts from free judgment and retains the power of being inclined to various things. For reason in contingent matters may follow opposite courses, as we see in dialectical syllogisms and rhetorical arguments. Now particular operations are contingent, and therefore in such matters the judgment of reason may follow opposite courses, and is not determinate to one. And in that man is rational, it is necessary that he have free choice.

Reply Obj. 1. As we have said above, the sensitive appetite, though it obeys the reason, yet in a given case can resist by desiring what the reason forbids.[29] This is therefore the good which man does not when he wishes—namely, *not to desire against reason*, as Augustine says.[30]

Reply Obj. 2. Those words of the Apostle are not to be taken as though man does not wish or does not run of his free choice, but because free choice is not sufficient thereto unless it be moved and helped by God.

Reply Obj. 3. Free choice is the cause of its own movement, because by his free choice man moves himself to act. But it does not of necessity belong to liberty that what is free should be the first cause of itself, as neither for one thing to be cause of another need it be the first cause. God, therefore, is the first cause, Who moves causes both natural and voluntary. And just as by moving natural causes He does not prevent their actions from being natural, so by moving voluntary causes He does not deprive their actions of being voluntary; but rather is He the cause of this very thing in them, for He operates in each thing according to its own nature.

---

[29]Q. 81, a. 3, ad 2.   [30]*Glossa interl.*, super *Rom.*, VIII, 19 (vI, 17r).—Cf. St. Augustine, *Serm. ad Popul.*, serm. CLIV, 3 (PL 38, 834).

Reply Obj. 4. *Man's way* is said *not to be his* in the execution of his choice, wherein he may be impeded, whether he will or not. The choice itself, however, is in us, but presupposes the help of God.

Reply Obj. 5. Quality in man is of two kinds: natural and adventitious. Now the natural quality may be in the intellectual part, or in the body and its powers. From the very fact, therefore, that man is such by virtue of a natural quality which is in the intellectual part, he naturally desires his last end, which is happiness. This desire is, indeed, a natural desire, and is not subject to free choice, as is clear from what we have said above.[31] But on the part of the body and its powers, man may be such by virtue of a natural quality, inasmuch as he is of such a temperament or disposition due to any impression whatever produced by corporeal causes, which cannot affect the intellectual part, since it is not the act of a corporeal organ. And such as a man is by virtue of a corporeal quality, such also does his end seem to him, because from such a disposition a man is inclined to choose or reject something. But these inclinations are subject to the judgment of reason, which the lower appetite obeys, as we have said.[32] Therefore this is in no way prejudicial to free choice.

The adventitious qualities are habits and passions, by virtue of which a man is inclined to one thing rather than to another. And yet even these inclinations are subject to the judgment of reason. Such qualities, too, are subject to reason, as it is in our power either to acquire them, whether by causing them or disposing ourselves to them, or to reject them. And so there is nothing in this that is repugnant to free choice.

SECOND ARTICLE
Whether Free Choice Is a Power?

We proceed thus to the Second Article:—

Objection 1. It would seem that free choice is not a power. For free choice is nothing but a free judgment. But judgment denominates an act, not a power. Therefore free choice is not a power.

Obj. 2. Further, free choice is defined as *the faculty of the will and reason.*[33] But faculty denominates the facility of power, which is due to a habit. Therefore free choice is a habit. Moreover Bernard says that free choice is *the soul's habit of disposing of itself.*[34] Therefore it is not a power.

Obj. 3. Further, no natural power is forfeited through sin. But free choice is forfeited through sin, for Augustine says that *man, by abusing free*

---

[31]Q. 82, a. 1 and 2.   [32]Q. 81, a. 3.   [33]Peter Lombard, *Sent.*, II, xxiv, 3 (I, 421).   [34]St. Bernard, *De Gratia et Libero Arbitrio*, I (PL 182, 1002).

choice, loses both it and himself.[35] Therefore free choice is not a power.

On the contrary, Nothing but a power, seemingly, is the subject of a habit. But free choice is the subject of grace, by the help of which it chooses what is good. Therefore free choice is a power.

I answer that, Although *free choice,* in its strict sense, denotes an act, in the common manner of speaking we call free choice that which is the principle of the act by which man judges freely. Now in us the principle of an act is both power and habit; for we say that we know something both by science and by the intellectual power. Therefore free choice must be either a power,[36] or a habit,[37] or a power with a habit.[38] That it is neither a habit nor a power together with a habit can be clearly proved in two ways. First of all, because, if it is a habit, it must be a natural habit; for it is natural to man to have free choice. But there is no natural habit in us with respect to those things which come under free choice, for we are naturally inclined to those things of which we have natural habits, for instance, to assent to first principles. Now those things to which we are naturally inclined are not subject to free choice, as we have said in the case of the desire of happiness.[39] Therefore it is against the very notion of free choice that it should be a natural habit; and that it should be a non-natural habit is against its nature. Therefore in no sense is it a habit.

Secondly, this is clear because habits are defined as that *by reason of which we are well or ill disposed with regard to actions and passions.*[40] For by temperance we are well-disposed as regards concupiscences, and intemperance ill-disposed; and by science we are well-disposed to the act of the intellect when we know the truth, and by the contrary habit ill-disposed. But free choice is indifferent to choosing well or ill, and therefore it is impossible that it be a habit. Therefore it is a power.

Reply Obj. 1. It is not unusual for a power to be named from its act. And so from this act, which is a free judgment, is named the power which is the principle of this act. Otherwise, if free choice denominated an act, it would not always remain in man.

Reply Obj. 2. *Faculty* sometimes denominates a power ready for operation, and in this sense faculty is used in the definition of free choice. But Bernard takes habit, not as divided against power, but as signifying any aptitude by which a man is somehow disposed to an act.[41] This may be

---

[35]*Enchir.*, XXX (PL 40, 246).   [36]St. Albert, *Summa de Creatur.*, II, q. 70, a. 2 (XXXV, 575).   [37]St. Bonaventure, *In II Sent.*, d. xxv, pt. I, a. 1, q. 4 (II, 601).   [38]Alex. of Hales, *Summa Theol.*, II, I, no. 390 (II, 486).   [39]Q. 82, a. 1 and 2.   [40]Aristotle, *Eth.*, II, 5 (1105b 25).   [41]*De Grat. et Lib. Arb.*, I (PL 182, 1002).

both by a power and by a habit, for by a power man is, as it were, empowered to do the action, and by the habit he is apt to act well or ill.

Reply Obj. 3. Man is said to have lost free choice by falling into sin, not as to natural liberty, which is freedom from coercion, but as regards freedom from fault and unhappiness. Of this we shall treat later in the treatise on Morals in the second part of this work.[42]

THIRD ARTICLE
Whether Free Choice Is an Appetitive Power?

We proceed thus to the Third Article:—

Objection 1. It would seem that free choice is not an appetitive, but a cognitive power. For Damascene says that *free choice straightway accompanies the rational power.*[43] But reason is a cognitive power. Therefore free choice is a cognitive power.

Obj. 2. Further, free choice is so called as though it were a free judgment. But to judge is an act of a cognitive power. Therefore free choice is a cognitive power.

Obj. 3. Further, the principal function of free choice is election. But election seems to belong to knowledge, because it implies a certain comparison of one thing to another; which belongs to the cognitive power. Therefore free choice is a cognitive power.

On the contrary, The Philosopher says that election is *the desire of those things which are in our power.*[44] But desire is an act of the appetitive power. Therefore election is also. But free choice is that by which we elect. Therefore free choice is an appetitive power.

I answer that, The proper act of free choice is election, for we say that we have a free choice because we can take one thing while refusing another; and this is to elect. Therefore we must consider the nature of free choice by considering the nature of election. Now two things concur in election: one on the part of the cognitive power, the other on the part of the appetitive power. On the part of the cognitive power, counsel is required, by which we judge one thing to be preferred to another; on the part of the appetitive power, it is required that the appetite should accept the judgment of counsel. Therefore Aristotle leaves it in doubt whether election belongs principally to the appetitive or the cognitive power: since he says that election is either *an appetitive intellect or an intellectual appetite.*[45] But he inclines to its being an intellectual appetite when he describes

---

[42]*S. T.,* I-II, q. 85; q. 109.   [43]*De Fide Orth.,* II, 27 (PG 94, 949).
[44]*Eth.,* III, 3 (1113a 11).   [45]*Op. cit.,* VI, 2 (1139b 4).

election as *a desire proceeding from counsel*.[46] And the reason of this is because the proper object of election is the means to the end. Now the means, as such, has the nature of that good which is called *useful*; and since the good, as such, is the object of the appetite, it follows that election is principally an act of an appetitive power. And thus free choice is an appetitive power.

Reply Obj. 1. The appetitive powers accompany the apprehensive, and in this sense Damascene says that free choice straightway accompanies the rational power.

Reply Obj. 2. Judgment, as it were, concludes and terminates counsel. Now counsel is terminated, first, by the judgment of reason; secondly, by the acceptance of the appetite. Hence the Philosopher says that, *having formed a judgment by counsel, we desire in accordance with that counsel*.[47] And in this sense election itself is a judgment from which free choice takes its name.

*Reply Obj.*3. This comparison which is implied in the term election belongs to the preceding counsel, which is an act of reason. For though the appetite does not make comparisons, yet inasmuch as it is moved by the apprehensive power which does compare, it has some likeness of comparison, by choosing one in preference to another.

FOURTH ARTICLE
Whether Free Choice Is a Power Distinct from the Will?

We proceed thus to the Fourth Article:—

Objection 1. It would seem that free choice is a power distinct from the will.[48] For Damascene says that θέλησις is one thing and βούλησις, another.[49] But θέλησις is will, while βούλησις seems to be free choice, because βούλησις, according to him, is the will as concerning an object by way of comparison between two things. Therefore it seems that free choice is a power distinct from the will.

Obj. 2. Further, powers are known by their acts. But election, which is the act of free choice, is distinct from the will, because *the will regards the end, whereas choice regards the means to the end*.[50] Therefore free choice is a power distinct from the will.

Obj. 3. Further, the will is the intellectual appetite. But on the part of the intellect there are two powers—agent and possible. Therefore, also on

---

[46]*Op. cit.*, III, 3 (1113a 11).   [47]*Ibid.*   [48]Cf. St. Albert, *Summa de Creatur.*, II, q. 70, a. 2 (XXXV, 577).   [49]*De Fide Orth.*, XXII (PG 94, 944).
[50]Aristotle, *Eth.*, III, 2 (1111b 26).

the part of the intellectual appetite there must be another power besides the will. And this, seemingly, can be only free choice. Therefore free choice is a power distinct from the will.

On the contrary, Damascene says free choice is nothing else than the will.[51]

I answer that, The appetitive powers must be proportionate to the apprehensive powers, as we have said above.[52] Now, as on the part of intellectual apprehension we have intellect and reason, so on the part of the intellectual appetite we have will and free choice, which is nothing else but the power of election. And this is clear from their relations to their respective objects and acts. For the act of *understanding* implies the simple acceptation of something, and hence we say that we understand first principles, which are known of themselves without any comparison. But to *reason,* properly speaking, is to come from one thing to the knowledge of another, and so, properly speaking, we reason about conclusions, which are known from the principles. In like manner, on the part of the appetite, to *will* implies the simple appetite for something, and so the will is said to regard the end, which is desired for itself. But to *elect* is to desire something for the sake of obtaining something else, and so, properly speaking, it regards the means to the end. Now in appetitive matters, the end is related to the means, which is desired for the end, in the same way as, in knowledge, principles are related to the conclusion to which we assent because of the principles. Therefore it is evident that as *intellect* is to *reason,* so *will* is to the *elective power,* which is free choice. But it has been shown above that it belongs to the same power both to understand and to reason,[53] even as it belongs to the same power to be at rest and to be in movement. Hence it belongs also to the same power to will and to elect. And on this account will and the free choice are not two powers, but one.

Reply Obj. 1. βούλησις is distinct from θέλησις because of a distinction not of powers, but of acts.

Reply Obj. 2. Election and will—that is, the act of willing—are different acts, yet they belong to the same power, as do *to understand* and *to reason,* as we have said.

Reply Obj. 3. The intellect is compared to the will as moving the will. And therefore there is no need to distinguish in the will an *agent* and a *possible* will.

---

[51]*De Fide Orth.*, XIV (PG 94, 1037).   [52]Q. 64, a. 2; q. 80, a. 2.   [53]Q. 79, a. 8.

Summa Theologica

First Part of Part Two
Question 8
On the Will, in Regard to What It Wills

We must now consider the different acts of the will; and in the first place, those acts which belong to the will itself immediately, as being elicited by the will; secondly, those acts which are commanded by the will.

First Article
Whether the Will Is of Good Only?

We proceed thus to the First Article.—

Objection 1. It would seem that the will is not of good only. For the same power regards opposites; for instance, sight regards white and black. But good and evil are opposites. Therefore the will is not only of good, but also of evil.

Obj. 2. Further, rational powers can be directed to opposite purposes, according to the Philosopher.[54] But the will is a rational power, since it is *in the reason*, as is stated in *De Anima* iii. 9. Therefore the will can be directed to opposites, and consequently its volition is not confined to good, but extends to evil.

Obj. 3. Further; good and being are convertible. But volition is directed not only to beings, but also to non-beings. For sometimes we wish *not to walk*, or *not to speak*; and again at times we wish for future things, which are not actual beings. Therefore the will is not of good only.

On the contrary, Dionysius says that *evil is outside the scope of the the will*, and that *all things desire good.*[55]

I answer that, The will is a rational appetite. Now every appetite is only of something good. The reason of this is that the appetite is nothing else than an inclination of a person desirous of a thing towards that thing. Now every inclination is to something like and suitable to the thing inclined. Since, therefore, everything, inasmuch as it is being and substance, is a

---

Selections on pp. 209–230 reprinted from St. Thomas Aquinas, *Summa Theologica*, translated by the Fathers of the English Dominican Province (New York: Benzinger Bros., 1948).

[54]*Metaph.* ix. 2.   [55]*De Div. Nom.* iv.

good, it must needs be that every inclination is to something good. And hence it is that the Philosopher says that *the good is that which all desire.*[56]

But it must be noted that, since every inclination results from a form, the natural appetite results from a form existing in the nature of things: while the sensitive appetite, as also the intellective or rational appetite, which we call the will, follows from an apprehended form. Therefore, just as the natural appetite tends to good existing in a thing; so the animal or voluntary appetite tends to a good which is apprehended. Consequently, in order that the will tend to anything, it is requisite, not that this be good in very truth, but that it be apprehended as good. Wherefore the Philosopher says that *the end is a good, or an apparent good.*[57]

Reply Obj. 1. The same power regards opposites, but it is not referred to them in the same way. Accordingly, the will is referred both to good and to evil: but to good by desiring it: to evil, by shunning it. Wherefore the actual desire of good is called *volition*,[58] meaning thereby the act of the will; for it is in this sense that we are now speaking of the will. On the other hand, the shunning of evil is better described as *nolition*: wherefore, just as volition is of good, so nolition is of evil.

Reply Obj. 2. A rational power is not to be directed to all opposite purposes, but to those which are contained under its proper object; for no power seeks other than its proper object. Now, the object of the will is good. Wherefore the will can be directed to such opposite purposes as are contained under good, such as to be moved or to be at rest, to speak or to be silent, and such like: for the will can be directed to either under the aspect of good.

Reply Obj. 3. That which is not a being in nature, is considered as a being in the reason, wherefore negations and privations are said to be *beings of reason.* In this way, too, future things, in so far as they are apprehended, are beings. Accordingly, in so far as such like are beings, they are apprehended under the aspect of good; and it is thus that the will is directed to them. Wherefore the Philosopher says that *to lack evil is considered as a good.*[59]

SECOND ARTICLE
Whether Volition Is of the End Only, or Also of the Means?

We proceed thus to the Second Article:—

---

[56]*Eth.* i. 1.　　　[57]*Phys.* ii. 3.　　　[58]In Latin,—*voluntas.* To avoid confusion with *voluntas* (the will) St. Thomas adds a word of explanation, which in the translation may appear superfluous.　　　[59]*Eth.* v. 1.

Objection 1. It would seem that volition is not of the means, but of the end only. For the Philosopher says that *volition is of the end, while choice is of the means.*[60]

Obj. 2. Further, *For objects differing in genus there are corresponding different powers of the soul.*[61] Now, the end and the means are in different genera of good: because the end, which is a good either of rectitude or of pleasure, is in the genus *quality*, or *action*, or *passion*; whereas the good which is useful, and is directed to an end, is in the genus *relation.*[62] Therefore, if volition is of the end, it is not of the means.

Obj. 3. Further, habits are proportionate to powers, since they are perfections thereof. But in those habits which are called practical arts, the end belongs to one, and the means to another art; thus the use of a ship, which is its end, belongs to the (art of the) helmsman; whereas the building of the ship, which is directed to the end, belongs to the art of the shipwright. Therefore, since volition is of the end, it is not of the means.

On the contrary, In natural things, it is by the same power that a thing passes through the middle space, and arrives at the terminus. But the means are a kind of middle space, through which one arrives at the end or terminus. Therefore, if volition is of the end, it is also of the means.

I answer that, The word *voluntas* sometimes designates the power of the will, sometimes its act. Accordingly, if we speak of the will as a power, thus it extends both to the end and to the means. For every power extends to those things in which may be considered the aspect of the object of that power in any way whatever: thus the sight extends to all things whatsoever that are in any way colored. Now the aspect of good, which is the object of the power of will, may be found not only in the end, but also in the means.

If, however, we speak of the will in regard to its act, then, properly speaking, volition is of the end only. Because every act denominated from a power, designates the simple act of that power; thus *to understand* designates the simple act of the understanding. Now the simple act of a power is referred to that which is in itself the object of that power. But that which is good and willed in itself is the end. Wherefore volition, properly speaking, is of the end itself. On the other hand, the means are good and willed, not in themselves, but as referred to the end. Wherefore the will is directed to them, only in so far as it is directed to the end: so that what it wills in them, is the end. Thus, to understand, is properly directed to things that are known in themselves, *i.e.*, first principles: but we do not speak of understanding with regard to things known through first princi-

---

[60]*Eth.* iii. 2.   [61]*Eth.* vi. 1.   [62]*Eth.* i. 6.

ples, except in so far as we see the principles in those things. For in morals the end is what principles are in speculative science.[63]

Reply Obj. 1. The Philosopher is speaking of the will in reference to the simple act of the will; not in reference to the power of the will.

Reply Obj. 2. There are different powers for objects that differ in genus and are on an equality; for instance, sound and color are different genera of sensibles, to which are referred hearing and sight. But the useful and the righteous are not on an equality, but are as that which is of itself, and that which is in relation to another. Now such like objects are always referred to the same power; for instance, the power of sight perceives both color and light by which color is seen.

Reply Obj. 3. Not everything that diversifies habits, diversifies the powers: since habits are certain determinations of powers to certain special acts. Moreover, every practical art considers both the end and the means. For the art of the helmsman does indeed consider the end, as that which it effects; and the means, as that which it commands. On the other hand, the ship-building art considers the means as that which it effects; but it considers that which is the end, as that to which it refers what it effects. And again, in every practical art there is an end proper to it and means that belong properly to that art.

THIRD ARTICLE
Whether the Will Is Moved by the Same
Act to the End and to the Means?

We proceed thus to the Third Article:—

Objection 1. It would seem that the will is moved by the same act, to the end and to the means. Because according to the Philosopher *where one thing is on account of another there is only one.*[64] But the will does not will the means save on account of the end. Therefore it is moved to both by the same act.

Obj. 2. Further, the end is the reason for willing the means, just as light is the reason of seeing colors. But light and colors are seen by the same act. Therefore it is the same movement of the will, whereby it wills the end and the means.

Obj. 3. Further, it is one and the same natural movement which tends through the middle space to the terminus. But the means are in comparison to the end, as the middle space is to the terminus. Therefore it is the same movement of the will whereby it is directed to the end and to the means.

---

[63]Cf. *Eth.* vii. 8.   [64]*Top.* iii. 2.

On the contrary, Acts are diversified according to their objects. But the end is a different species of good from the means, which are a useful good. Therefore the will is not moved to both by the same act.

I answer that, Since the end is willed in itself, whereas the means, as such, are only willed for the end, it is evident that the will can be moved to the end, without being moved to the means; whereas it cannot be moved to the means, as such, unless it is moved to the end. Accordingly the will is moved to the end in two ways: first, to the end absolutely and in itself; secondly, as the reason for willing the means. Hence it is evident that the will is moved by one and the same movement,—to the end, as the reason for willing the means; and to the means themselves. But it is another act whereby the will is moved to the end absolutely. And sometimes this act precedes the other in time; for example when a man first wills to have health, and afterwards deliberating by what means to be healed, wills to send for the doctor to heal him. The same happens in regard to the intellect: for at first a man understands the principles in themselves; but afterwards he understands them in the conclusions, inasmuch as he assents to the conclusions on account of the principles.

Reply Obj. 1. This argument holds in respect of the will being moved to the end as the reason for willing the means.

Reply Obj. 2. Whenever color is seen, by the same act the light is seen; but the light can be seen without the color being seen. In like manner whenever a man wills the means, by the same act he wills the end; but not conversely.

Reply Obj. 3. In the execution of a work, the means are as the middle space, and the end, as the terminus. Wherefore just as natural movement sometimes stops in the middle and does not reach the terminus; so sometimes one is busy with the means, without gaining the end. But in willing it is the reverse: for the will through (willing) the end comes to will the means; just as the intellect arrives at the conclusions through the principles which are called *means*. Hence it is that sometimes the intellect understands a mean, and does not proceed thence to the conclusion. And in like manner the will sometimes wills the end, and yet does not proceed to will the means.

The solution to the argument in the contrary sense is clear from what has been said above.[65] For the useful and the righteous are not species of good in an equal degree, but are as that which is for its own sake and that which is for the sake of something else: wherefore the act of the will can be directed to one and not to the other; but not conversely.

---

[65]A. 2 ad 2.

Summa Theologica

FIRST PART OF PART TWO
QUESTION 9
Of That Which Moves the Will

FIRST ARTICLE
Whether the Will Is Moved by the Intellect?

We proceed thus to the First Article:—

Objection 1. It would seem that the will is not moved by the intellect. For Augustine says on Ps. cxviii. 20: *My soul hath coveted to long for Thy justifications:*—*The intellect flies ahead, the desire follows sluggishly or not at all: we know what is good, but deeds delight us not.* But it would not be so, if the will were moved by the intellect: because movement of the movable results from motion of the mover. Therefore the intellect does not move the will.

Obj. 2. Further, the intellect in presenting the appetible object to the will, stands in relation to the will, as the imagination in representing the appetible object to the sensitive appetite. But the imagination, in presenting the appetible object, does not move the sensitive appetite: indeed sometimes our imagination affects us no more than what is set before us in a picture, and moves us not at all.[66] Therefore neither does the intellect move the will.

Obj. 3. Further, the same is not mover and moved in respect of the same thing. But the will moves the intellect; for we exercise the intellect when we will. Therefore the intellect does not move the will.

On the contrary, The Philosopher says that *the appetible object is a mover not moved, whereas the will is a mover moved.*[67]

I answer that, A thing requires to be moved by something in so far as it is in potentiality to several things; for that which is in potentiality needs to be reduced to act by something actual; and to do this is to move. Now a power of the soul is seen to be in potentiality to different things in two ways: first, with regard to acting and not acting; secondly, with regard to this or that action. Thus the sight sometimes sees actually, and sometimes sees not: and sometimes it sees white, and sometimes black. It needs

---

[66]*De An.* ii. 3.   [67]*De An.* iii. 10.

therefore a mover in two respects, viz., as to the exercise or use of the act, and as to the determination of the act. The first of these is on the part of the subject, which is sometimes acting, sometimes not acting: while the other is on the part of the object, by reason of which the act is specified.

The motion of the subject itself is due to some agent. And since every agent acts for an end, as was shown above,[68] the principle of this motion lies in the end. And hence it is that the art which is concerned with the end, by its command moves the art which is concerned with the means; just as the *art of sailing commands the art of shipbuilding*.[69] Now good in general, which has the nature of an end, is the object of the will. Consequently, in this respect, the will moves the other powers of the soul to their acts, for we make use of the other powers when we will. For the end and perfection of every other power, is included under the object of the will as some particular good: and always the art or power to which the universal end belongs, moves to their acts the arts or powers to which belong the particular ends included in the universal end. Thus the leader of an army, who intends the common good—*i.e.*, the order of the whole army—by his command moves one of the captains, who intends the order of one company.

On the other hand, the object moves, by determining the act, after the manner of a formal principle, whereby in natural things actions are specified, as heating by heat. Now the first formal principle is universal *being* and *truth*, which is the object of the intellect. And therefore by this kind of motion the intellect moves the will, as presenting its object to it.

Reply Obj. 1. The passage quoted proves, not that the intellect does not move, but that it does not move of necessity.

Reply Obj. 2. Just as the imagination of a form without estimation of fitness or harmfulness, does not move the sensitive appetite; so neither does the apprehension of the true without the aspect of goodness and desirability. Hence it is not the speculative intellect that moves, but the practical intellect.[70]

Reply Obj. 3. The will moves the intellect as to the exercise of its act; since even the true itself which is the perfection of the intellect, is included in the universal good, as a particular good. But as to the determination of the act, which the act derives from the object, the intellect moves the will; since the good itself is apprehended under a special aspect as contained in the universal true. It is therefore evident that the same is not mover and moved in the same respect.

---

[68] Q. 1, A. 2.   [69] *Phys.* ii. 2.   [70] *De An.* iii. 9.

SECOND ARTICLE
Whether the Will Is Moved by the Sensitive Appetite?

We proceed thus to the Second Article:—

Objection 1. It would seem that the will cannot be moved by the sensitive appetite. For *to move and to act is more excellent than to be passive*, as Augustine says.[71] But the sensitive appetite is less excellent than the will which is the intellectual appetite; just as sense is less excellent than intellect. Therefore the sensitive appetite does not move the will

Obj. 2. Further, no particular power can produce a universal effect. But the sensitive appetite is a particular power, because it follows the particular apprehension of sense. Therefore it cannot cause the movement of the will, which movement is universal, as following the universal apprehension of the intellect.

Obj. 3. Further, as is proved in *Phys.* viii. 5, the mover is not moved by that which it moves, in such a way that there be reciprocal motion. But the will moves the sensitive appetite, inasmuch as the sensitive appetite obeys the reason. Therefore the sensitive appetite does not move the will.

On the contrary, It is written: *Every man is tempted by his own concupiscence, being drawn away and allured.*[72] But man would not be drawn away by his concupiscence, unless his will were moved by the sensitive appetite, wherein concupiscence resides. Therefore the sensitive appetite moves the will.

I answer that, As stated above that which is apprehended as good and fitting, moves the will by way of object.[73] Now, that a thing appear to be good and fitting, happens from two causes: namely, from the condition, either of the thing proposed, or of the one to whom it is proposed. For fitness is spoken of by way of relation; hence it depends on both extremes. And hence it is that taste, according as it is variously disposed, takes to a thing in various ways, as being fitting or unfitting. Wherefore as the Philosopher says: *According as a man is, such does the end seem to him.*[74]

Now it is evident that according to a passion of the sensitive appetite man is changed to a certain disposition. Wherefore according as man is affected by a passion, something seems to him fitting, which does not seem so when he is not so affected: thus that seems good to a man when angered, which does not seem good when he is calm. And in this way, the sensitive appetite moves the will, on the part of the object.

Reply Obj. 1. Nothing hinders that which is better simply and in itself, from being less excellent in a certain respect. Accordingly the will is sim-

---

[71]*De Genesi ad Lit.* xii. 16. [72]James i. 14. [73]A. 1. [74]*Eth.* iii. 5.

ply more excellent than the sensitive appetite: but in respect of the man in whom a passion is predominant, in so far as he is subject to that passion, the sensitive appetite is more excellent.

Reply Obj. 2. Men's acts and choices are in reference to singulars. Wherefore from the very fact that the sensitive appetite is a particular power, it has great influence in disposing man so that something seems to him such or otherwise, in particular cases.

Reply Obj. 3. As the Philosopher says, the reason, in which resides the will, moves, by its command, the irascible and concupiscible powers, not, indeed, *by a despotic sovereignty,* as a slave is moved by his master, but by a *royal and politic sovereignty,* as free men are ruled by their governor, and can nevertheless act counter to his commands.[75] Hence both irascible and concupiscible can move counter to the will: and accordingly nothing hinders the will from being moved by them at times.

THIRD ARTICLE
Whether the Will Moves Itself?

We proceed thus to the Third Article:—

Objection 1. It would seem that the will does not move itself. For every mover, as such, is in act: whereas what is moved, is in potentiality; since *movement is the act of that which is in potentiality, as such.*[76] Now the same is not in potentiality and in act, in respect of the same. Therefore nothing moves itself. Neither, therefore, can the will move itself.

Obj. 2. Further, the movable is moved on the mover being present. But the will is always present to itself. If, therefore, it moved itself, it would always be moving itself, which is clearly false.

Obj. 3. Further, the will is moved by the intellect, as stated above.[77] If, therefore, the will move itself, it would follow that the same thing is at once moved immediately by two movers; which seems unreasonable. Therefore the will does not move itself.

On the contrary, The will is mistress of its own act, and to it belongs to will and not to will. But this would not be so, had it not the power to move itself to will. Therefore it moves itself.

I answer that, As stated above,[78] it belongs to the will to move the other powers, by reason of the end which is the will's object. Now, as stated above, the end is in things appetible, what the principle is in things intelligible.[79] But it is evident that the intellect, through its knowledge of the

---

[75] *Polit.* i. 2.   [76] Aristotle, *Phys.* iii. 1.   [77] A. 1.   [78] A. 1.   [79] Q. 8, A. 2.

principle, reduces itself from potentiality to act, as to its knowledge of the conclusions; and thus it moves itself. And, in like manner, the will, through its volition of the end, moves itself to will the means.

Reply Obj. 1. It is not in respect of the same that the will moves itself and is moved: wherefore neither is it in act and in potentiality in respect of the same. But forasmuch as it actually wills the end, it reduces itself from potentiality to act, in respect of the means, so as, in a word, to will them actually.

Reply Obj. 2. The power of the will is always actually present to itself; but the act of the will, whereby it wills an end, is not always in the will. But it is by this act that it moves itself. Accordingly it does not follow that it is always moving itself.

Reply Obj. 3. The will is moved by the intellect, otherwise than by itself. By the intellect it is moved on the part of the object: whereas it is moved by itself, as to the exercise of its act, in respect of the end.

FOURTH ARTICLE
Whether the Will Is Moved by an Exterior Principle?

We proceed thus to the Fourth Article:—

Objection 1. It would seem that the will is not moved by anything exterior. For the movement of the will is voluntary. But it is essential to the voluntary act that it be from an intrinsic principle, just as it is essential to the natural act. Therefore the movement of the will is not from anything exterior.

Obj. 2. Further, the will cannot suffer violence, as was shown above,[80] But the violent act is one *the principle of which is outside the agent.*[81] Therefore the will cannot be moved by anything exterior.

Obj. 3. Further, that which is sufficiently moved by one mover, needs not to be moved by another. But the will moves itself sufficiently. Therefore it is not moved by anything exterior.

On the contrary, The will is moved by the object, as stated above.[82] But the object of the will can be something exterior, offered to the sense. Therefore the will can be moved by something exterior.

I answer that, As far as the will is moved by the object, it is evident that it can be moved by something exterior. But in so far as it is moved in the exercise of its act, we must again hold it to be moved by some exterior principle.

---

[80]Q. 6, A. 4.   [81]Aristotle, *Ethic.* iii. 1.   [82]A. 1.

For everything that is at one time an agent actually, and at another time an agent in potentiality, needs to be moved by a mover. Now it is evident that the will begins to will something, whereas previously it did not will it. Therefore it must, of necessity, be moved by something to will it. And, indeed, it moves itself, as stated above, in so far as through willing the end it reduces itself to the act of willing the means.[83] Now it cannot do this without the aid of counsel: for when a man wills to be healed, he begins to reflect how this can be attained, and through this reflection he comes to the conclusion that he can be healed by a physician: and this he wills. But since he did not always actually will to have health, he must, of necessity, have begun, through something moving him, to will to be healed. And if the will moved itself to will this, it must, of necessity, have done this with the aid of counsel following some previous volition. But this process could not go on to infinity. Wherefore we must, of necessity, suppose that the will advanced to its first movement in virtue of the instigation of some exterior mover, as Aristotle concludes in a chapter of the *Eudemian Ethics*.[84]

Reply Obj. 1. It is essential to the voluntary act that its principle be within the agent: but it is not necessary that this inward principle be the first principle unmoved by another. Wherefore though the voluntary act has an inward proximate principle, nevertheless its first principle is from without. Thus, too, the first principle of the natural movement is from without, that, to wit, which moves nature.

Reply Obj. 2. For an act to be violent it is not enough that its principle be extrinsic, but we must add *without the concurrence of him that suffers violence*. This does not happen when the will is moved by an exterior principle: for it is the will that wills, though moved by another. But this movement would be violent, if it were counter to the movement of the will: which in the present case is impossible; since then the will would will and not will the same thing.

Reply Obj. 3. The will moves itself sufficiently in one respect, and in its own order, that is to say as proximate agent; but it cannot move itself in every respect, as we have shown. Wherefore it needs to be moved by another as first mover.

FIFTH ARTICLE
Whether the Will Is Moved by a Heavenly Body?

We proceed thus to the Fifth Article:—

---

[83]A. 3.   [84]vii. 14.

Objection 1. It would seem that the human will is moved by a heavenly body. For all various and multiform movements are reduced, as to their cause, to a uniform movement which is that of the heavens, as is proved in *Phys.* viii. 9. But human movements are various and multiform, since they begin to be, whereas previously they were not. Therefore they are reduced, as to their cause, to the movement of the heavens, which is uniform according to its nature.

Obj. 2. Further, according to Augustine *the lower bodies are moved by the higher.*[85] But the movements of the human body, which are caused by the will, could not be reduced to the movement of the heavens, as to their cause, unless the will too were moved by the heavens. Therefore the heavens move the human will.

Obj. 3. Further, by observing the heavenly bodies astrologers foretell the truth about future human acts, which are caused by the will. But this would not be so, if the heavenly bodies could not move man's will. Therefore the human will is moved by a heavenly body.

On the contrary, Damascene says that *the heavenly bodies are not the causes of our acts.*[86] But they would be, if the will, which is the principle of human acts, were moved by the heavenly bodies. Therefore the will is not moved by the heavenly bodies.

I answer that, It is evident that the will can be moved by the heavenly bodies in the same way as it is moved by its object; that is to say; in so far as exterior bodies, which move the will, through being offered to the senses, and also the organs themselves of the sensitive powers, are subject to the movements of the heavenly bodies.

But some have maintained that heavenly bodies have an influence on the human will, in the same way as some exterior agent moves the will, as to the exercise of its act.—But this is impossible. For the *will*, as stated in *De Anima* iii. 9, *is in the reason*. Now the reason is a power of the soul, not bound to a bodily organ: wherefore it follows that the will is a power absolutely incorporeal and immaterial. But it is evident that no body can act on what is incorporeal, but rather the reverse: because things incorporeal and immaterial have a power more formal and more universal than any corporeal things whatever. Therefore it is impossible for a heavenly body to act directly on the intellect or the will.—For this reason Aristotle ascribed to those who held that intellect differs not from sense, the theory that *such is the will of men, as is the day which the father of men and of gods*

---

[85]*De Trin.* iii. 4.   [86]*De Fide Ortho.* ii. 7.

bring on[87] (referring to Jupiter, by whom they understand the entire heavens).[88] For all the sensitive powers, since they are acts of bodily organs, can be moved accidentally, by the heavenly bodies—*i.e.*, through those bodies being moved, whose acts they are.

But since it has been stated that the intellectual appetite is moved,[89] in a fashion, by the sensitive appetite, the movements of the heavenly bodies have an indirect bearing on the will; in so far as the will happens to be moved by the passions of the sensitive appetite.

Reply Obj. 1. The multiform movements of the human will are reduced to some uniform cause, which, however, is above the intellect and will. This can be said, not of any body, but of some superior immaterial substance. Therefore there is no need for the movement of the will to be referred to the movement of the heavens, as to its cause.

Reply Obj. 2. The movements of the human body are reduced, as to their cause, to the movement of a heavenly body in so far as the disposition suitable to a particular movement, is somewhat due to the influence of heavenly bodies;—also, in so far as the sensitive appetite is stirred by the influence of heavenly bodies;—and again, in so far as exterior bodies are moved in accordance with the movement of heavenly bodies, at whose presence, the will begins to will or not to will something; for instance, when the body is chilled, we begin to wish to make the fire. But this movement of the will is on the part of the object offered from without: not on the part of an inward instigation.

Reply Obj. 3. As stated above the sensitive appetite is the act of a bodily organ.[90] Wherefore there is no reason why man should not be prone to anger or concupiscence, or some like passion, by reason of the influence of heavenly bodies, just as by reason of his natural complexion. But the majority of men are led by the passions, which the wise alone resist. Consequently, in the majority of cases predictions about human acts, gathered from the observation of heavenly bodies, are fulfilled. Nevertheless, as Ptolemy says, *the wise man governs the stars*[91]: which is as though to say that by resisting his passions, he opposes his will, which is free and nowise subject to the movement of the heavens, to such like effects of the heavenly bodies.

Or, as Augustine says: *We must confess that when the truth is foretold by astrologers, this is due to some most hidden inspiration, to which the human*

---

[87]*Odyssey* xviii. 135.   [88]*De An.* iii. 3.   [89]A. 2.   [90]Cf. P. I, Q. 84, AA. 6, 7.   [91]*Centiloquium* v.

mind is subject without knowing it. And since this is done in order to deceive man, it must be the work of the lying spirits.[92]

SIXTH ARTICLE

Whether the Will Is Moved by God Alone, as Exterior Principle?

We proceed thus to the Sixth Article:—

Objection 1. It would seem that the will is not moved by God alone as exterior principle. For it is natural that the inferior be moved by its superior: thus the lower bodies are moved by the heavenly bodies. But there is something which is higher than the will of man and below God, namely, the angel. Therefore man's will can be moved by an angel also, as exterior principle.

Obj. 2. Further, the act of the will follows the act of the intellect. But man's intellect is reduced to act, not by God alone, but also by the angel who enlightens it, as Dionysius says.[93] For the same reason, therefore, the will also is moved by an angel.

Obj. 3. Further, God is not cause of other than good things, according to Gen. i. 31: *God saw all the things that He had made, and they were very good.* If, therefore man's will were moved by God alone, it would never be moved to evil: and yet it is the will whereby *we sin and whereby we do right,* as Augustine says.[94]

On the contrary, It is written[95]: *It is God Who worketh in us*[96] *both to will and to accomplish.*

I answer that, The movement of the will is from within, as also is the movement of nature. Now although it is possible for something to move a natural thing, without being the cause of the thing moved, yet that alone, which is in some way the cause of a thing's nature, can cause a natural movement in that thing. For a stone is moved upwards by a man, who is not the cause of the stone's nature, but this movement is not natural to the stone; but the natural movement of the stone is caused by no other than the cause of its nature. Wherefore it is said in *Phys.* viii. 4, that the generator moves locally heavy and light things. Accordingly man endowed with a will is sometimes moved by something that is not his cause; but that his voluntary movement be from an exterior principle that is not the cause of his will, is impossible.

Now the cause of the will can be none other than God. And this is evident for two reasons. First, because the will is a power of the rational soul,

---

[92]*De Genesi ad Lit.* ii. 17.   [93]*De Cael. Hier.* iv.   [94]*Retract.* i. 9.
[95]Phil. ii. 13.   [96]Vulg.,—*you.*

which is caused by God alone, by creation, as was stated above in the First Part.[97]—Secondly, it is evident from the fact that the will is ordained to the universal good. Wherefore nothing else can be the cause of the will, except God Himself, Who is the universal good: while every other good is good by participation, and is some particular good: and a particular cause does not give universal inclination. Hence neither can primary matter, which is potentiality to all forms, be created by some particular agent.

Reply Obj 1. An angel is not above man in such a way as to be the cause of his will, as the heavenly bodies are the causes of natural forms, from which result in the natural movements of natural bodies.

Reply Obj. 2. Man's intellect is moved by an angel, on the part of the object, which by the power of the angelic light is proposed to man's knowledge. And in this way the will also can be moved by a creature from without, as stated above.[98]

Reply Obj. 3. God moves man's will, as the Universal Mover, to the universal object of the will, which is good. And without this universal motion, man cannot will anything. But man determines himself by his reason to will this or that, which is true or apparent good.—Nevertheless, sometimes God moves some specially to the willing of something determinate, which is good; as in the case of those whom He moves by grace, as we shall state later on.[99]

---

[97]Q. 90, A. 2.   [98]A. 4.   [99]Q. 109, A. 2.

FIRST PART OF PART TWO
QUESTION 10
Of the Manner in Which the Will Is Moved

FIRST ARTICLE
Whether the Will Is Moved to Anything Naturally?

We proceed thus to the First Article.—

Objection 1. It would seem that the will is not moved to anything naturally. For the natural agent is condivided with the voluntary agent, as stated at the beginning of *Phys.* ii. 1. Therefore the will is not moved to anything naturally.

Obj. 2. Further, that which is natural is in a thing always: as *being hot* is in fire. But no movement is always in the will. Therefore no movement is natural to the will.

Obj. 3. Further, nature is determinate to one thing: whereas the will is referred to opposites. Therefore the will wills nothing naturally.

On the contrary, The movement of the will follows the movement of the intellect. But the intellect understands some things naturally. Therefore the will, too, wills some things naturally.

I answer that, As Boethius says[100] and the Philosopher also[101] the word *nature* is used in a manifold sense. For sometimes it stands for the intrinsic principle in movable things. In this sense nature is either matter or the material form, as stated in *Phys.* ii. 1.—In another sense nature stands for any substance, or even for any being. And in this sense, that is said to be natural to a thing which befits it in respect of its substance. And this is that which of itself is in a thing. Now all things that do not of themselves belong to the thing which they are, are reduced to something which belongs of itself to that thing, as to their principle. Wherefore, taking nature in this sense, it is necessary that the principle of whatever belongs to a thing, be a natural principle. This is evident in regard to the intellect: for the principles of the intellectual knowledge are naturally known. In like manner the principle of voluntary movements must be something naturally willed.

---

[100]*De Duabus Nat.*   [101]*Metaph.* v. 4.

Now this is good in general, to which the will tends naturally, as does each power to its object; and again it is the last end, which stands in the same relation to things appetible, as the first principles of demonstrations to things intelligible: and, speaking generally, it is all those things which belong to the willer according to his nature. For it is not only things pertaining to the will that the will desires, but also that which pertains to each power, and to the entire man. Wherefore man wills naturally not only the object of the will, but also other things that are appropriate to the other powers; such as the knowledge of truth, which befits the intellect; and to be and to live and other like things which regard the natural well-being; all of which are included in the object of the will, as so many particular goods.

Reply Obj. 1. The will is distinguished from nature as one kind of cause from another; for some things happen naturally and some are done voluntarily. There is, however, another manner of causing that is proper to the will, which is mistress of its act, besides the manner proper to nature, which is determinate to one thing. But since the will is founded on some nature, it is necessary that the movement proper to nature be shared by the will, to some extent: just as what belongs to a previous cause is shared by a subsequent cause. Because in every thing, being itself, which is from nature, precedes volition, which is from the will. And hence it is that the will wills something naturally.

Reply Obj. 2. In the case of natural things, that which is natural, as a result of the form only, is always in them actually, as heat is in fire. But that which is natural as a result of matter, is not always in them actually, but sometimes only in potentiality: because form is act, whereas matter is potentiality. Now movement is *the act of that which is in potentiality*.[102] Wherefore that which belongs to, or results from, movement, in regard to natural things, is not always in them. Thus fire does not always move upwards, but only when it is outside its own place.[103] And in like manner it is not necessary that the will (which is reduced from potentiality to act, when it wills something), should always be in the act of volition; but only when it is in a certain determinate disposition. But God's will, which is pure act, is always in the act of volition.

Reply Obj. 3. To every nature there is one thing corresponding, proportionate, however, to that nature. For to nature considered as a genus, there corresponds something one generically; and to nature as species there corresponds something one specifically; and to the individualized

---

[102]Aristotle, *Phys*. iii. 1.   [103]The Aristotelian theory was that fire's proper place is the fiery heaven, *i.e.*, the *Empyrean*.

nature there corresponds some one individual. Since, therefore, the will is an immaterial power like the intellect, some one general thing corresponds to it, naturally which is the good; just as to the intellect there corresponds some one general thing, which is the true, or being, or *what a thing is*. And under good in general are included many particular goods, to none of which is the will determined.

SECOND ARTICLE
Whether the Will Is Moved, of Necessity, by Its Object?

We proceed thus to the Second Article:—

Objection 1. It seems that the will is moved of necessity, by its object. For the object of the will is compared to the will as mover to movable, as stated in *De Anima* iii. 10. But a mover, if it be sufficient, moves the movable of necessity. Therefore the will can be moved of necessity by its object.

Obj. 2. Further, just as the will is an immaterial power, so is the intellect: and both powers are ordained to a universal object, as stated above.[104] But the intellect is moved, of necessity, by its object: therefore the will also, by its object.

Obj. 3. Further, whatever one wills, is either the end, or something ordained to an end. But, seemingly, one wills an end necessarily: because it is like the principle in speculative matters, to which principle one assents of necessity. Now the end is the reason for willing the means; and so it seems that we will the means also necessarily. Therefore the will is moved of necessity by its object.

On the contrary, The rational powers, according to the Philosopher are directed to opposites.[105] But the will is a rational power, since it is in the reason, as stated in *De Anima* iii. 9. Therefore the will is directed to opposites. Therefore it is not moved, of necessity, to either of the opposites.

I answer that, The will is moved in two ways: first, as to the exercise of its act; secondly, as to the specification of its act, derived from the object. As to the first way, no object moves the will necessarily, for no matter what the object be, it is in man's power not to think of it, and consequently not to will it actually. But as to the second manner of motion, the will is moved by one object necessarily, by another not. For in the movement of a power by its object, we must consider under what aspect the object moves the power. For the visible moves the sight, under the aspect of color actually visible. Wherefore if color be offered to the sight, it

---

[104]A. 1 ad 3.   [105]*Metaph.* ix. 2.

moves the sight necessarily: unless one turns one's eyes away; which belongs to the exercise of the act. But if the sight were confronted with something not in all respects colored actually, but only so in some respects, and in other respects not, the sight would not of necessity see such an object: for it might look at that part of the object which is not actually colored, and thus it would not see it. Now just as the actually colored is the object of sight, so is good the object of the will. Wherefore if the will be offered an object which is good universally and from every point of view, the will tends to it of necessity, if it wills anything at all; since it cannot will the opposite. If, on the other hand, the will is offered an object that is not good from every point of view, it will not tend to it of necessity. And since lack of any good whatever, is a non-good, consequently, that good alone which is perfect and lacking in nothing, is such a good that the will cannot not-will it: and this is Happiness. Whereas any other particular goods, in so far as they are lacking in some good, can be regarded as non-goods: and from this point of view, they can be set aside or approved by the will, which can tend to one and the same thing from various points of view.

Reply Obj 1. The sufficient mover of a power is none but that object that in every respect presents the aspect of the mover of that power. If, on the other hand, it is lacking in any respect, it will not move of necessity, as stated above.

Reply Obj. 2. The intellect is moved, of necessity, by an object, which is such as to be always and necessarily true: but not by that which may be either true or false—viz., by that which is contingent: as we have said of the good.

Reply Obj. 3. The last end moves the will necessarily, because it is the perfect good. In like manner whatever is ordained to that end, and without which the end cannot be attained, such as *to be* and *to live*, and the like. But other things without which the end can be gained, are not necessarily willed by one who wills the end: just as he who assents to the principle, does not necessarily assent to the conclusions, without which the principles can still be true.

THIRD ARTICLE
Whether the Will Is Moved, of Necessity, by the Lower Appetite?

We proceed thus to the Third Article:—

Objection 1. It would seem that the will is moved of necessity by a passion of the lower appetite. For the Apostle says: *The good which I will I do not; but the evil which I will not, that I do:* and this is said by reason of concupiscence, which is a passion.[106] Therefore the will is moved of necessity by a passion.

Obj. 2. Further, as stated in *Ethic.* iii. 5, *according as a man is, such does the end seem to him.* But it is not in man's power to cast aside a passion at once. Therefore it is not in man's power not to will that to which the passion inclines him.

Obj. 3. Further, a universal cause is not applied to a particular effect, except by means of a particular cause: wherefore the universal reason does not move save by means of a particular estimation, as stated in *De Anima* iii. 11. But as the universal reason is to the particular estimation, so is the will to the sensitive appetite. Therefore the will is not moved to will something particular, except through the sensitive appetite. Therefore, if the sensitive appetite happen to be disposed to something, by reason of a passion, the will cannot be moved in a contrary sense.

On the contrary, It is written[107]: *Thy lust[108] shall be under thee, and thou shalt have dominion over it.* Therefore man's will is not moved of necessity by the lower appetite.

I answer that, As stated above, the passion of the sensitive appetite moves the will, in so far as the will is moved by its object[109]: inasmuch as, to wit, man through being disposed in such and such a way by a passion, judges something to be fitting and good, which he would not judge thus were it not for the passion. Now this influence of a passion on man occurs in two ways. First, so that his reason is wholly bound, so that he has not the use of reason: as happens in those who through a violent access of anger or concupiscence become furious or insane, just as they may from some other bodily disorder; since such like passions do not take place without some change in the body. And of such the same is to be said as of irrational animals, which follow, of necessity, the impulse of their passions: for in them there is neither movement of reason, nor, consequently, of will.

Sometimes, however, the reason is not entirely engrossed by the passion, so that the judgment of reason retains, to a certain extent, its freedom: and thus the movement of the will remains in a certain degree. Accordingly in so far as the reason remains free, and not subject to the passion, the will's movement, which also remains, does not tend of necessity to that whereto the passion inclines it. Consequently, either there is no movement of the will in that man, and the passion alone holds its sway: or if there be a movement of the will, it does not necessarily follow the passion.

---

[106]Rom. vii. 19.   [107]Gen. iv. 7.   [108]Vulg.,—*The lust thereof.*
[109]Q. 9, A. 2.

Reply Obj. 1. Although the will cannot prevent the movement of concupiscence from arising, of which the Apostle says: *The evil which I will not, that I do—i.e., I desire*; yet it is in the power of the will not to will to desire, or not to consent to concupiscence. And thus it does not necessarily follow the movement of concupiscence.

Reply Obj. 2. Since there is in man a twofold nature, intellectual and sensitive; sometimes man is such and such uniformly in respect of his whole soul: either because the sensitive part is wholly subject to his reason, as in the virtuous; or because reason is entirely engrossed by passion, as in a madman. But sometimes, although reason is clouded by passion, yet something of the reason remains free. And in respect of this, man can either repel the passion entirely, or at least hold himself in check so as not to be led away by the passion. For when thus disposed, since man is variously disposed according to the various parts of the soul, a thing appears to him otherwise according to his reason, than it does according to a passion.

Reply Obj. 3. The will is moved not only by the universal good apprehended by the reason, but also by good apprehended by sense. Wherefore he can be moved to some particular good independently of a passion of the sensitive appetite. For we will and do many things without passion, and through choice alone; as is most evident in those cases wherein reason resists passion.

FOURTH ARTICLE
Whether the Will Is Moved of Necessity by the Exterior Mover Which Is God?

We proceed thus to the Fourth Article:—

Objection 1. It would seem that the will is moved of necessity by God. For every agent that cannot be resisted moves of necessity. But God cannot be resisted, because His power is infinite; wherefore it is written: *Who resisteth His will?*[110] Therefore God moves the will of necessity.

Obj. 2. Further, the will is moved of necessity to whatever it wills naturally, as stated above.[111] But *whatever God does in a thing is natural to it*, as Augustine says.[112] Therefore the will wills of necessity everything to which God moves it.

Obj. 3. Further, a thing is possible, if nothing impossible follows from its being supposed. But something impossible follows from the supposition that the will does not will that to which God moves it: because in that

---

[110]Rom. ix. 19.   [111]A. 2 ad 3.   [112]*Contra Faust.* xxvi. 3.

case God's operation would be ineffectual. Therefore it is not possible for the will not to will that to which God moves it. Therefore it wills it of necessity.

On the contrary, It is written: *God made man from the beginning, and left him in the hand of his own counsel.*[113] Therefore He does not of necessity move man's will.

I answer that, As Dionysius says *it belongs to Divine providence, not to destroy but to preserve the nature of things.*[114] Wherefore it moves all things in accordance with their conditions; so that from necessary causes through the Divine motion, effects follow of necessity; but from contingent causes, effects follow contingently. Since, therefore, the will is an active principle, not determinate to one thing, but having an indifferent relation to many things, God so moves it, that He does not determine it of necessity to one thing, but its movement remains contingent and not necessary, except in those things to which it is moved naturally.

Reply Obj. 1. The Divine will extends not only to the doing of something by the thing which He moves, but also to its being done in a way which is fitting to the nature of that thing. And therefore it would be more repugnant to the Divine motion, for the will to be moved of necessity, which is not fitting to its nature; than for it to be moved freely, which is becoming to its nature.

Reply Obj. 2. That is natural to a thing, which God so works in it that it may be natural to it: for thus is something becoming to a thing, according as God wishes it to be becoming. Now He does not wish that whatever He works in things should be natural to them, for instance, that the dead should rise again. But this He does wish to be natural to each thing,—that it be subject to the Divine power.

Reply Obj. 3. If God moves the will to anything, it is incompatible with this supposition, that the will be not moved thereto. But it is not impossible simply. Consequently it does not follow that the will is moved by God necessarily.

---

[113]Ecclus. xv. 14.   [114]*De Div. Nom.* iv.

8

THE PASSIONS OF THE SOUL

Summa Theologica

PART ONE
QUESTION 80
The Appetitive Powers in General

Next we consider the appetitive powers, concerning which there are four heads of consideration: first, the appetitive powers in general; second, sensuality[1]; third, the will[2]; fourth, free choice.[3]

FIRST ARTICLE
Whether the Appetite Is a Special Power of the Soul?

We proceed thus to the First Article:—

Objection 1. It would seem that the appetite is not a special power of the soul. For no power of the soul is to be assigned for those things which are common to animate and to inanimate beings. But appetite is common to animate and inanimate beings, since *all desire good*, as the Philosopher says.[4] Therefore the appetite is not a special power of the soul.

Obj. 2. Further, powers are differentiated by their objects. But what we desire is the same as what we know. Therefore the appetitive power is not distinct from the apprehensive power.

Obj. 3. Further, the common is not divided from the proper. But each power of the soul desires some particular desirable thing—namely, its own suitable object. Therefore, with regard to the object which is the desirable in general, we should not assign some particular power distinct from the others, called the appetitive power.

On the contrary, The Philosopher distinguishes the appetitive from the

---

Selections on pp. 231–240 reprinted from *Basic Writings of Saint Thomas Aquinas*, edited and annotated by Anton C. Pegis (Indianapolis: Hackett Publishing Company, 1997). Reprinted by permission of the publisher.

[1]Q. 81.   [2]Q. 82.   [3]Q. 83.   [4]Aristotle, *Eth.*, I, 1 (1092a 3).

other powers.[5] Damascene also distinguishes the appetitive from the cognitive powers.[6]

I answer that, It is necessary to assign an appetitive power to the soul. To make this evident, we must observe that some inclination follows every form: for example, fire, by its form, is inclined to rise, and to generate its like. Now, the form is found to have a more perfect existence in those things which participate in knowledge than in those which lack knowledge. For in those which lack knowledge, the form is found to determine each thing only to its own being—that is, to the being which is natural to each. Now this natural form is followed by a natural inclination, which is called the natural appetite. But in those things which have knowledge, each one is determined to its own natural being by its natural form, but in such a manner that it is nevertheless receptive of the species of other things. For example, sense receives the species of all sensible things, and the intellect, of all intelligible things; so that the soul of man is, in a way, all things by sense and intellect. In this way, those beings that have knowledge approach, in a way, to a likeness to God, *in Whom all things pre-exist*, as Dionysius says.[7]

Therefore, just as in those beings that have knowledge forms exist in a higher manner and above the manner of natural forms, so there must be in them an inclination surpassing the natural inclination, which is called the natural appetite. And this superior inclination belongs to the appetitive power of the soul, through which the animal is able to desire what it apprehends, and not only that to which it is inclined by its natural form. And so it is necessary to assign an appetitive power to the soul.

Reply Obj. 1. Appetite is found in things which have knowledge, above the common manner in which it is found in all things, as we have said above. Therefore it is necessary to assign to the soul a particular power.

Reply Obj. 2. What is apprehended and what is desired are the same in reality, but differ in aspect; for a thing is apprehended as something sensible or intelligible, whereas it is desired as suitable or good. Now, it is diversity of aspect in the objects, and not material diversity, which demands a diversity of powers.

Reply Obj. 3. Each power of the soul is a form or nature, and has a natural inclination to something. Hence each power desires, by natural appetite, that object which is suitable to itself. Above this natural appetite is the animal appetite, which follows the apprehension, and by which something

---

[5]*De An.*, II, 3 (414a 31); cf. *op. cit.*, III, 10 (433a 9). [6]*De Fide Orth.*, II, 22 (PG 94, 941). [7]*De Div. Nom.*, V, 5 (PG 3, 820).

is desired, not as suitable to this or that power (such as sight for seeing, or sound for hearing), but as suitable absolutely to the animal.

SECOND ARTICLE

**Whether the Sensitive and Intellectual
Appetites Are Distinct Powers?**

We proceed thus to the Second Article:—

Objection 1. It would seem that the sensitive and intellectual appetites are not distinct powers. For powers are not differentiated by accidental differences, as we have seen above.[8] But it is accidental to the appetible object whether it be apprehended by the sense or by the intellect. Therefore the sensitive and intellectual appetites are not distinct powers.

Obj. 2. Further, intellectual knowledge is of universals, and is thereby distinguished from sensitive knowledge, which is of individuals. But there is no place for this distinction in the appetitive part. For since the appetite is a movement of the soul to individual things, every act of the appetite seems to be towards individual things. Therefore the intellectual appetite is not distinguished from the sensitive.

Obj. 3. Further, just as under the apprehensive power the appetitive is subordinate as a lower power, so also is the motive power. But the motive power which in man follows the intellect is not distinct from the motive power which in animals follows sense. Therefore, for a like reason, neither is there distinction in the appetitive part.

On the contrary, The Philosopher distinguishes a double appetite, and says that the higher appetite moves the lower.[9]

I answer that, We must needs say that the intellectual appetite is a distinct power from the sensitive appetite. For the appetitive power is a passive power, which is naturally moved by the thing apprehended. Therefore *the apprehended appetible is a mover which is not moved, while the appetite is a moved mover,* as the Philosopher says in *De Anima* iii. and in *Metaph.* xii.[10] Now things passive and movable are differentiated according to the distinction of the corresponding active and motive principles, for the motive must be proportionate to the movable, and the active to the passive. Indeed, the passive power itself has its very nature from its relation to its active principle. Therefore, since what is apprehended by the intellect and what is apprehended by sense are generically different, consequently, the intellectual appetite is distinct from the sensitive.

---

[8]Q. 77, a. 3.   [9]*De An.*, III, 9 (432b 5); 10 (433a 23); 11 (434a 12).   [10]*Op. cit.*, III, 10 (433b 16); *Metaph.*, XI, 7 (1072a 26).

Reply Obj. 1. It is not accidental to the thing desired to be apprehended by the sense or the intellect. On the contrary, this belongs to it by its nature, for the appetible does not move the appetite except as it is apprehended. Hence differences in the thing apprehended are of themselves differences in the appetible. And so the appetitive powers are distinguished according to the distinction of the things apprehended as according to their proper objects.

Reply Obj. 2. The intellectual appetite, though it tends to individual things which exist outside the soul, yet it tends to them as standing under the universal; as when it desires something because it is good. Therefore the Philosopher says that hatred can be of a universal, as when *we hate every kind of thief*.[11] In the same way, by the intellectual appetite we may desire the immaterial good, which is not apprehended by sense, such as knowledge, virtue and the like.

Reply Obj. 3. As the Philosopher says, a universal opinion does not move except by means of a particular opinion[12]; and in like manner the higher appetite moves by means of the lower. Therefore, there are not two distinct motive powers following the intellect and the sense.

---

[11]*Rhetor.*, II, 4 (1382a 5).   [12]Aristotle, *De An.*, III, 11 (434a 16).

Summa Theologica

PART ONE

QUESTION 81

The Power of Sensuality

FIRST ARTICLE
Whether Sensuality Is Only Appetitive?

We proceed thus to the First Article:—

Objection 1. It would seem that sensuality is not only appetitive, but also cognitive. For Augustine says that *the sensual movement of the soul which is directed to the bodily senses is common to us and beasts.*[13] But the bodily senses belong to the apprehensive powers. Therefore sensuality is a cognitive power.

Obj. 2. Further, things which come under one division seem to be of one genus. But Augustine divides sensuality against the higher and lower reason, which belong to knowledge.[14] Therefore sensuality also is apprehensive.

Obj. 3. Further, in man's temptations sensuality stands in the place of the *serpent.* But in the temptation of our first parents, the serpent presented himself as one giving information and proposing sin, which belong to the cognitive power. Therefore sensuality is a cognitive power.

On the contrary, Sensuality is defined as *the appetite of things belonging to the body.*[15]

I answer that, The name *sensuality* seems to be taken from the sensual movement, of which Augustine speaks,[16] just as the name of a power is taken from its act, for instance, sight from seeing. Now the sensual movement is an appetite following sensible apprehension. For the act of the apprehensive power is not so properly called a movement as the act of the appetite; since the operation of the apprehensive power is completed in the very fact that the thing apprehended is in the one that apprehends, while the operation of the appetitive power is completed in the fact that he who desires is borne towards the desirable thing. Hence it is that the operation of the apprehensive power is likened to rest; whereas the operation of the appetitive power is rather likened to movement. Therefore by sen-

---

[13]*De Trin.,* XII, 12 (PL 42, 1007).   [14]*Ibid.*   [15]Cf. Peter Lombard, *Sent.,* II, xxiv, 4 (I, 421).   [16]*De Trin.,* XII, 12; 13 (PL 42, 1007; 1009).

sual movement we understand the operation of the appetitive power. Thus, sensuality is the name of the sensitive appetite.

Reply Obj. 1. By saying that the sensual movement of the soul is directed to the bodily senses, Augustine does not give us to understand that the bodily senses are included in sensuality, but rather that the movement of sensuality is a certain inclination to the bodily senses, since we desire things which are apprehended through the bodily senses. And thus the bodily senses pertain to sensuality as a sort of gateway.

Reply Obj. 2. Sensuality is divided against higher and lower reason, as having in common with them the act of movement; for the apprehensive power, to which belong the higher and lower reason, is a motive power; as is appetite, to which sensuality pertains.

Reply Obj. 3. The serpent not only showed and proposed sin, but also incited to the commission of sin. And in this, sensuality is signified by the serpent.

SECOND ARTICLE
Whether the Sensitive Appetite Is Divided into the Irascible and Concupiscible as Distinct Powers?

We proceed thus to the Second Article:—

Objection 1. It would seem that the sensitive appetite is not divided into the irascible and concupiscible as distinct powers. For the same power of the soul regards both sides of a contrariety, as sight regards both black and white, according to the Philosopher.[17] But suitable and harmful are contraries. Since, then, the concupiscible power regards what is suitable, while the irascible is concerned with what is harmful, it seems that irascible and concupiscible are the same power in the soul.

Obj. 2. Further, the sensitive appetite regards only what is suitable according to the senses. But such is the object of the concupiscible power. Therefore there is no sensitive appetite differing from the concupiscible.

Obj. 3. Further, hatred is in the irascible part, for Jerome says on *Matt.* xiii. 33: *We ought to have the hatred of vice in the irascible power.*[18] But hatred is contrary to love, and is in the concupiscible part. Therefore the concupiscible and irascible are the same powers.

On the contrary, Gregory of Nyssa and Damascene assign two parts to the sensitive appetite, the irascible and the concupiscible.[19]

---

[17]Aristotle, *De An.*, II, 11 (422b 23). [18]*In Matt.*, I, super XIII, 33 (PL 26, 94). [19]Cf. Nemesius, *De Nat. Hom.*, XVI; XVI; XVII (PL 40, 672; 676); Damascene, *De Fide Orth.*, II, 12 (PG 94, 928).

I answer that, The sensitive appetite is one generic power, and is called sensuality; but it is divided into two powers, which are species of the sensitive appetite—the irascible and the concupiscible. In order to make this clear, we must observe that in natural corruptible things there is needed an inclination not only to the acquisition of what is suitable and to the avoiding of what is harmful, but also to resistance against corruptive and contrary forces which are a hindrance to the acquisition of what is suitable, and are productive of harm. For example, fire has a natural inclination, not only to rise from a lower place, which is unsuitable to it, towards a higher place, which is suitable, but also to resist whatever destroys or hinders its action. Therefore, since the sensitive appetite is an inclination following sensitive apprehension (just as natural appetite is an inclination following the natural form), there must needs be in the sensitive part two appetitive powers:—one, through which the soul is inclined absolutely to seek what is suitable, according to the senses, and to fly from what is hurtful, and this is called the *concupiscible*; and another, whereby an animal resists the attacks that hinder what is suitable, and inflict harm, and this is called the *irascible*. Whence we say that its object is something arduous, because its tendency is to overcome and rise above obstacles.

Now these two inclinations are not to be reduced to one principle. For sometimes the soul busies itself with unpleasant things, against the inclination of the concupiscible appetite, in order that, following the impulse of the irascible appetite, it may fight against obstacles. And so even the passions of the irascible appetite counteract the passions of the concupiscible appetite; since concupiscence, on being roused, diminishes anger, and anger, being roused, very often diminishes concupiscence. This is clear also from the fact that the irascible is, as it were, the champion and defender of the concupiscible, when it rises up against what hinders the acquisition of the suitable things which the concupiscible desires, or against what inflicts harm, from which the concupiscible flies. And for this reason all the passions of the irascible appetite rise from the passions of the concupiscible appetite and terminate in them. For instance, anger rises from sadness, and, having wrought vengeance, terminates in joy. For this reason also the quarrels of animals are about things concupiscible—namely, food and sex, as the Philosopher says.[20]

Reply Obj. 1. The concupiscible power regards both what is suitable and what is unsuitable. But the object of the irascible power is to resist the onslaught of the unsuitable.

---

[20] Aristotle, *Hist. Anim.*, VIII, 1 (589a 2).

Reply Obj. 2. Just as in the apprehensive powers of the sensitive part there is an estimative power, which perceives those things which do not impress the senses, as we have said above,[21] so also in the sensitive appetite there is an appetitive power which regards something as suitable, not because it pleases the senses, but because it is useful to the animal for self-defense. And this is the irascible power.

Reply Obj. 3. Hatred belongs absolutely to the concupiscible appetite, but by reason of the strife which arises from hatred it may belong to the irascible appetite.

THIRD ARTICLE
Whether the Irascible and Concupiscible Appetites Obey Reason?

We proceed thus to the Third Article:—

Objection 1. It would seem that the irascible and concupiscible appetites do not obey reason. For irascible and concupiscible are parts of sensuality. But sensuality does not obey reason; which is why it is signified by the serpent, as Augustine says.[22] Therefore the irascible and concupiscible appetites do not obey reason.

Obj. 2. Further, what obeys a certain thing does not resist it. But the irascible and concupiscible appetites resist reason, according to the Apostle (*Rom.* vii. 23): *I see another law in my members fighting against the law of my mind.* Therefore the irascible and concupiscible appetites do not obey reason.

Obj. 3. Further, as the appetitive power is inferior to the rational part of the soul, so also is the sensitive power. But the sensitive part of the soul does not obey reason, for we neither hear nor see just when we wish. Therefore, in like manner, neither do the powers of the sensitive appetite, the irascible and concupiscible, obey reason.

On the contrary, Damascene says that *the part of the soul which is obedient and amenable to reason is divided into concupiscence and anger.*[23]

I answer that, In two ways do the irascible and concupiscible powers obey the higher part, in which are the intellect or reason, and the will: first, as to the reason, and secondly, as to the will. They obey the reason in their own acts, because in other animals the sensitive appetite is naturally moved by the estimative power; for instance, a sheep, esteeming the wolf as an enemy, is afraid. In man the estimative power, as we have said above, is replaced by the cogitative power, which is called by some *the particular*

---

[21]Q. 78, a. 2.   [22]*De Trin.*, XII, 12; 13 (PL 42, 1007; 1009).   [23]*De Fide Orth.*, II, 12 (PG 94, 928).

reason, because it compares individual intentions.[24] Hence, in man the sensitive appetite is naturally moved by this particular reason. But this same particular reason is naturally guided and moved according to the universal reason; and that is why in syllogisms particular conclusions are drawn from universal propositions. Therefore it is clear that the universal reason directs the sensitive appetite, which is divided into concupiscible and irascible, and that this appetite obeys it. But because to draw particular conclusions from universal principles is not the work of the intellect, as such, but of the reason, hence it is that the irascible and concupiscible are said to obey the reason rather than to obey the intellect. Anyone can experience this in himself; for by applying certain universal considerations, anger or fear or the like may be lessened or increased.

To the will also is the sensitive appetite subject in execution, which is accomplished by the motive power. For in other animals movement follows at once the concupiscible and irascible appetites. For instance, the sheep, fearing the wolf, flies at once, because it has no superior counteracting appetite. On the contrary, man is not moved at once according to the irascible and concupiscible appetites; but he awaits the command of the will, which is the superior appetite. For wherever there is order among a number of motive powers, the second moves only by virtue of the first; and so the lower appetite is not sufficient to cause movement, unless the higher appetite consents. And this is what the Philosopher says, namely, that *the higher appetite moves the lower appetite, as the higher sphere moves the lower.*[25] In this way, therefore, the irascible and concupiscible are subject to reason.

Reply Obj. 1. Sensuality is signified by the serpent in what is proper to it as a sensitive power. But the irascible and concupiscible powers denominate the sensitive appetite rather on the part of the act, to which they are led by the reason, as we have said.

Reply Obj. 2. As the Philosopher says: *We observe in an animal a despotic and a politic principle; for the soul dominates the body by a despotic rule, but the intellect dominates the appetite by a politic and royal rule.*[26] For that rule is called despotic whereby a man rules his slaves, who have not the means to resist in any way the orders of the one that commands them, since they have nothing of their own. But that rule is called politic and royal by which a man rules over free subjects, who, though subject to the government of the ruler, have nevertheless something of their own, by reason of which they can resist the orders of him who commands. And so, the soul

---

[24]Q. 78, a. 4.   [25]*De An.*, III, 11 (434a 12).   [26]*Polit.*, I, 2 (1254b 2).

is said to rule the body by a despotic rule, because the members of the body cannot in any way resist the sway of the soul, but at the soul's command both hand and foot, and whatever member is naturally moved by voluntary movement, are at once moved. But the intellect or reason is said to govern the irascible and concupiscible by a politic rule because the sensitive appetite has something of its own, by virtue whereof it can resist the commands of reason. For the sensitive appetite is naturally moved, not only by the estimative power in other animals, and in man by the cogitative power which the universal reason guides, but also by the imagination and the sense. Whence it is that we experience that the irascible and concupiscible powers do resist reason, inasmuch as we sense or imagine something pleasant, which reason forbids, or unpleasant, which reason commands. And so from the fact that the irascible and concupiscible resist reason in something, we must not conclude that they do not obey it.

Reply Obj. 3. The exterior senses require for their acts exterior sensible things by which to be immuted, whose presence does not lie in the power of the reason. But the interior powers, both appetitive and apprehensive, do not require exterior things. Therefore they are subject to the command of reason, which can not only incite or modify the affections of the appetitive power, but can also form the phantasms of the imagination.

Summa Theologica

FIRST PART OF PART TWO
QUESTION 22
Of the Subject of the Soul's Passions

FIRST ARTICLE
Whether Any Passion Is in the Soul?

We proceed thus to the First Article:—

Objection 1. It would seem that there is no passion in the soul. Because passivity belong to matter. But the soul is not composed of matter and form, as stated in the First Part.[27] Therefore there is no passion in the soul.

Obj. 2. Further, passion is movement, as is stated in *Phys.* iii. 3. But the soul is not moved, as is proved in *De Anima* i. 3. Therefore passion is not in the soul.

Obj. 3. Further, passion is the road to corruption; since *every passion, when increased, alters the substance*, as is stated in *Topic.* vi. 6. But the soul is incorruptible. Therefore no passion is in the soul.

On the contrary, The Apostle says[28]: *When we were in the flesh, the passions of sins which were by the law, did the work in our members.* Now sins are, properly speaking, in the soul. Therefore passions also, which are described as being *of sins,* are in the soul.

I answer that, The word *passive* is used in three ways. First, in a general way, according as whatever receives something is passive, although nothing is taken from it: thus we may say that the air is passive when it is lit up. But this is to be perfected rather than to be passive. Secondly, the word *passive* is employed in its proper sense, when something is received, while something else is taken away: and this happens in two ways. For sometimes that which is lost is unsuitable to the thing: thus when an animal's body is healed, it is said to be passive, because it receives health, and loses sickness.—At other times the contrary occurs:

Selections on pp. 241–267 reprinted from St. Thomas Aquinas, *Summa Theologica*, translated by the Fathers of the English Dominican Province (New York: Benzinger Bros., 1948).

[27]Q. 75, A. 5.   [28]Rom. vii. 5.

thus to ail is to be passive; because the ailment is received and health is lost. And here we have passion in its most proper acceptation. For a thing is said to be passive from its being drawn to the agent: and when a thing recedes from what is suitable to it, then especially does it appear to be drawn to something else. Moreover in *De Generat.* i. 3, it is stated that when a more excellent thing is generated from a less excellent, we have generation simply, and corruption in a particular respect: whereas the reverse is the case, when from a more excellent thing, a less excellent is generated. In these three ways it happens that passions are in the soul. For in the sense of mere reception, we speak of *feeling and understanding as being a kind of passion.*[29] But passion, accompanied by the loss of something, is only in respect of a bodily transmutation; wherefore passion properly so called cannot be in the soul, save accidentally, in so far, to wit, as the *composite* is passive. But here again we find a difference; because when this transmutation is for the worse, it has more of the nature of a passion, than when it is for the better: hence sorrow is more properly a passion than joy.

Reply Obj. 1. It belongs to matter to be passive in such a way as to lose something and to be transmuted: hence this happens only in those things that are composed of matter and form. But passivity, as implying mere reception, need not be in matter, but can be in anything that is in potentiality. Now, though the soul is not composed of matter and form, yet it has something of potentiality, in respect of which it is competent to receive or to be passive, according as the act of understanding is a kind of passion, as stated in *De Anima* iii. 4.

Reply Obj. 2. Although it does not belong to the soul in itself to be passive and to be moved, yet it belongs accidentally, as stated in *De Anima* i. 3.

Reply Obj. 3. This argument is true of passion accompanied by transmutation to something worse. And passion, in this sense, is not found in the soul, except accidentally: but the composite, which is corruptible, admits of it by reason of its own nature.

SECOND ARTICLE
Whether Passion Is in the Appetitive Rather Than in the Apprehensive Part?

We proceed thus to the Second Article.—

Objection 1. It would seem that passion is in the apprehensive part of the soul rather than in the appetitive. Because that which is first in any

---

[29]*De An.* i. 5.

genus, seems to rank first among all things that are in that genus, and to be their cause, as is stated in *Metaph.* ii. 1. Now passion is found to be in the apprehensive, before being in the appetitive part: for the appetitive part is not affected unless there be a previous passion in the apprehensive part. Therefore passion is in the apprehensive part more than in the appetitive.

Obj. 2. Further, what is more active is less passive; for action is contrary to passion. Now the appetitive part is more active than the apprehensive. Therefore it seems that passion is more in the apprehensive part.

Obj. 3. Further, just as the sensitive appetite is the power of a corporeal organ, so is the power of sensitive apprehension. But passion in the soul occurs, properly speaking, in respect of a bodily transmutation. Therefore passion is not more in the sensitive appetitive than in the sensitive apprehensive part.

On the contrary, Augustine says that *the movements of the soul, which the Greeks call* πάθη *are styled by some of our writers, Cicero for instance,*[30] *disturbances; by some, affections or emotions; while others rendering the Greek more accurately, call them passions.*[31] From this it is evident that the passions of the soul are the same as affections. But affections manifestly belong to the appetitive, and not to the apprehensive part. Therefore the passions are in the appetitive rather than in the apprehensive part.

I answer that, As we have already stated the word *passion* implies that the patient is drawn to that which belongs to the agent.[32] Now the soul is drawn to a thing by the appetitive power rather than by the apprehensive power: because the soul has, through its appetitive power, an order to things as they are in themselves: hence the Philosopher says that *good and evil, i.e.,* the objects of the appetitive power, *are in things themselves.*[33] On the other hand the apprehensive power is not drawn to a thing, as it is in itself; but knows it by reason of an *intention* of the thing, which *intention* it has in itself, or receives in its own way. Hence we find it stated that *the true and the false,* which pertain to knowledge, *are not in things, but in the mind.*[34] Consequently it is evident that the nature of passion is consistent with the appetitive, rather than with the apprehensive part.

Reply Obj. 1. In things relating to perfection the case is the opposite, in comparison to things that pertain to defect. Because in things relating to perfection, intensity is in proportion to the approach to one first princi-

---

[30]*Those things which the Greeks call* πάθη, *we prefer to call disturbances rather than diseases* (Tusc. iv. 5).   [31]*De Civit. Dei* ix. 4.   [32]A. 1.   [33]*Metaph.* vi. 4.   [34]*Ibid.*

ple; to which the nearer a thing approaches, the more intense it is. Thus the intensity of a thing possessed of light depends on its approach to something endowed with light in a supreme degree, to which the nearer a thing approaches the more light it possesses. But in things that relate to defect, intensity depends, not on approach to something supreme, but in receding from that which is perfect; because therein consists the very notion of privation and defect. Wherefore the less a thing recedes from that which stands first, the less intense it is: and the result is that at first we always find some small defect, which afterwards increases as it goes on. Now passion pertains to defect, because it belongs to a thing according as it is in potentiality. Wherefore in those things that approach to the Supreme Perfection, *i.e.*, to God, there is but little potentiality and passion: while in other things, consequently, there is more. Hence also, in the supreme, *i.e.*, the apprehensive, power of the soul, passion is found less than in the other powers.

Reply Obj. 2. The appetitive power is said to be more active, because it is, more than the apprehensive power, the principle of the exterior action: and this for the same reason that it is more passive, namely, its being related to things as existing in themselves: since it is through the external action that we come into contact with things.

Reply Obj. 3. As stated in the First Part the organs of the soul can be changed in two ways.[35] First, by a spiritual change, in respect of which the organ receives an *intention* of the object. And this is essential to the act of the sensitive apprehension: thus is the eye changed by the object visible. not by being colored, but by receiving an intention of color. But the organs are receptive of another and natural change, which affects their natural disposition; for instance, when they become hot or cold, or undergo some similar change. And whereas this kind of change is accidental to the act of the sensitive apprehension; for instance, if the eye be wearied through gazing intently at something, or be overcome by the intensity of the object: on the other hand, it is essential to the act of the sensitive appetite; wherefore the material element in the definitions of the move meets of the appetitive part, is the natural change of the organ; for instance, *anger* is said to be *a kindling of the blood about the heart*. Hence it is evident that the notion of passion is more consistent with the act of the sensitive appetite, than with that of the sensitive apprehension, although both are actions of a corporeal organ.

---

[35]Q. 78, A. 3.

THIRD ARTICLE

Whether Passion Is in the Sensitive Appetite Rather Than in the Intellectual Appetite, Which Is Called the Will?

We proceed thus to the Third Article:—

Objection 1. It would seem that passion is not more in the sensitive than in the intellectual appetite. For Dionysius declares Hierotheus *to be taught by a kind of yet more Godlike instruction; not only by learning Divine things, but also by suffering (patiens) them.*[36] But the sensitive appetite cannot *suffer* Divine things, since its object is the sensible good. Therefore passion is in the intellect appetite, just as it is also in the sensitive appetite.

Obj. 2. Further, the more powerful the active force, the more intense the passion. But the object of the intellectual appetite, which is the universal good, is a more powerful active force than the object of the sensitive appetite, which is a particular good. Therefore passion is more consistent with the intellectual than with the sensitive appetite.

Obj. 3. Further, joy and love are said to be passions. But these are to be found in the intellectual and not only in the sensitive appetite: else they would not be ascribed by the Scriptures to God and the angels. Therefore the passions are not more in the sensitive than in the intellectual appetite.

On the contrary, Damascene says while describing the animal passions: *Passion is a movement of the sensitive appetite when we imagine good or evil: in other words, passion is a movement of the irrational soul, when we think of good or evil.*[37]

I answer that, As stated above passion is properly to be found where there is corporeal transmutation.[38] This corporeal transmutation is found in the act of the sensitive appetite, and is not only spiritual, as in the sensitive apprehension, but also natural. Now there is no need for corporeal transmutation in the act of the intellectual appetite: because this appetite is not exercised by means of a corporeal organ. It is therefore evident that passion is more properly in the act of the sensitive appetite, than in that of the intellectual appetite; and this is again evident from the definitions of Damascene quoted above.

Reply Obj. 1. By *suffering* Divine things is meant being well affected towards them, and united to them by love: and this takes place without any alteration in the body.

Reply Obj 2. Intensity of passion depends not only on the power of the agent, but also on the possibility of the patient: because things that are disposed to passion, suffer much even from petty agents. Therefore although

---

[36]*De Div. Nom.* ii.   [37]*De Fide Orthod.* ii. 22.   [38]A. 1.

the object of the intellectual appetite has greater activity than the object of the sensitive appetite, yet the sensitive appetite is more passive.

Reply Obj. 3. When love and joy and the like are ascribed to God or the angels, or to man in respect of his intellectual appetite, they signify simple acts of the will having like effects, but without passion. Hence Augustine says: *The holy angels feel no anger while they punish . . . , no fellow-feeling with misery while they relieve the unhappy: and yet ordinary human speech is wont to ascribe to them also these passions by name, because, although they have none of our weakness, their acts bear a certain resemblance to ours.*[39]

---

[39] *De Civit. Dei* ix. 5.

Summa Theologica

QUESTION 23

How the Passions Differ from One Another

FIRST ARTICLE
Whether the Passions of the Concupiscible Part
Are Different from Those of the Irascible Part?

We proceed thus to the First Article:—

Objection 1. It would seem that the same passions are in the irascible and concupiscible parts. For the Philosopher says that the passions of the soul are those emotions *which are followed by joy or sorrow.*[40] But joy and sorrow are in the concupiscible part. Therefore all the passions are in the concupiscible part, and not some in the irascible, others in the concupiscible part.

Obj. 2. Further, on the words of Matth. xiii. 33, *The kingdom of heaven is like to leaven,* etc., Jerome's gloss says: *We should have prudence in the reason; hatred of vice, in the irascible faculty; desire of virtue, in the concupiscible part.* But hatred is in the concupiscible faculty, as also is love, of which it is the contrary, as is stated in *Topic.* ii. 7. Therefore the same passion is in the concupiscible and irascible faculties.

Obj. 3. Further, passions and actions differ specifically according to their objects. But the objects of the irascible and concupiscible passions are the same, viz., good and evil. Therefore the same passions are in the irascible and concupiscible faculties.

On the contrary, The acts of different powers differ in species; for instance, to see, and to hear. But the irascible and the concupiscible are two powers into which the sensitive appetite is divided, as stated in the First Part.[41] Therefore, since the passions are movements of the sensitive appetite, as stated above,[42] the passions of the irascible faculty are specifically distinct from those of the concupiscible part.

I answer that, The passions of the irascible part differ in species from those of the concupiscible faculty. For since different powers have different objects, as stated in the First Part,[43] the passions of different powers

---

[40]*Eth.* ii. 5.   [41]Q. 81, A. 2.   [42]Q. 22, A. 3.   [43]Q. 77, A. 3.

must of necessity be referred to different objects. Much more, therefore, do the passions of different faculties differ in species; since a greater difference in the object is required to diversify the species of the powers, than to diversify the species of passions or actions. For just as in the physical order, diversity of genus arises from diversity in the potentiality of matter, while diversity of species arises from diversity of form in the same matter; so in the acts of the soul, those that belong to different powers, differ not only in species but also in genus, while acts and passions regarding different specific objects, included under the one common object of a single power, differ as the species of that genus.

In order, therefore, to discern which passions are in the irascible, and which in the concupiscible, we must take the object of each of these powers. For we have stated in the First Part that the object of the concupiscible power is sensible good or evil, simply apprehended as such, which causes pleasure or pain.[44] But, since the soul must, of necessity, experience difficulty or struggle at times, in acquiring some such good, or in avoiding some such evil, in so far as such good or evil is more than our animal nature can easily acquire or avoid; therefore this very good or evil, inasmuch as it is of an arduous or difficult nature, is the object of the irascible faculty. Therefore whatever passions regard good or evil absolutely, belong to the concupiscible power; for instance, joy, sorrow, love, hatred and such like: whereas those passions which regard good or bad as arduous, through being difficult to obtain or avoid, belong to the irascible faculty; such are daring, fear, hope and the like.

Reply Obj. 1. As stated in the First Part, the irascible faculty is bestowed on animals, in order to remove the obstacles that hinder the concupiscible power from tending towards its object, either by making some good difficult to obtain, or by making some evil hard to avoid.[45] The result is that all the irascible passions terminate in the concupiscible passions: and thus it is that even the passions which are in the irascible faculty are followed by joy and sadness which are in the concupiscible faculty.

Reply Obj. 2. Jerome ascribes hatred of vice to the irascible faculty, not by reason of hatred, which is properly a concupiscible passion; but on account of the struggle, which belongs to irascible power.

Reply Obj. 3. Good, inasmuch as it is delightful, moves the concupiscible power. But if it prove difficult to obtain, from this very fact it has a certain contrariety to the concupiscible power: and hence the need of

---

[44]Q. 81. A. 2.   [45]*Loc. cit.*

another power tending to that good. The same applies to evil. And this power is the irascible faculty. Consequently the concupiscible passions are specifically different from the irascible passions.

SECOND ARTICLE

Whether the Contrariety of the Irascible Passions Is Based on the Contrariety of Good and Evil?

We proceed thus to the Second Article:—

Objection 1. It would seem that the contrariety of the irascible passions is based on no other contrariety than that of good and evil. For the irascible passions are ordained to the concupiscible passions, as stated above.[46] But the contrariety of the concupiscible passions is no other than that of good and evil; take, for instance, love and hatred, joy and sorrow. Therefore the same applies to the irascible passions.

Obj. 2. Further, passions differ according to their objects; just as movements differ according to their termini. But there is no other contrariety of movements, except that of the termini, as is stated in *Phys.* v. 3. Therefore there is no other contrariety of passions, save that of the objects. Now the object of the appetite is good or evil. Therefore in no appetitive power can there be contrariety of passions other than that of good and evil.

Obj. 3. Further, *every passion of the soul is by way of approach and withdrawal*, as Avicenna declares in his sixth book of *Physics*. Now approach results from the apprehension of good; withdrawal, from the apprehension of evil: since just as *good is what all desire,*[47] so evil is what all shun. Therefore, in the passions of the soul, there can be no other contrariety than that of good and evil.

On the contrary, Fear and daring are contrary to one another, as stated in *Ethic.* iii. 7. But fear and daring do not differ in respect of good and evil: because each regards some kind of evil. Therefore not every contrariety of the irascible passions is that of good and evil.

I answer that, Passion is a kind of movement, as stated in *Phys.* iii. 3. Therefore contrariety of passions is based on contrariety of movements or changes. Now there is a twofold contrariety in changes and movements, as stated in *Phys.* v. 5. One is according to approach and withdrawal in respect of the same term: and this contrariety belongs properly to changes, *i.e.*, to generation, which is a change *to being*, and to corruption, which is change *from being*. The other contrariety is according to opposi-

---

[46]A. 1 ad 1.   [47]*Eth.* i. 1.

tion of termini, and belongs properly to movements: thus whitening, which is movement from black to white, is contrary to blackening, which is movement from white to black.

Accordingly there is a twofold contrariety in the passions of the soul: one, according to contrariety of objects, *i.e.*, of good and evil; the other, according to approach and withdrawal in respect of the same term. In the concupiscible passions the former contrariety alone is to be found; viz., that which is based on the objects: whereas in the irascible passions, we find both forms of contrariety. The reason of this is that the object of the concupiscible faculty, as stated above, is sensible good or evil considered absolutely.[48] Now good, as such, cannot be a term wherefrom, but only a term whereto, since nothing shuns good as such; on the contrary, all things desire it. In like manner, nothing desires evil, as such; but all things shun it: wherefore evil cannot have the aspect of a term whereto, but only of a term wherefrom. Accordingly every concupiscible passion in respect of good, tends to it, as love, desire and joy; while every concupiscible passion in respect of evil, tends from it, as hatred, avoidance or dislike, and sorrow. Wherefore, in the concupiscible passion there can be no contrariety of approach and withdrawal in respect of the same object.

On the other hand, the object of the irascible faculty is sensible good or evil, considered not absolutely, but under the aspect of difficulty or arduousness. Now the good which is difficult or arduous, considered as good, is of such a nature as to produce in us a tendency to it, which tendency pertains to the passion of *hope*; whereas, considered as arduous or difficult, it makes us turn from it; and this pertains to the passion of *despair*. In like manner the arduous evil, considered as an evil, has the aspect of something to be shunned; and this belongs to the passion of *fear*: but it also contains a reason for tending to it, as attempting something arduous, whereby to escape being subject to evil; and this tendency is called *daring*. Consequently, in the irascible passions we find contrariety in respect of good and evil (as between hope and fear): and also contrariety according to approach and withdrawal in respect of the same term (as between daring and fear).

From what has been said the replies to the objections are evident.

Third Article
Whether Any Passion of the Soul Has No Contrary?

We proceed thus to the Third Article:—

---

[48]A. 1.

Objection 1. It would seem that every passion of the soul has a contrary. For every passion of the soul is either in the irascible or in the concupiscible faculty, as stated above.[49] But both kinds of passions have their respective modes of contrariety. Therefore every passion of the soul has its contrary.

Obj. 2. Further, every passion of the soul has either good or evil for its object; for these are the common objects of the appetitive part. But a passion having good for its object, is contrary to a passion having evil for its object. Therefore every passion has a contrary.

Obj. 3. Further, every passion of the soul is in respect of approach or withdrawal, as stated above.[50] But every approach has a corresponding contrary withdrawal, and vice versa. Therefore every passion of the soul has a contrary.

On the contrary, Anger is a passion of the soul. But no passion is set down as being contrary to anger, as stated in *Ethic.* iv. 5. Therefore not every passion has a contrary.

I answer that, The passion of anger is peculiar in this, that it cannot have a contrary, either according to approach and withdrawal, or according to the contrariety of good and evil. For anger is caused by a difficult evil already present: and when such an evil is present, the appetite must needs either succumb, so that it does not go beyond the limits of *sadness,* which is a concupiscible passion; or else it has a movement of attack on the hurtful evil, which movement is that of *anger.* But it cannot have a movement of withdrawal: because the evil is supposed to be already present or past. Thus no passion is contrary to anger according to contrariety of approach and withdrawal.

In like manner neither can there be according to contrariety of good and evil. Because the opposite of present evil is good obtained, which can no longer have the aspect of arduousness or difficulty. Nor, when once good is obtained, does there remain any other movement, except the appetite's repose in the good obtained; which repose belongs to joy, which is a passion of the concupiscible faculty.

Accordingly no movement of the soul can be contrary to the movement of anger, and nothing else than cessation from its movement is contrary thereto; thus the Philosopher says that *calm is contrary to anger,* by opposition not of contrariety but of negation or privation.[51]

From what has been said the replies to the objections are evident.

---

[49]A. 1.   [50]A. 2.   [51]*Rhetor.* ii. 3.

FOURTH ARTICLE
Whether in the Same Power, There Are Any Passions, Specifically Different, but Not Contrary to One Another?

We proceed thus to the Fourth Article:—

Objection 1. It would seem that there cannot be, in the same power, specifically different passions that are not contrary to one another. For the passions of the soul differ according to their objects. Now the objects of the soul's passions are good and evil; and on this distinction is based the contrariety of the passions. Therefore no passions of the same power, that are not contrary to one another, differ specifically.

Obj. 2. Further, difference of species implies a difference of form. But every difference of form is in respect of some contrariety, as stated in *Metaph.* x. 8. Therefore passions of the same power, that are not contrary to one another, do not differ specifically.

Obj. 3. Further, since every passion of the soul consists in approach or withdrawal in respect of good or evil, it seems that every difference in the passions of the soul must needs arise from the difference of good and evil; or from the difference of approach and withdrawal; or from degrees in approach or withdrawal. Now the first two differences cause contrariety in the passions of the soul, as stated above[52]: whereas the third difference does not diversify the species; else the species of the soul's passions would be infinite. Therefore it is not possible for passions of the same power to differ in species, without being contrary to one another.

On the contrary, Love and joy differ in species, and are in the concupiscible power; and yet they are not contrary to one another; rather, in fact, one causes the other. Therefore in the same power there are passions that differ in species without being contrary to one another.

I answer that, Passions differ in accordance with their active causes, which, in the case of the passions of the soul, are their objects. Now the difference in active causes may be considered in two ways: first, from the point of view of their species or nature, as fire differs from water; secondly, from the point of view of the difference in their active power. In the passions of the soul we can treat the difference of their active or motive causes in respect of their motive power, as if they were natural agents. For every mover, in a fashion, either draws the patient to itself, or repels it from itself. Now in drawing it to itself, it does three things in the patient. Because, in the first place, it gives the patient an inclination or aptitude to tend to the mover: thus a light body, which is above, bestows lightness on

---

[52]A. 2.

the body generated, so that it has an inclination or aptitude to be above. Secondly, if the generated body be outside its proper place, the mover gives it movement towards that place.

Thirdly, it makes it to rest, when it shall have come to its proper place: since to the same cause are due, both rest in a place, and the movement to that place. The same applies to the cause of repulsion.

Now, in the movements of the appetitive faculty, good has, as it were, a force of attraction, while evil has a force of repulsion. In the first place, therefore, good causes, in the appetitive power, a certain inclination, aptitude or connaturalness in respect of good: and this belongs to the passion of *love*: the corresponding contrary of which is *hatred* in respect of evil.— Secondly, if the good be not yet possessed, it causes in the appetite a movement towards the attainment of the good beloved: and this belongs to the passion of *desire* or *concupiscence*: and contrary to it, in respect of evil, is the passion of *aversion* or *dislike*. Thirdly, when the good is obtained, it causes the appetite to rest, as it were, in the good obtained: and this belongs to the passion of *delight* or *joy*: the contrary of which, in respect of evil, is *sorrow* or *sadness*.

On the other hand, in the irascible passions, the aptitude, or inclination to seek good, or to shun evil, is presupposed as arising from the concupiscible faculty, which regards good or evil absolutely. And in respect of good not yet obtained, we have *hope* and *despair*. In respect of evil not yet present we have *fear* and *daring*. But in respect of good obtained there is no irascible passion: because it is no longer considered in the light of something arduous, as stated above.[53] But evil already present gives rise to the passion of *anger*.

Accordingly it is clear that in the concupiscible faculty there are three couples of passion; viz., love and hatred, desire and aversion, joy and sadness. In like manner there are three groups in the irascible faculty; viz., hope and despair, fear and daring, and anger which has no contrary passion.

Consequently there are altogether eleven passions differing specifically; six in the concupiscible faculty, and five in the irascible; and under these all the passions of the soul are contained.

From this the replies to the objections are evident.

---

[53] A. 3.

FIRST PART OF PART TWO
QUESTION 24
Of Good and Evil in the Passions of the Soul

FIRST ARTICLE
Whether Moral Good and Evil Can Be
Found in the Passions of the Soul?

We proceed thus to the First Article:—

Objection 1. It would seem that no passion of the soul is morally good or evil. For moral good and evil are proper to man: since *morals are properly predicated of man*, as Ambrose says.[54] But passions are not proper to man, for he has them in common with other animals. Therefore no passion of the soul is morally good or evil.

Obj. 2. Further, the good or evil of man consists in *being in accord, or in disaccord with reason*, as Dionysius says.[55] Now the passions of the soul are not in the reason, but in the sensitive appetite, as stated above.[56] Therefore they have no connection with human, *i.e.*, moral, good or evil.

Obj. 3. Further, the Philosopher says that *we are neither praised nor blamed for our passions.*[57] But we are praised and blamed for moral good and evil. Therefore the passions are not morally good or evil.

On the contrary, Augustine says while speaking of the passions of the soul: *They are evil if our love is evil; good if our love is good.*[58]

I answer that, We may consider the passions of the soul in two ways: first, in themselves; secondly, as being subject to the command of the reason and will.—If then the passions be considered in themselves, to wit, as movements of the irrational appetite, thus there is no moral good or evil in them, since this depends on the reason, as stated above.[59] If, however, they be considered as subject to the command of the reason and will, then moral good and evil are in them. Because the sensitive appetite is nearer than the outward members to the reason and will; and yet the movements and actions of the outward members are morally good or evil, inasmuch as they are voluntary. Much more, therefore, may the passions, in so far as

---

[54]*Super Luc., Prolog.*   [55]*De Div. Nom.* iv.   [56]Q. 22, A. 3.   [57]*Eth.* ii. 5.   [58]*De Civit. Dei* xiv. 7.   [59]Q. 18, A. 5.

they are voluntary, be called morally good or evil. And they are said to be voluntary, either from being commanded by the will, or from not being checked by the will.

Reply Obj. 1. These passions, considered in themselves, are common to man and other animals: but, as commanded by the reason, they are proper to man.

Reply Obj. 2. Even the lower appetitive powers are called rational, in so far as *they partake of reason in some sort.*[60]

Reply Obj. 3. The Philosopher says that we are neither praised nor blamed for our passions considered absolutely; but he does not exclude their becoming worthy of praise or blame, in so far as they are subordinate to reason. Hence he continues: *For the man who fears or is angry, is not praised . . . or blamed, but the man who is angry in a certain way, i.e., according to, or against reason.*

SECOND ARTICLE
Whether Every Passion of the Soul Is Evil Morally?

We proceed thus to the Second Article:—

Objection 1. It would seem that all the passions of the soul are morally evil. For Augustine says that *some call the soul's passions diseases or disturbances of the soul.*[61] But every disease or disturbance of the soul is morally evil. Therefore every passion of the soul is evil morally.

Obj. 2. Further, Damascene says that *movement in accord with nature is an action, but movement contrary to nature is passion.*[62] But in movements of the soul, what is against nature is sinful and morally evil: hence he says elsewhere that *the devil turned from that which is in accord with nature to that which is against nature.*[63] Therefore these passions are morally evil.

Obj. 3. Further, whatever leads to sin, has an aspect of evil. But these passions lead to sin: wherefore they are called *the passions of sins.*[64] Therefore it seems that they are morally evil.

On the contrary, Augustine says that *all these emotions are right in those whose love is rightly placed. . . . For they fear to sin, they desire to persevere; they grieve for sin, they rejoice in good works.*[65]

I answer that, On this question the opinion of the Stoics differed from that of the Peripatetics: for the Stoics held that all passions are evil, while the Peripatetics maintained that moderate passions are good. This difference, although it appears great in words, is nevertheless, in reality, none at

[60]*Eth.* i. 13.   [61]*De Civit. Dei* ix. 4. *Cf.* Q. 22, A. 2, footnote 30.   [62]*De Fide Orthod.* ii. 22.   [63]*Ibid.* 4.   [64]Rom. vii. 5.   [65]*De Civit. Dei* xiv. 9.

all, or but little, if we consider the intent of either school. For the Stoics did not discern between sense and intellect; and consequently neither between the intellectual and sensitive appetite. Hence they did not discriminate the passions of the soul from the movements of the will, in so far as the passions of the soul are in the sensitive appetite, while the simple movements of the will are in the intellectual appetite: but every rational movement of the appetitive part they call will, while they called passion, a movement that exceeds the limits of reason. Wherefore Cicero, following their opinion calls all passions *diseases of the soul:* whence he argues that *those who are diseased are unsound; and those who are unsound are wanting in sense.*[66] Hence we speak of those who are wanting in sense as being *unsound.*

On the other hand, the Peripatetics give the name of *passions* to all the movements of the sensitive appetite. Wherefore they esteem them good, when they are controlled by reason; and evil when they are not controlled by reason. Hence it is evident that Cicero was wrong in disapproving of the Peripatetic theory of a mean in the passions, when he says that *every evil, though moderate, should be shunned; for, just as a body, though it be moderately ailing, is not sound; so, this mean in the diseases or passions of the soul, is not sound.*[67] For passions are not called *diseases* or *disturbances* of the soul, save when they are not controlled by reason.

Hence the reply to the First Objection is evident.

Reply Obj. 2. In every passion there is an increase or decrease in the natural movement of the heart, according as the heart is moved more or less intensely by contraction and dilatation; and hence it derives the character of passion. But there is no need for passion to deviate always from the order of natural reason.

Reply Obj. 3. The passions of the soul, in so far as they are contrary to the order of reason, incline us to sin: but in so far as they are controlled by reason, they pertain to virtue.

THIRD ARTICLE
Whether Passion Increases or Decreases the Goodness or Malice of an Act?

We proceed thus to the Third Article:—

Objection 1. It would seem that every passion decreases the goodness of a moral action. For anything that hinders the judgment of reason, on which depends the goodness of a moral act, consequently decreases the

---

[66]*De Tusc. Quaest.* iii. 4.   [67]*Ibid.*

goodness of the moral act. But every passion hinders the judgment of reason: for Sallust says: *All those that take counsel about matters of doubt, should be free from hatred, anger, friendship and pity.*[68] Therefore passion decreases the goodness of a moral act.

Obj. 2. Further, the more a man's action is like to God, the better it is: hence the Apostle says: *Be ye followers of God, as most dear children.* But *God and the holy angels feel no anger when they punish . . . no fellow-feeling with misery when they relieve the unhappy,* [69] as Augustine says.[70] Therefore it is better to do such like deeds without than with a passion of the soul.

Obj. 3. Further, just as moral evil depends on its relation to reason, so also does moral good. But moral evil is lessened by passion: for he sins less, who sins from passion, than he who sins deliberately. Therefore he does a better deed, who does well without passion, than he who does with passion.

On the contrary, Augustine says that *the passion of pity is obedient to reason, when pity is bestowed without violating right, as when the poor are relieved, or the penitent forgiven.*[71] But nothing that is obedient to reason lessens the moral good. Therefore a passion of the soul does not lessen moral good.

I answer that, As the Stoics held that every passion of the soul is evil, they consequently held that every passion of the soul lessens the goodness of an act; since the admixture of evil either destroys good altogether, or makes it to be less good. And this is true indeed, if by passions we understand none but the inordinate movements of the sensitive appetite, considered as disturbances or ailments. But if we give the name of passions to all the movements of the sensitive appetite, then it belongs to the perfection of man's good that his passions be moderated by reason. For since man's good is founded on reason as its root, that good will be all the more perfect, according as it extends to more things pertaining to man. Wherefore no one questions the fact that it belongs to the perfection of moral good, that the actions of the outward members be controlled by the law of reason. Hence, since the sensitive appetite can obey reason, as stated above,[72] it belongs to the perfection of moral or human good, that the passions themselves also should be controlled by reason.

Accordingly just as it is better that man should both will good and do it in his external act; so also does it belong to the perfection of moral good, that man should be moved unto good, not only in respect of his will, but also in respect of his sensitive appetite; according to Ps. lxxxiii. 3: *My*

---

[68]*Catilin.*   [69]*Eph.* v. 1.   [70]*De Civit. Dei* ix. 5.   [71]*De Civit. Dei.*
ix. 5.   [72]Q. 17, A. 7.

heart and my flesh have rejoiced in the living God: where by *heart* we are to understand the intellectual appetite, and by *flesh* the sensitive appetite.

Reply Obj. 1. The passions of the soul may stand in a twofold relation to the judgment of reason. First, antecedently: and thus, since they obscure the judgment of reason, on which the goodness of the moral act depends, they diminish the goodness of the act; for it is more praiseworthy to do a work of charity from the judgment of reason than from the mere passion of pity.—In the second place, consequently: and this in two ways. First, by way of redundance: because, to wit, when the higher part of the soul is intensely moved to anything, the lower part also follows that movement; and thus the passion that results in consequence, in the sensitive appetite, is a sign of the intensity of the will, and so indicates greater moral goodness.—Secondly, by way of choice; when, to wit, a man, by the judgment of his reason, chooses to be affected by a passion in order to work more promptly with the co-operation of the sensitive appetite. And thus a passion of the soul increases the goodness of an action.

Reply Obj. 2. In God and the angels there is no sensitive appetite, nor again bodily members: and so in them good does not depend on the right ordering of passions or of bodily actions, as it does in us.

Reply Obj. 3. A passion that tends to evil, and precedes the judgment of reason, diminishes sin; but if it be consequent in either of the ways mentioned above[73] it aggravates the sin, or else it is a sign of its being more grievous.

FOURTH ARTICLE
Whether Any Passion Is Good or Evil in Its Species?

We proceed thus to the Fourth Article:—

Objection 1. It would seem that no passion of the soul is good or evil morally according to its species. Because moral good and evil depend on reason. But the passions are in the sensitive appetite; so that accordance with reason is accidental to them. Since, therefore, nothing accidental belongs to a thing's species, it seems that no passion is good or evil according to its species.

Obj. 2. Further, acts and passions take their species from their object. If, therefore, any passion were good or evil, according to its species, it would follow that those passions the object of which is good, are specifically good, such as love, desire and joy: and that those passions, the object

---

[73]*Reply Obj.* 1.

of which is evil, are specifically evil, as hatred, fear and sadness. But this is clearly false. Therefore no passion is good or evil according to its species.

Obj. 3. Further, there is no species of passion that is not to be found in other animals. But moral good is in man alone. Therefore no passion of the soul is good or evil according to its species.

On the contrary, Augustine says that *pity is a kind of virtue.*[74] Moreover, the Philosopher says that modesty is a praiseworthy passion.[75] Therefore some passions are good or evil according to their species.

I answer that, We ought, seemingly, to apply to passions what has been said in regard to acts—viz., that the species of a passion, as the species of an act, can be considered from two points of view.[76] First, according to its natural genus; and thus moral good and evil have no connection with the species of an act or passion. Secondly, according to its moral genus, inasmuch as it is voluntary and controlled by reason. In this way moral good and evil can belong to the species of a passion, in so far as the object to which a passion tends, is, of itself, in harmony or in discord with reason: as is clear in the case of *shame* which is base fear; and of *envy* which is sorrow for another's good: for thus passions belong to the same species as the external act.

Reply Obj. 1 This argument considers the passions in their natural species, in so far as the sensitive appetite is considered in itself. But in so far as the sensitive appetite obeys reason, good and evil of reason are no longer accidentally in the passions of the appetite, but essentially.

Reply Obj. 2. Passions having a tendency to good, are themselves good, if they tend to that which is truly good, and in like manner, if they turn away from that which is truly evil. On the other hand, those passions which consist in aversion from good, and a tendency to evil are themselves evil.

Reply Obj. 3. In irrational animals the sensitive appetite does not obey reason. Nevertheless, in so far as they are led by a kind of estimative power, which is subject to a higher, *i.e.*, the Divine, reason, there is a certain likeness of moral good in them, in regard to the soul's passions.

---

[74]*De Civit. Dei* ix. 5.   [75]*Eth.* ii. 7.   [76]Q. 18, AA. 5, 6; Q. 20, A. 1.

Summary Theologica

FIRST PART OF PART TWO
QUESTION 25
Of the Order of the Passions to One Another

FIRST ARTICLE
Whether the Irascible Passions Precede the Concupiscible Passions, or Vice Versa?

We proceed thus to the First Article:—

Objection 1. It would seem that the irascible passions precede the concupiscible passions. For the order of the passions is that of their objects. But the object of the irascible faculty is the difficult good, which seems to be the highest good. Therefore the irascible passions seem to precede the concupiscible passions.

Obj. 2. Further, the mover precedes that which is moved. But the irascible faculty is compared to the concupiscible, as mover to that which is moved; since it is given to animals, for the purpose of removing the obstacles that hinder the concupiscible faculty from enjoying its object, as stated above.[77] Now *that which removes an obstacle, is a kind of mover.*[78] Therefore the irascible passions precede the concupiscible passions.

Obj. 3. Further, joy and sadness are concupiscible passions. But joy and sadness succeed to the irascible passions: for the Philosopher says that *retaliation causes anger to cease, because it produces pleasure instead of the previous pain.*[79] Therefore concupiscible passions follow the irascible passions.

On the contrary, The concupiscible passions regard the absolute good, while the irascible regard a restricted, viz., the difficult, good. Since, therefore, the absolute good precedes the restricted good, it seems that the concupiscible passions precede the irascible.

I answer that, In the concupiscible passions there is more diversity then in the passions of the irascible faculty. For the former we find something relating to movement—*e.g.,* desire; and something belonging to repose, *e.g.,* joy and sadness. But in the irascible passions there is nothing pertaining to repose, and only that which belongs to movement. The rea-

---

[77]Q. 23; A. 1 ad 1; P. 1, Q. 81, A. 2.   [78]*Phys.* viii. 4.   [79]*Eth.* iv. 5.

son of this is that when we find rest in a thing, we no longer look upon it as something difficult or arduous; whereas such is the object of the irascible faculty.

Now since rest is the end of movement, it is first in the order of intention, but last in the order of execution. If, therefore, we compare the passions of the irascible faculty with those concupiscible passions that denote rest in good, it is evident that in the order of execution, the irascible passions take precedence of such like passions of the concupiscible faculty: thus hope precedes joy, and hence causes it according to the Apostle: *Rejoicing in hope.*[80] But the concupiscible passion which denotes rest in evil, viz., sadness, comes between two irascible passions: because it follows fear; since we become sad when we are confronted by the evil that we feared: while it precedes the movement of anger; since the movement of self-vindication, that results from sadness, is the movement of anger. And because it is looked upon as a good thing to pay back the evil done to us; when the angry man has achieved this he rejoices. Thus it is evident that every passion of the irascible faculty terminates in a concupiscible passion denoting rest, viz., either in joy or in sadness.

But if we compare the irascible passions to those concupiscible passions that denote movement, then it is clear that the latter take precedence: because the passions of the irascible faculty add something to those of the concupiscible faculty; just as the object of the irascible adds the aspect of arduousness or difficulty to the object of the concupiscible faculty. Thus hope adds to desire a certain effort, and a certain raising of the spirits to the realization of the arduous good. In like manner fear adds to aversion or detestation a certain lowness of spirits, on account of difficulty in shunning the evil.

Accordingly the passions of the irascible faculty stand between those concupiscible passions that denote movement towards good or evil, and those concupiscible passions that denote rest in good or evil. And it is therefore evident that the irascible passions both arise from and terminate in the passions of the concupiscible faculty.

Reply Obj. 1. This argument would prove, if the formal object of the concupiscible faculty were something contrary to the arduous, just as the formal object of the irascible faculty is that which is arduous. But because the object of the concupiscible faculty is good absolutely, it naturally precedes the object of the irascible, as the common precedes the proper.

---

[80]Rom. xii. 12.

Reply Obj. 2. The remover of an obstacle is not a direct but an accidental mover: and here we are speaking of passions as directly related to one another.—Moreover, the irascible passion removes the obstacle that hinders the concupiscible from resting in its object. Wherefore it only follows that the irascible passions precede those concupiscible passions that connote rest.—The third objection leads to the same conclusion.

SECOND ARTICLE

Whether Love Is the First of the Concupiscible Passions?

We proceed thus to the Second Article:—

Objection 1. It would seem that love is not the first of the concupiscible passions. For the concupiscible faculty is so called from concupiscence, which is the same passion as desire. But *things are named from their chief characteristic.*[81] Therefore desire takes precedence of love.

Obj. 2. Further, love implies a certain union; since it is a *uniting and binding force*, as Dionysius states.[82] But concupiscence or desire is a movement towards union with the thing coveted or desired. Therefore desire precedes love.

Obj. 3. Further, the cause precedes its effect. But pleasure is sometimes the cause of love: since some love on account of pleasure.[83] Therefore pleasure precedes love; and consequently love is not the first of the concupiscible passions.

On the contrary, Augustine says that all the passions are caused by love since *love yearning for the beloved object, is desire; and, having and enjoying it, is joy.*[84] Therefore love is the first of the concupiscible passions.

I answer that, Good and evil are the object of the concupiscible faculty. Now good naturally precedes evil; since evil is the privation of good. Wherefore all the passions, the object of which is good, are naturally before those, the object of which is evil,—that is to say, each precedes its contrary passion: because the quest of a good is the reason for shunning the opposite evil.

Now good has the aspect of an end, and the end is indeed first in the order of intention, but last in the order of execution. Consequently the order of the concupiscible passions can be considered either in the order of intention or in the order of execution. In the order of execution, the first place belongs to that which takes place first in the thing that tends to the end. Now it is evident that whatever tends to an end, has, in the first

---

[81]*De An.* ii. 4.   [82]*De Div. Nom.* iv.   [83]*Eth.* viii. 3, 4.   [84]*De Civit. Dei* xiv. 7, 9.

place, an aptitude or proportion to that end, for nothing tends to a dispro-
portionate end; secondly, it is moved to that end; thirdly, it rests in the
end, after having attained it. And this very aptitude or proportion of the
appetite to good is love, which is complacency in good; while movement
towards good is desire or concupiscence; and rest in good is joy or pleasure. Accordingly in this order, love precedes desire, and desire precedes
pleasure.—But in the order of intention, it is the reverse: because the
pleasure intended causes desire and love. For pleasure is the enjoyment of
the good, which enjoyment is, in a way, the end, just as the good itself is,
as stated above.[85]

Reply Obj. 1. We name a thing as we understand it, for *words are signs of
thoughts,* as the Philosopher states.[86] Now in most cases we know a cause
by its effect. But the effect of love, when the beloved object is possessed, is
pleasure: when it is not possessed, it is desire or concupiscence: and, as
Augustine says, *we are more sensible to love, when we lack that which we
love.*[87] Consequently of all the concupiscible passions, concupiscence is
felt most; and for this reason the power is named after it.

Reply Obj. 2. The union of lover and beloved is twofold. There is real
union, consisting in the conjunction of one with the other. This union
belongs to joy or pleasure, which follows desire. There is also an affective
union, consisting in an aptitude or proportion, in so far as one thing, from
the very fact of its having an aptitude for and an inclination to another,
partakes of it: and love betokens such a union. This union precedes the
movement of desire.

Reply Obj. 3. Pleasure causes love, in so far as it precedes love in the
order of intention.

THIRD ARTICLE
Whether Hope Is the First of the Irascible Passions?

We proceed thus to the Third Article:—

Objection 1. It would seem that hope is not the first of the irascible passions. Because the irascible faculty is denominated from anger. Since,
therefore, *things are named from their chief characteristic,*[88] it seems that
anger precedes and surpasses hope.

Obj. 2. Further, the object of the irascible faculty is something arduous. Now it seems more arduous to strive to overcome a contrary evil that
threatens soon to overtake us, which pertains to daring; or an evil actually

---

[85]Q. 11, A. 3 ad 3.   [86]*Peri Herm.* i. 1.   [87]*De Trin.* x. 12.   [88]*Cf.* A.
2, *Obj.* 1.

present, which pertains to anger; than to strive simply to obtain some good. Again, it seems more arduous to strive to overcome a present evil, than a future evil. Therefore anger seems to be a stronger passion than daring, and daring, than hope. And consequently it seems that hope does not precede them.

Obj. 3. Further, when a thing is moved towards an end, the movement of withdrawal precedes the movement of approach. But fear and despair imply withdrawal from something; while daring and hope imply approach towards something. Therefore fear and despair precede hope and daring.

On the contrary, The nearer a thing is to the first, the more it precedes others. But hope is nearer to love, which is the first of the passions. Therefore hope is the first of the passions in the irascible faculty.

I answer that, As stated above all the irascible passions imply movement towards something.[89] Now this movement of the irascible faculty towards something may be due to two causes: one is the mere aptitude or proportion to the end; and this pertains to love or hatred, those whose object is good, or evil; and this belongs to sadness or joy. As a matter of fact, the presence of good produces no passion in the irascible, as stated above[90]; but the presence of evil gives rise to the passion of anger.

Since then in the order of generation or execution, proportion or aptitude to the end precedes the achievement of the end; it follows that, of all the irascible passions, anger is the last in the order of generation. And among the other passions of the irascible faculty, which imply a movement arising from love of good or hatred of evil, those whose object is good, viz., hope and despair, must naturally precede those whose object is evil, viz., daring and fear: yet so that hope precedes despair; since hope is a movement towards good as such which is essentially attractive, so that hope tends to good directly; whereas despair is a movement away from good, a movement which is consistent with good, not as such, but in respect of something else, wherefore its tendency from good is accidental, as it were. In like manner fear, through being a movement from evil, precedes daring.—And that hope and despair naturally precede fear and daring is evident from this,—that as the desire of good is the reason for avoiding evil, so hope and despair are the reason for fear and daring: because daring arises from the hope of victory, and fear arises from the despair of overcoming. Lastly, anger arises from daring: for no one is angry while seeking vengeance, unless he dare to avenge himself, as Avi-

---

[89]A. 1.   [90]Q. 23, AA. 3, 4.

cenna observes in the sixth book of his *Physics*. Accordingly, it is evident that hope is the first of all the irascible passions.

And if we wish to know the order of all the passions in the way of generation, love and hatred are first; desire and aversion, second; hope and despair, third; fear and daring, fourth; anger, fifth; sixth and last, joy and sadness, which follow from all the passions, as stated in *Ethic*. ii. 5: yet so that love precedes hatred; desire precedes aversion; hope precedes despair; fear precedes daring; and joy precedes sadness, as may be gathered from what has been stated above.

Reply Obj. 1. Because anger arises from the other passions, as an effect from the causes that precede it, it is from anger, as being more manifest than the other passions, that the power takes its name.

Reply Obj. 2. It is not the arduousness but the good that is the reason for approach or desire. Consequently hope, which regards good more directly, takes precedence: although at times daring or even anger regards something more arduous.

Reply Obj. 3. The movement of the appetite is essentially and directly towards the good as towards its proper object; its movement from evil results from this. For the movement of the appetitive part is in proportion, not to natural movement, but to the intention of nature, which intends the end before intending the removal of a contrary, which removal is desired only for the sake of obtaining the end.

Fourth Article
Whether These Are the Four Principal Passions,—Joy, Sadness, Hope, and Fear?

We proceed thus to the Fourth Article:—

Objection 1. It would seem that joy, sadness, hope and fear are not the four principal passions. For Augustine omits hope and puts desire in its place.[91]

Obj. 2. Further, there is a twofold order in the passions of the soul: the order of intention, and the order of execution or generation. The principal passions should therefore be taken, either in the order of intention; and thus joy and sadness, which are the final passions, will be the principal passions; or in the order of execution or generation, and thus love will be the principal passion. Therefore joy and sadness, hope and fear should in no way be called the four principal passions.

---

[91]*De Civit. Dei* xiv. 3, 7 *sqq*.

Obj. 3. Further, just as daring is caused by hope, so fear is caused by despair. Either, therefore, hope and despair should be reckoned as principal passions, since they cause others: or hope and daring, from being akin to one another.

On the contrary, Boethius in enumerating the four principal passions, says[92]:

> Banish joys: banish fears:
> Away with hope: away with tears.

I answer that, These four are commonly called the principal passions. Two of them, viz., joy and sadness, are said to be principal because in them all the other passions have their completion and end; wherefore they arise from all the other passions, as is stated in *Ethic.* ii. 5.—Fear and hope are principal passions, not because they complete the others simply, but because they complete them as regards the movement of the appetite towards something: for in respect of good, movement begins in love, goes forward to desire, and ends in hope; while in respect of evil, it begins in hatred, goes on to aversion, and ends in fear.—Hence it is customary to distinguish these four passions in relation to the present and the future: for movement regards the future, while rest is in something present: so that joy relates to present good, sadness relates to present evil; hope regards future good, and fear, future evil.

As to the other passions that regard good or evil, present or future, they all culminate in these four. For this reason some have said that these four are the principal passions, because they are general passions; and this is true, provided that by hope and fear we understand the appetite's common tendency to desire or shun something.

Reply Obj. 1. Augustine puts desire or covetousness in place of hope, in so far as they seem to regard the same object, viz., some future good.

Reply Obj. 2. These are called principal passions, in the order of intention and completion. And though fear and hope are not the last passions simply, yet they are the last of those passions that tend towards something as future. Nor can the argument be pressed any further except in the case of anger: yet neither can anger be reckoned a principal passion, because it is an effect of daring, which cannot be a principal passion, as we shall state further on.[93]

---

[92]*De Consol.* i.   [93]*Reply Obj.* 3.

Reply Obj. 3. Despair implies movement away from good; and this is, as it were, accidental: and daring implies movement towards evil; and this too is accidental. Consequently these cannot be principal passions, because that which is accidental cannot be said to be principal. And so neither can anger be called a principal passion, because it arises from daring.

WORKS CITED

Albert the Great
In Sent.   Commentary on the Sentences
Summa de Creatur.   Summa on Creatures

Alcher of Clairvaux
  (Pseudo-
    Augustine)
De Spir. et An.   On Spirit and Soul

Alexander of
  Aphrodisias
De Intellectu et Intellecto   On the Intellect and Its Object

Alexander of Hales
Summa Theol.   Summa of Theology

Ambrose
Super Luc.   Commentary on the Gospel of Luke

Aristotle
De An.   On the Soul
De Caelo   On the Heaven
De Gener. Anim.   On the Generation of Animals
De Mem. et Rem.   On Memory and Reminiscence
De Somno   On Sleep
Eth., E.N.   Nicomachean Ethics
Eth. Eudem.   Eudemian Ethics
Hist. Anim.   History of Animals
Metaph.   Metaphysics
Peri Herm.   On Interpretation
Phys.   Physics
Polit.   Politics
Post. Anal.   Posterior Analytics
Rhetor.   Rhetoric
Top.   Topics

Augustine
Confess.   Confessions
Contra Faust.   Against Faustus
De Civit. Dei   On the City of God

De Doc. Christ.	On Christian Doctrine
De Genesi ad Litt.	On the Literal Interpretation of Genesis
De Musica	On Music
De Quant. An.	On the Quantity of the Soul
De Trin.	On the Trinity
De Vera Relig.	On the True Religion
Enchir.	Enchiridion on Faith, Hope, and Love
Epist.	Letters
Lib. 83 Quaest.	On Eighty-Three Questions
Retract.	Retractations
Solil.	Soliloquies

Averroes

De An. Beatitud.	On the Blessedness of the Soul
De Sensu et Sensibili.	On Sense and Sensibles
In De An.	Commentary on Aristotle's On the Soul
In De Caelo	Commentary on Aristotle's On the Heaven
In De Gener.	Commentary on Aristotle's On Generation and Corruption
In De Gener. Anim.	Commentary on Aristotle's On the Generation of Animals
In Metaph.	Commentary on Aristotle's Metaphysics

Avicenna

De An.	On the Soul
Metaphys.	Metaphysics

Bernard of Clairvaux

De Gratia et Libera Arbitrio	On Grace and Free Choice

Boethius

De Consol.	On the Consolation of Philosophy
De Duabus Nat.	On the Two Natures
De Trin.	On the Trinity

Bonaventure

In Sent.	Commentary on the Sentences
Itin. Mentis in Deum	Journey of the Mind to God
Quaest. Disp. de Scientia Dei	Disputed Questions on the Knowledge of God

Cicero

Tusc. Disp.	Tusculan Disputations
De Tusc. Quaest.	Tusculan Questions

Damascene
De Fide Orthod.   On the Orthodox Faith

Democritus
De Divinat.   On Divination

Dionysius
De Cael. Hier.   On the Celestial Hierarchy
De Div. Nom.   On the Divine Names
De Myst. Theol.   On Mystical Theology

Eadmer
De Similit.   On Likenesses

Gennadius
De Eccles. Dogm.   On the Teachings of the Church

Gregory
In Evang.   Homilies on the Gospels

Jerome
In Matth.   On the Gospel of Matthew

Lombard, Peter
Sent.   Sentences

Macrobius
In Somn. Scipion.   On the Dream of Scipio

Nemesius
De Nat. Hom.   On the Nature of Man

Origen
Peri Archon   On the Principles

Plato
Alcib.   Alcibiades
Meno   Meno
Phaedo   Phaedo
Republic   Republic
Theaetet.   Theaetetus
Timaeus   Timaeus

Proclus
Elem. of Theol.   Elements of Theology

Sallust
Catilin.   Catiline

Themistius
In De An.   Commentary on Aristotle's On the Soul

William of Auvergne
De An.   On the Soul
De Univ.   On the Universe of Creatures

Biblical Texts
Eccles.   Ecclesiastes
Ecclus.   Ecclesiasticus
Eph.   Letters to Ephesians
Gen.   Genesis
Jo.   John
Matth.   Matthew
Ps.   Psalms
Rom.   Romans

BIBLIOGRAPHY FOR WORKS CITED

PL stands for *Patrologia Latina* (J. P. Migne, Patrologiae Cursus Completus, Series II, 221 vols., Paris, 1844–1864, with later reprints).

PG stands for *Patrologia Graeca* (J. P. Migne, Patrologiae Cursus Completus, Series I, 162 vols., Paris, 1857–1866, with later reprints).

Albert the Great, St.: *Opera Omnia*, 38 vols., ed. A. Borgnet (Paris: Vivès, 1890–1899).

Alcher of Clairvaux (Pseudo-Augustine): *De Spiritu et Anima Liber Unus*, PL 40, coll. 779–832.

Alexander of Aphrodisias: *De Intellectu et Intellecto* (in G. Théry, Alexandre d'Aphrodise [Autor du décret de 1210, II] Bibliothèque Thomiste, vol. VII, Kain: La Saulchoir, 1926, pp. 74–82).

Alexander of Hales: *Summa Theologica*, 3 vols. (Quaracchi: Ex Typographia Collegii S. Bonaventurae, 1924–1930).

Ambrose, St.: *Opera Omnia*, PL 14–17.

Aristotle: *Aristotelis Opera*, 5 vols., edidit Academia Regia Borussica, ex recognitione I. Bekker (Berlin: G. Reimer, 1831).

Augustine, St.: *Opera Omnia*, PL 32–47.

Averroes: *Aristotelis Stagiritae Libri Omnes . . . cum Averrois Cordubensis variis in eosdem Commentariis*, II vols. Venetiis apud Juntas, 1550–1552.

Avicenna: *Opera in lucem redacta ac nuper quantum ars niti potuit per canonicos emendata*, Venetiis, 1508.

Bernard of Clairvaux, St.: *Opera Omnia*, PL 182–184.

Boethius: *Opera Omnia*, PL 63–64.

Bonaventure, St.: *Opera Omnia*, 10 vols. (Quaracchi: Ex Typographia Collegii S. Bonaventurae, 1882–1902).

Cicero: *Oeuvres Complètes* (Firmin-Didot [DD], Paris, 1881).

Cicero: *Tusculanae Disputationes*, ed. M. Pohlenz (Leipsig: B. G. Teubner, 1918).

Damascene, John, St.: *Expositio Accurata Fidei Orthodoxae*, PG 94, coll. 789–1228.

Dionysius the Pseudo-Areopagite: *Opera Omnia*, PG 3–4.

Eadmer: *Liber de Sancti Anselmi Similitudinibus*, PL 159, coll. 605–708.

Gennadius: *Liber de Ecclesiasticis Dogmatibus*, PL 42, coll. 1213–1222; PL 58, coll. 979–1000.

Gregory the Great: *Opera Omnia*, PL 75–79.

Jerome, St.: *Opera Omnia*, PL 22–30.

Lombard, Peter: *Libri VI Sententiarum*, 2 vols. (Quarrechi [QR], 1916).

Macrobius: *Commentarius ex Cicerone in Somnum Scipionis* (Firmin-Didot [DD], Paris, 1875). Macrobius, ed. F. Eyssenhardt (Leipsig: B. G. Teubner, 1893).

Nemesius: *De Natura Hominis*, PG 40, coll. 503–818.

Origen: *Opera Omnia*, PG 11–17.

Plato: *Platonis Opera*, 5 vols., ed. J. Burnet (Oxford: Clarendon Press, 1905–1913).

Proclus: *Institutio Theologica*, ed. F. Dubner (Firmin-Didot [DD] Paris, 1855). *The Elements of Theology*, ed. E. R. Dodds (Oxford: Clarendon Press, 1933).

Sallust: *Conjuration de Catilina—Guerre de Jugurthia*, ed. and trans. by J. Roman (éditions Budé [BU], Paris, 1924).

Themistius: *Paraphrases Aristotelis*, 2 Vols., ed. L. Spengel (Leipsig: B. G. Teubner, 1866).

William of Auvergne: *Opera Omnia*, 2 vols. (Paris, 1674).

BIBLIOGRAPHY FOR
AQUINAS ON HUMAN NATURE

Adler, Mortimer. *The Difference of Man and the Difference It Makes* (New York: Holt, Rinehart and Winston, 1967).

Brock, Stephen L. *Action and Conduct: Thomas Aquinas and the Theory of Action* (Edinburgh: T&T Clark, 1998).

Elders, Leo. *The Philosophy of Nature of St. Thomas Aquinas: Nature, The Universe, Man* (New York: P. Lang, 1997).

Gilson, Etienne. *Thomist Realism and the Critique of Knowledge*, trans. by Mark A. Wauk (San Francisco: St. Ignatius Press, 1986).

Jenkins, John. *Knowledge and Faith in Thomas Aquinas* (New York: Cambridge University Press, 1997).

Kenny, Anthony. *Aquinas on Mind* (New York: Routledge, 1993).

Lonergan, Bernard. *Verbum: Word and Idea in Aquinas*, ed. David Burrell (Notre Dame, Ind.: University of Notre Dame Press, 1967).

Nussbaum, Martha and Hilary Putnam. "Changing Aristotle's Mind," in *Essays on Aristotle's De Anima*, ed. A. Rorty and M. Nussbaum (Oxford: Clarendon Press, 1992).

O'Callaghan, John. "The Problem of Language and Mental Representation in Aristotle and St. Thomas," *The Review of Metaphysics* 50 (1997), pp. 499–541.

Pegis, Anton. *St. Thomas and the Problem of the Soul in the Thirteenth-Century* (Toronto: The Pontifical Institute of Medieval Studies, 1976).

Pieper, Josef. *Guide to Thomas Aquinas*, trans. by Richard and Clara Winston (San Francisco: St. Ignatius Press, 1991).

Rosen, Stanley. "Thought and Touch: A Note on Aristotle's *De Anima*," *Phronesis* 6 (1961), pp. 127–137.

Simon, Yves. *Freedom of Choice* (New York: Fordham University Press, 1969).

Wilhelmsen, Frederick. *Man's Knowledge of Reality* (Englewood Cliffs, N.J.: Prentice Hall, 1956).